Narrative Spirituality

Mirror and Window: Reading Scripture with an Integrative Mindset

KEN MACKLIN, PHD

CLAY BRIDGES
PRESS

Narrative Spirituality
Mirror and Window: Reading Scripture with an Integrative Mindset.

Published by Clay Bridges in Houston, TX
www.claybridgespress.com

ISBN: 978-1-68488-165-9 (Paperback)
ISBN: 978-1-68488-174-1 (Hardback)
eISBN: 978-1-68488-166-6

Special Sales: Most Clay Bridges titles are available in special quantity discounts. Custom imprinting or excerpting can also be done to fit special needs. For standard bulk orders, go to www.claybridgesbulk.com. For specialty press or large orders, contact Clay Bridges at info@claybridgespress.com.

"In this new volume, Ken Macklin shows himself to be not only a pastor, with a pastor's heart, but also a prophet, a storyteller, and a poet. The book fairly throbs with a poetic heart, by which I do not mean the ability to put together clever rhyme schemes or interesting phrasing. The poetic voice with which Macklin writes begins on the level of perception long before it reaches expression in language. It is the ability to see two realities at the same time, and then, profoundly, to use language to probes the relationships between them. The title — *Mirror and Window* — captures that dynamic nicely.

Mirror and Window could not be released at a timelier moment. In our world, right now, the dissonances are cacophonous, ragged, hostile even — the opposite of poetry. Macklin asks us to quiet ourselves, to listen attentively — poetically! — to the scripture, to develop eyes that see beyond surfaces, and ears that hear beyond cacophonies. Macklin is inviting us to develop poetic hearts."

—Dr. Jerry Camery-Hoggatt
Professor New Testament and Story Telling
Vanguard University
Author of *A Death of Splendid Daring: A Novel Approach to the Gospel of Mark* 2 volumes

"Pastor Ken Macklin's *Narrative Spirituality: Mirror and Window: Reading Scripture with an Integrative Mindset* is a transformative work shaped by more than fifty years of pastoral ministry. Drawing on his life as a pastor, teacher, and spiritual director, Pastor Macklin offers readers a unique invitation to experience Scripture not only as written text, but as a mirror – reflecting who we are – and a window—opening into who God is. The book unfolds in ten movements called graphia, each blending theological reflection and biblical imagination. With pastoral wisdom and spiritual insight, Pastor Macklin writes with grace and honesty, inviting readers to see life's complexities through the lens of integration. His integrative approach shines through every page, drawing from decades of personal wrestling with Scripture, pastoral conversations, and deeply rooted spiritual practice. Both seasoned believers and curious seekers will find themselves captivated and refreshed, eager to read a book the author himself longed to discover. *Narrative Spirituality: Mirror and Window: Reading Scripture with an integrative Mindset*, promises to be an inspiring companion for all who yearn to read Scripture where God's narrative and our narrative meet."

Rev. Kapp L. Johnson, J.D.
Retired Senior Lecturer Business Ethics and Law
California Lutheran University.

"Ken Macklin brings spiritual insight and a lifetime of experience to his interpretation of scripture. Though readers are sometimes cautioned against reading themselves into scripture, Macklin begins with the assumption that readers cannot do otherwise. The spiritual invitation, then, is to let scriptures read the reader—to reflect back to the reader their belovedness in God's eyes as well as to surface a wider truth about their assumptions. Receiving themselves thus, as in a mirror, readers are led to confession, lament, and deeper communion with Christ. Drawn inward to the heart of God in this way, readers are released outwardly into the world God loves, with greater capacity to share in the work of the gospel."

—Rev. Dr. Colleen Windham-Hughes
Rector of Pacific Lutheran Theological Seminary
Cal Lutheran University

"*Narrative Spirituality: Mirror and Window* offers a new way to read Scripture—both as a mirror to our lives and a window into God's presence. This interpretation goes beyond questions about whether the Bible should be interpreted literally or symbolically, guiding readers to understand their own narratives in the context of God's love and guidance. Dr. Macklin's integrative approach invites readers into a deeper, transformative encounter with scripture and their own faith."

—Dr. Kate Bono
Higher Ed Leader, Professor of Child and Adolescent Studies,
Early Childhood Advocate
Former Lay Leader of the La Mirada,
United Methodist Chruch

"As Ken Macklin's former District Superintendent, I came to know him as a pastor who listens deeply—to Scripture, to people, and to the Spirit. His pastoral presence has always been marked by deep reflection, compassionate leadership, and a sincere love for the proclamation of the Word.

In this book, Ken brings those same gifts to the written page. He invites readers to encounter Scripture not merely as text, but as a living dialogue — a mirror that reflects who we are, and a window that opens us to God's ever-expanding horizon of grace and justice.

Written with both pastoral warmth and theological depth, this book offers a fresh way of engaging Scripture that is contemplative, integrative, and deeply human. It is a gift for pastors, teachers, and seekers who long to rediscover the transforming power of God's Word."

—Rev. J. Mark Galang
District Superintendent
Puget Sound Missional District
Pacific Northwest Conference of the UMC

To Rev. Dr. Leonard Evans, my first pastor,
who preached not just the Word but the Word of love and
showed me what it means to shepherd with compassion.
Your life is the mirror and window through which
I first glimpsed the mercy of God.

Table of Contents

Preface

This book has been a long time coming. Some stories take shape in a season; others take shape across a lifetime. These ten graphia belong to the latter.

For years I have wrestled with Scripture, not only as text but as mirror and window—a mirror reflecting who I am and a window opening into who God is. Along the way, I have discovered that Scripture does not merely invite us to read it. Scripture also reads us. It interprets us, confronts us, and re-images us through reframing our stories.

The journey began in the quiet practice of reflection where I noticed how Scripture mirrored my own longings, fears, and questions. From there, the path widened. The text became a window opening me beyond myself into God's greater story of love, justice, reconciliation, and hope.

This book is the fruit of that journey. It unfolds in ten movements—ten scriptural pathways that I have come to call *graphia*. The first five graphia explore the inward journey: confession, lament, awakening, and communion. The second five move outward: justice, compassion, reconciliation, creation's healing, and the vision of God's beloved community.

Taken together, they form a single tapestry—not ten separate books but one story of love—God's love reflected and refracted through our lives.

I write as one who is still learning. I do not claim to have exhausted Scripture's meaning, nor do I pretend to have tied every thread neatly. What I offer instead is testimony—how the Word has spoken to me, mirrored me, and opened me to God's horizon.

My hope is simple—that as you walk through these pages, you too will find yourself mirrored honestly, and through that mirror you will see the window opening wide. And perhaps in the process you will discover that you are already part of the story Scripture is telling.

A Dance of Words: Why Did I Begin to Write a Book After I Retired from Parish Ministry?

When I was ten years old, my father brought home a set of encyclopedias. Nestled among them was a two-volume edition of the Bible. Although I was not raised in a church environment, I quickly became captivated by the stories within its pages. The illustrations drew me in first—images that became windows into worlds of faith, struggle, and hope. I followed those pictures like signposts, letting them guide me into the heart of the narratives.

Growing up with deaf parents meant that my first language was sign. My world was shaped not by sound but by sight, expression, and gesture. This visual language taught me early on that stories are not simply told; they are shown. Every movement of a hand, every nuance of expression in sign language carries a depth that words on their own cannot hold. From that perspective, storytelling became for me a dance of words, a rhythm of thought and feeling that invites others to see what I see.

Then, in high school, another door opened. I was a sophomore when Anna Ruffini placed a book in my hands: *The Three Musketeers*. It was my first real novel. As I turned the pages, I felt transported to another world of adventure, loyalty, and daring. My eyes were opened to the power of narrative in a new way, and from that moment, I never stopped reading. That gift—one book freely offered—changed the course of my imagination. It taught me that stories could carry me beyond myself into places I might never walk and into lives I might never live yet still feel deeply.

When I write, I strive to bring that same rhythm into prose. Each word is a step, each sentence a gesture, and each paragraph a movement in the dance. I want readers not only to hear the story but to watch it unfold before them, alive with imagery and emotion.

Great storytellers have inspired this path. Charles Dickens, for instance, showed me what it means to write characters and worlds so vividly that readers can see and feel them as if they were present. Dickens had a gift for making social struggles real, compelling readers to engage the world differently. His challenge to "make me see" became a challenge I took upon myself—to write in such a way that readers cannot remain passive but must enter the story with eyes wide open.

From another place of inspiration, Mother Teresa's words echo in my heart: "I am a little pencil in God's hands." Her life reminds me that writing, too, can be an act of service—an offering of hope, love, and compassion. Like her, I long to create works that uplift others, to tell stories that remind people of their worth, their beloved, and their place in the grander story of grace. In that sense, my words are less of my own and more an instrument of a greater purpose.

David McCullough also shaped my vision of writing. His approach to history—accessible, passionate, and deeply human—taught me to "write a book you want to read." That phrase became a guiding star. I realized that authenticity is found when a writer follows their own passions and curiosities. When I write stories that I hunger for, I know they will resonate with others who share that same desire for meaning, truth, and beauty.

Looking back, I can see how those early encounters—encyclopedias on the shelf, pictures in the Bible, the silence and gestures of my parents' world—planted seeds that grew into a lifelong calling. Storytelling for me is not just about arranging words on a page; it is about creating a space where thoughts and feelings dance together, where readers are invited to see, feel, and step into the beauty of the journey.

Poetry in its essence is writing to see. It is like a little finger in the hand of transcendence, pointing beyond itself toward something greater. That is what I seek in every word I write, not only to tell a story but to share in the dance of meaning—one that I, too, would want to read and one that invites others to dance along.

Looking back now, I can trace the thread from that ten-year-old boy with a two-volume Bible in his lap to the writer I am becoming. Those pictures, those stories, and those silent yet expressive hands around me were my teachers. They showed me that storytelling is more than communication; it is communion. It's a weaving together of sight and sound, thought and feeling, the ordinary and the divine.

For me, poetry is the purest expression of this truth. Poetry is writing to see. It is the little finger pointing toward transcendence, the gesture that reminds us we are part of something larger than ourselves. In every story I write, I hope to share that dance of words, the rhythm of thought and feeling that invites others not only to read but to join the dance themselves.

But in truth, Anna Ruffini's gift of *The Three Musketeers* was the spark that ignited it all. That first novel taught me that reading is itself a kind of travel and that every story can open a window into a greater world. In the dance of words that has marked my life, that moment was the first true step.

With gratitude for Anna whose love has been my constant mirror and window.

And for all who dare to let Scripture read them, may you find in its reflection the truth of who you are and through its window the wideness of God's horizon.

Scripture is more than text. It is a living Word, breathing through the centuries and meeting us anew in every generation. But how we encounter it matters. As author Anaïs Nin wrote, "We do not see the world as it is; we see it as we are." The same is true of Scripture. We do not read the Bible as it is; we read it as we are.

Charles Dickens once offered a simple but profound admonition to all writers—in essence to "make me see." Those three words carry the weight of the writer's calling—to open eyes, to pierce veils, to reveal what is hidden.

That is the goal of my Mirror and Window. The mirror helps me see myself—not only the parts I prefer but the wounds, fears, and prejudices I might rather ignore. The window opens me outward, helping me see beyond myself into God's greater story into the neighbor who waits by the well and into the wide landscape of possibility where growth and transformation can unfold.

To read Scripture in this way is to honor Dickens' charge. It is to see my reflection in the mirror and to see through the window the great possibilities of becoming—becoming more human, more compassionate, and more awake to God's presence and purposes. This book is my invitation to you to let Scripture help you see more clearly who you are and who, by grace, you are called to be. This book was born from a simple conviction: Scripture is both a mirror and a window.

I have arranged the reflections in ten sets of readings, not as isolated meditations but as a journey. Together they form a rhythm—from self-reflection to communal encounter, from lament to hope, from inner healing to outward justice. The first half of the journey (Mirror and Window: Reading Scripture with an Integrative

Mindset) turns us inward to see ourselves more truthfully, to confess, to lament, and to discover communion with Christ. The second half (Mirror and Window: Reading Scripture with an Integrative Spiritual Worldview) turns us outward to confront distorted power, to embrace paradox, to cultivate an open mindset, and to envision our lives as the next chapter of the gospel.

The choice of ten readings was intentional. They mirror the rhythm of discipleship: reflection, struggle, encounter, and response. They invite us to move beyond fragmented or closed ways of reading the Bible and to step into an integrative spiritual worldview—one that embraces both personal transformation and social justice, and both the depth of our stories and the breadth of God's story.

This book is written for all who find themselves caught between two worlds. It is for those who grew up with a rigid, literalist reading of the Bible that no longer speaks to the questions of their heart. It is for those who have been told the Bible is little more than ancient literature, stripped of its living voice. And it is for those who ache for Scripture to become a living encounter again.

If you are a lay reader longing for fresh devotion, a pastor or teacher seeking a new resource for guiding your community, or a seeker who wonders if the Bible can still hold meaning in a fractured world, this book is for you.

May these ten windows and mirrors offer you not answers to every question but rather a path of discovery. May you find here an invitation to see yourself more clearly, to see God more deeply, and to glimpse a vision of the world transformed by love.

I chose ten sets of readings because together they form a journey—not simply a collection of passages but a narrative arc. The first five (Mirror and Window: Reading Scripture with an Integrative Mindset) explore the inner life of faith: self-reflection, confession, lament, and communion. The second five (Mirror and Window:

Reading Scripture with an Integrative Spiritual Worldview) widen the lens outward into justice, worldview, community, and hope.

Each set hangs together around movement: from mirror to window, from self to neighbor, from inner transformation to outward action. By weaving these passages in sequence, the book mirrors the rhythm of discipleship: reflection, struggle, encounter, and response.

How the Readings Hang Together

- Samaria (Luke 10; John 4): Encountering the stranger in the mirror and the window
- Echoes of Innocence (Matt. 2; Mark 4; John 11): Facing grief and learning lament
- Night Conversations (John 3): Awakening to new birth
- Confession and the Gap (Mark 8; Exod. 3; John 17): Wrestling with faith and fragility
- From Confession to Communion (Luke 24; Acts 2): Discovering shared life
- The Prophetic Mirror (Amos 5; Isa. 58; Luke 4): Worship and justice bound together
- Grace and Paradox (2 Cor. 12; Phil. 2): Divine affirmation and affront
- Worldview and Mindsets (Rom. 12; John 1): Open versus closed vision
- Broken Mirror, Broken Window (1 Sam. 8; contemporary echoes): Power, distortion, and truth
- The Next Chapter (John 20; Rev. 21): Our lives becoming gospel story

The Personal Invitation

What if every time you opened the Bible, you were also opening a mirror (seeing yourself more clearly) and a window (catching a glimpse of God's greater vision)? This book is an invitation to read Scripture not as a rulebook or relic, but as a living story that can heal, challenge, and transform the way we see ourselves, others, and God.

The Problem Statement

Many people feel torn between two ways of reading the Bible: either as rigid literalism or as distant symbolism. But what if there were a third way—one that honors the depth of Scripture, our personal stories, and the Spirit's movement? Mirror and Window explore this integrative mindset, showing how our narratives and God's narrative meet.

The Narrative Hook

A Samaritan woman came to the well one afternoon, carrying nothing more than a clay jar and her shame. In her encounter with Jesus, the well became a mirror (reflecting her wounds) and a window (opening onto living water). That story is not hers alone. It is ours. This book is about discovering how Scripture can do the same for us.

The Transformative Question

What stories shape the way you see yourself, your neighbor, and God? Mirror and Window ask this question and guide you through Scripture's stories so you can discover your own reflection and glimpse a greater horizon of grace, justice, and love.

To be relational in being is to love others into being. At the heart of our humanity is this call: to awaken one another and to mirror back the truth that we are created for connection, not isolation. Love does not leave us as we are; it calls us forth and makes us more whole.

From this conviction arises an integrative mindset, which serves as an anchor for a spiritual worldview. Such a mindset resists fragmentation, polarization, and reduction. Instead, it holds together what is often torn apart: reason and imagination, faith and inquiry, and personal story and shared history. It sees life not as a fixed state but as a process of becoming—becoming fully human and fully alive, and therefore having a life worth living.

Socrates once declared, "The unexamined life is not worth living." While this remains true, I would add that a life worth living is not only examined but embraced, integrated, and shared. It is a life that allows space for mystery, listens across differences, and gathers wisdom wherever it may be found.

This book is an invitation into such a journey. It does not offer final answers but seeks to open windows of understanding and hold mirrors of reflection. It is a conversation—a weaving together of narrative and natural spirituality, of ancient voices and contemporary experience. Its purpose is simple yet profound: to help us live in a world where being relational, dialogical, and interdisciplinary is not an exception but the very rhythm of life.

That is why the image of mirror and window is so central. The Bible is first a mirror, reflecting us back to ourselves—our fears and hopes, our prejudices and longings, and our failures and faith. Sometimes what we see unsettles us. It's been said, "If a donkey looks in the mirror, you can't expect an apostle to look back out." The text is honest, showing us what we bring to it.

Yet Scripture is also a window. When we allow the Word to read us, as one of my teachers once said, the mirror grows transparent. Suddenly we see through it—into God's larger story, God's greater horizon of love, justice, and grace. In that moment, we are not only reflected; we are reframed.

This book is built on that dynamic. It unfolds in ten graphia—ten scriptural journeys that are not separate volumes but woven threads in a single garment of grace. Each graphia is its own story, yet together they form one narrative arc.

- From Samaria's outsider to the Beloved Community
- From innocence lost to creation renewed
- From night conversations to Spirit's communion
- From confession's gap to prophetic justice
- From walls of division to tables of welcome

Prologue

Mirror and Window: One Story of Love

Scripture is more than words on a page. It is a living Word, breathing through history, meeting us anew each time we open its pages. But how we encounter it matters.

Remember Anaïs Nin's statement: "We do not see the world as it is; we see it as we are." Each of us comes with our fears, our hopes, our prejudices, and our longings—and they shape how we read Scripture. That is why the image of mirror and window is so vital.

In the stories of the Bible we see our pride and our pain, our resistance and our yearning. Sometimes the reflection comforts us, and sometimes it unsettles us—but always it calls us to honesty.

Yet Scripture is not only mirror. It is also a window, opening us to a horizon beyond our own. Through the window we glimpse God's greater story: the life of Christ, the work of the Spirit, the vision of justice and communion. As one of my teachers once said, "It is not how you read Scripture but how Scripture reads you that is decisive." When the Word reads us, the mirror grows transparent, and we begin to see the world as God sees it.

This book unfolds in the following two movements, woven together like threads in a single garment of grace:

1. ***Part One: Mirror and Window – Reading Scripture with an Integrative Mindset:*** Part One, the first half, explores how Scripture forms the inner journey. To read with an integrative mindset is to hold together head and heart, reason and devotion, reflection and action. In this movement,

Scripture reflects us truthfully and then reframes us in God's love. We discover the God who reads us even as we read the text, healing our divisions and calling us into wholeness.

2. ***Part Two: Mirror and Window – Reading Scripture with an Integrative Spiritual Worldview:*** Part Two, the second half, turns outward, expanding into the communal journey. Here we encounter the richness of Eastern Orthodox tradition that speaks of a hermeneutics of the Holy Spirit—a way of reading shaped by love. To interpret with the Spirit is to interpret with compassion, humility, and openness to the many layers of meaning: literal, allegorical, moral, and anagogical. In this movement, Scripture becomes not only mirror and window but also icon—a living image that draws us into God's presence. It teaches us that the Spirit safeguards truth through love, through the principle of doing no harm, and through the shared discernment of community. In this way, Scripture leads us into justice, reconciliation, renewal of creation, and the vision of the Beloved Community.

Together, these two halves form a single story: one of reflection and revelation, of transformation both personal and communal, of love that heals hearts and renews the world.

And so, dear reader, the invitation is this:

- Let Scripture be your mirror.
- Let it become your window.
- Let it draw you as an icon into the presence of God.

And may the spirit of love guide you into a life where faith and justice, devotion and action, mind and heart are woven together as one.

The first five graphia explore the inner journey: how Scripture mirrors our longings, laments, questions, confessions, and hopes.

The next five turn outward to the communal journey: how Scripture calls us into justice, reconciliation, stewardship of creation, and the vision of God's Beloved Community.

These ten pathways are not exhaustive—Scripture overflows with meaning—but they are representative. They trace movement from mirror to window, from self-reflection to social transformation, from personal faith to cosmic hope.

And so, dear reader, I invite you to walk these ten roads not as a spectator but as a participant. For every time you open the Bible with an integrative spiritual worldview—anchored in love, attuned to justice, open to mystery—you are not just reading the gospel story; you are becoming part of it.

A Narrative Spirituality: An Overview of the Book

When we open the Bible, we do not encounter a single flat story but a library of stories, voices, images, and encounters with God. Each one shines like a fragment of stained glass—beautiful but even more radiant when joined together.

This book is written in that same spirit. It is one book, yet within it you will find many books (graphia). Each gospel story could stand on its own as a small volume of wisdom, a mirror reflecting our lives and a window opening into God's kingdom. The Good Samaritan (Luke 10) could be a book on mercy. The grateful Samaritan leper (Luke 17) could be a book on gratitude. Nicodemus at night (John 3) could be a book on questions and searching for faith. The woman at the well (John 4) could be a book on identity, healing, and living water.

Yet when these stories are read together, they become more than separate lessons. They weave into a larger narrative of transformation, showing us how Scripture not only speaks to us but shapes us, inviting us to move from reflection to action, from mirror to window, from question to calling.

Why Mirror and Window?

The Scripture is not only a mirror, but it is also a window, opening us to the larger reality of God's story. Remember, it's not how we read Scripture but how Scripture reads us. When the Word reads us—questioning our assumptions, confronting our distortions, and offering us a truer vision of reality—the mirror becomes transparent. We are invited to see through it into the mystery of God. From mirror to window, from self-reflection to God's revelation is at the heart of this book. It is an invitation to allow Scripture not only to reflect our lives but also to read them, reframing us considering God's larger story.

From Single Story to Integrative Mindset

Our great temptation is to flatten the Bible into one story, one lens, one meaning. But a single story is dangerous. It shrinks God into our own image and turns Scripture into a weapon or a rule book.

Instead, we are called to an integrative mindset—a way of reading that welcomes many voices and perspectives, that holds together symbol and metaphor, that hears Scripture as both ancient word and living word. When we read integratively, Scripture becomes like stained glass: fragments of culture, history, and perspective lit by one Spirit, revealing a larger beauty.

This book will lead you into that kind of reading. It will move through the rhythm of construction, deconstruction, and reconstruction.

- *Construction:* The foundations of love for God and neighbor
- *Deconstruction:* The hard but necessary questions, like "Who is my neighbor?"
- *Reconstruction:* The rebuilding of faith on mercy, gratitude, and compassion

Along the way, you will practice mirror-reading and window-reading, learn to notice your own lenses, and allow Scripture to both unsettle you and renew you.

A Personal Word

My own journey with Scripture has been shaped not only by academic study but by deep encounters with narrative spirituality. As a pastor, professor, teacher, and spiritual director, I have seen how gospel stories—when read not just literally but symbolically—become living waters for those who are thirsty.

I sat with people who, like Nicodemus, came with questions they could not ask in daylight. I have walked with those who, like the Samaritan woman, carried shame until Jesus named them with dignity. I have witnessed gratitude burst forth from those who once felt like outsiders, echoing the Samaritan leper who fell at Jesus's feet. And I have seen mercy embodied in unexpected places, as in the Samaritan who stopped on the roadside.

These are not ancient tales alone. They are mirrors of our lives and windows into the Spirit's ongoing work. My hope is that through this book you will not only learn about these stories but enter them—and let them enter you.

How to Use This Book

Each chapter follows a rhythm:

- *Meditation:* A short reflection to draw you into the theme
- *Narrative:* A retelling or reimagining of a gospel story
- *Practice:* A simple exercise for engaging Scripture personally
- *Reflection Questions:* Prompts for journaling or group discussion
- *Prayer:* A closing prayer to gather the insights into your heart

You can read the book straight through as a journey of transformation or pause with one story at a time. Each chapter is a book in miniature—a complete conversation between Scripture and your life.

An Invitation

This is not a book of answers but a book of companions. It will not provide you with a single way to read Scripture but will invite you into a conversation that includes many ways. My hope is that as you read you will recognize yourself in the mirror, glimpse God's mercy through the window, and step more fully into the life Jesus names when he says, "Go and do likewise."

In the end, the question is not simply "What does the Bible say?" but "What do you read there?" (Luke 10:26).

This book is my attempt to walk with you in answering that question—one story, one mirror, one window at a time.

Book 'Graphe' One

The Greek word for Scripture (ypaøń) (graphe) signifies a writing or something written, and is found throughout the New Testament.

- The Woman at the Well: A spiritual narrative of healing
- Living Stories: Where denial, division, and wounds meet healing
- The Goal of This Spiritual Narrative: Becoming psychologically healthy and theologically sound
- Psychologically Healthy: We honor the woman's story not as pathology but as trauma lived by systemic injustice, distorted relationships, and wounded self-image. Jesus's presence becomes healing, not shaming.
- Theologically Sound: We anchor everything in the gospel's truth. Jesus must go through Samaria, not to expose the woman's weakness but to reveal God's inclusive love that crosses boundaries and restores dignity.
- A Spiritual Narrative: Told through first-person voices (the woman and the disciple) so readers not only understand the theology but also feel the story as their own.

Preface

The story of the woman at the well has always intrigued me, not because it is simple but because it is so layered, so human, and so holy. In John 4, we are not given a miracle of healing the blind or feeding the thousands. Instead, we are given an ordinary conversation at a well—and yet it changes everything.

For years, this story has whispered to me that the wells of our lives are not just physical places but spiritual ones. The well is wherever we come face to face with our thirst, our shame, our divisions, or our unspoken longings. It is the avoided place inside us, the "Samaria" we would rather walk around. And yet that is precisely where Christ waits.

I write this book as both a spiritual/theologian and a pilgrim. As a spiritual/theologian, I believe the Gospel of John is offering us far more than a travel itinerary or a moral lesson. It is revealing a God who must go through Samaria, who must meet us in the places we avoid because only there can living water flow.

As a pilgrim, I have known my own Samaria, places of brokenness, shame, and fear I would rather have bypassed. And yet I have also known the Christ who sat with me there, who saw me fully and did not turn away, who turned my jar of shame into a testimony of grace.

This book is not written as an academic commentary or a sermon series, although it draws from both. It is written as a narrative, weaving the voices of the Samaritan woman and the disciples, psychology and theology, shame and healing, Spirit and truth. My hope is that as you listen to their voices, you will hear your own.

If you find yourself in the "meanwhile"—caught between who you were and who you are becoming—this story is for you. If you find yourself carrying a jar too heavy with shame or secrecy, this story is for you. If you find yourself longing for living water that cannot be drawn from any well on this earth, this story is for you.

And if you find yourself wondering whether God could possibly meet you in the places you most want to avoid, I pray this book helps you hear the answer that has changed my life: Yes, He had to go through Samaria, and that Samaria includes yours.

Book Outline: A Spiritual Place of Connection

Part One – The Encounter

Where Christ Meets Us at the Well

Every story of healing begins with an encounter—not when we are ready, not when we are whole, but when we are thirsty. The woman came to the well at noon, carrying her jar and her shame. The disciples walked reluctantly through Samaria, burdened with prejudice and fear. Neither expected to meet God in that place.

But encounter is never about our readiness. It is about God's initiative. Jesus "had to go through Samaria" (John 4:4). He had to sit in the avoided places, to speak into the silences, and to meet both the woman and the disciples where they were least prepared.

These chapters invite us to step into our own encounter with Christ—to let ourselves be seen, known, and spoken to. The story begins not with answers but with the courage to draw near to the well.

Part Two – The Transformation

Where Stories Become Healing

An encounter with Christ is never static. Once living water begins to flow, it reshapes everything it touches. For the woman, transparency becomes testimony. For the disciples, narrowness is broken open into compassion. For the village, shame turns to joy.

Transformation is not about erasing the past but about reframing it. What was once a burden becomes witness. What was once silence becomes song. What was once division becomes community.

These chapters invite us to imagine our own stories differently. Where have we carried jars of shame? Where have our mindsets diminished us or others? And what would it mean to leave those jars behind and let our wounds become places of connection?

Part Three - The Abiding Presence

Where the Well Becomes a Font and a Table

The story does not end well. It widens into sacrament. What began as water becomes baptism, the leaving behind of an old life. What began as bread in ordinary homes becomes Eucharist, the abiding presence of Christ who dwells with His people.

In this part, we learn that the gospel is not only about one woman's healing or one village's awakening. It is about the abiding truth: Christ is the Savior of the world. He stays, He feeds, He baptizes us into belonging, and He gathers us at a table where no one is excluded.

These chapters invite us to discover the sacramental presence of Christ in our own lives—to drink living water, to break ordinary bread with holy gratitude, to let our testimony become an invitation for others to come and see.

Prologue

The Well We Carry

There is a well inside each of us.

Some days we draw from it quietly, hoping no one notices. Some days we avoid it because to approach it is to face the places in us we would rather forget. And yet it is at that very well—the one we carry within—that Christ waits.

The Gospel of John tells us that Jesus had to go through Samaria, not because it was the shortest path but because it was the path of love. He had to go where others would not. He had to sit where shame lingered. He had to meet a woman who had forgotten her own worth.

This book is her story. It is also ours.

It is a story of wounds and healing, of silence and voice, of shame and dignity, and of sin and grace. It is the story of Jesus meeting us in the places we avoid and showing us that those places can become wells of living water.

What follows is not simply commentary on John 4; it is a narrative journey. You will hear the woman's voice—raw, vulnerable, breaking open into hope. You will hear the disciple's voice—hesitant, surprised, slowly awakening to a God larger than he imagined. And between them, perhaps you will hear your own voice.

For the well is not just in Samaria; it is in you. And Christ waits there still.

Narrative Spirituality: Embracing Christian Mythology

The Story That Holds Us

Narrative spirituality begins with the conviction that truth is often best carried in story. Unlike propositions or doctrines, stories make room for mystery, ambiguity, imagination, and transformation. They are inclusive because they welcome all who are willing to listen, regardless of background, culture, or belief. Stories do not force assent; they invite participation. And in this sense, narrative spirituality does not exclude Christian mythology. Instead, it embraces mythology as a way of telling truths that cannot be said otherwise.

Myth as Doorway

Adrian van Kaam in his *Formative Spirituality* series helps us see how the encounter at the well unfolds as a spiritual journey. The Samaritan woman sees Jesus first as a man, then as a Jew, then as a prophet, then as Messiah, and at last as Savior of the world. This story is a movement from the exclusive to the inclusive, from limited recognition to a cosmic vision of Christ who transcends all boundaries.

Morton Kelsey in *Myth, History, and Faith* calls this the "remythologizing of Christianity." The gospel stories are not stripped of their historical meaning, but history itself becomes mythic when it points to the universal and eternal. The Christ event—life, death, and resurrection—is not only history but myth, truth that reverberates beyond time and place.

Thus, narrative spirituality honors myth as a doorway into mystery. It welcomes every story, Christian and otherwise, as a preparation for the greater story in which all stories find their meaning.

Narrative Reflection

In John's Gospel, Jesus is not merely a character in history but the Revealer, as John Ashton describes. He makes visible the invisible presence of God. John Sanford, in *Mystical Christianity*, shows us how the conversation with the Samaritan woman turns on the symbol of "living waters." What begins as a literal request for water deepens into a mythic exchange: the water of the Spirit, the eternal flow of life from God.

The woman's journey mirrors our own. She moves from misunderstanding to revelation, from exclusion to inclusion, from isolation to witness. In her story, we see humanity's story: every thirst, every exile, every longing for truth. Narrative spirituality invites us to see ourselves in her journey. It is not her story alone; it is the story of us all.

Symbolic Reading: The Cosmic Christ

Narrative spirituality widens our perspective to glimpse the Cosmic Christ. The progression from man, to Jew, to prophet, to Messiah, to Savior of the world is more than her recognition of Jesus. It is humanity's awakening to the universal Christ who transcends categories and embraces all creation.

Myth is the only language vast enough to hold this mystery. Myth allows history to speak universally. The Christ revealed at a Samaritan well is the Christ who holds galaxies together, the One in whom all things live and move and have their being.

Living the Story

Narrative spirituality is all-inclusive because it honors the way truth comes to us—through stories that are both historical and mythic, personal and universal, human and divine. It recognizes that Christian mythology is not an obstacle to faith but its very vehicle.

The woman at the well becomes more than a figure in history; she becomes our sister, our teacher, our mirror. Her story whispers the truth of our own thirst and the possibility of finding water that never runs dry. Myth, far from being a distraction, draws us into this truth.

Narrative spirituality is, therefore, a way of living the story-embracing myth as revelation, honoring history as mystery, and entering the inclusive embrace of the Cosmic Christ.

Prayer

O Christ, Revealer of the unseen God,
You meet us at the wells of our lives
where we come thirsty, weary, and uncertain.
You turn our emptiness into fullness,
our isolation into belonging,
our silence into witness.
Teach us to welcome every story as sacred,
to honor myth as a vessel of truth,
and to live into Your mystery:
the Living Water, the Cosmic Christ,
the Face of God revealed to the world.
Amen.

Reflection Questions

- How do you respond to the idea that myth is not falsehood but another way of telling truth?
- In what ways do you see yourself in the Samaritan woman's journey from exclusion to inclusion?

- How does the image of Jesus as Revealer deepen your understanding of the Gospel of John?
- What "living waters" might Christ be offering you in your current season of life?
- How does the vision of the Cosmic Christ expand your sense of God's presence beyond personal or cultural boundaries?

Benediction

May the Living Christ meet you at the wells of your life.
May His presence turn your thirst into living waters,
your solitude into belonging,
and your story into truth for the world.
Amen.

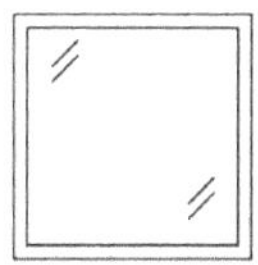

CHAPTER 1

Samaria: The Place We Avoid

"But he had to go through Samaria" (John 4:4).

The Gospel of John tells us that Jesus had to go through Samaria. On the map, it was the shortest route from Judea to Galilee, but devout Jews usually avoided it. They would walk for days out of their way rather than set foot on Samaritan soil. The enmity ran deep—centuries of mistrust, disputes over worship, and wounds of identity. To cross into Samaria was to cross into enemy territory.

But the text insists: Jesus had to go. Not for geography. Not for convenience. He had to go for love.

Samaria in Our Lives

We all have a Samaria.

It's that place inside us we don't want to visit—a memory we keep buried, a prejudice we pretend isn't there, a person we refuse to face, a wound we can't acknowledge. Like the Jews of old, we find detours around it. We build walls, excuses, and distractions—anything but going through.

Yet if the living Christ is to meet us, He will meet us there. The well of living water is not in Jerusalem's temple or in Galilee's comfort, but in Samaria—the place of tension, division, and pain.

Jesus Sits by the Well

John says Jesus, tired from his journey, sat down by Jacob's well. It was noon, the hottest time of day when no one else would come—except one woman. She, too, carried her Samaria within her: broken relationships, shame, and isolation. She came at the time when others would not see her.

Isn't it striking? The meeting happens not in a synagogue, not in a holy city, not in a moment of ritual, but in a weary, human pause—a thirsty Christ, a wounded woman, a deep well.

This is how God enters our Samaria: quietly, humanly, in the moments we least expect.

The Spiritual Geography of Healing

Samaria: It is the landscape of our hearts where prejudice and pain, shame and secrecy live. Jesus must go there because we cannot heal what we will not face. He must go there because living water cannot flow around our wounds; it must flow through them.

A Narrative Reflection on James 4:7–10 and the Woman at the Well

James speaks to us as a pastor, not merely a theologian. His call—"Submit yourselves therefore to God. Resist the devil. . . . Draw near to God, and he will draw near to you" (James 4:7–8)—is not a distant command but an invitation to a way of being. These verses are not abstract rules but rather imperatives woven into worship, reminding us that worship is not confined to sacred mountains or temples but is lived out in spirit and in truth, as Jesus once said to the woman at the well.

Worship here is not ritual for its own sake but for the congruence of heart and action. Joel B. Green, author and professor at Fuller Theological Seminary, notes that James offers five imperatives that anchor this way of life: submit to God, resist the devil, draw near to God, cleanse your hands, and purify your hearts. On the surface, they seem like moral commands. But when read as both mirror and window, they become deeper: a mirror revealing our tendency toward double-mindedness and a window opening us to a life aligned with the Spirit.

Submission is not weakness but humility—the recognition that our lives are not our own and that false narratives about God, self, and the world distort our vision. Resistance, then, is not only against some external tempter but also against diminished mindsets and thought distortions that fragment our humanity. To draw near to God is to step into the mystery of life as relationship, not as a puzzle to be solved.

"Cleanse your hands" and "purify your hearts" reach beyond ritual washing. Neuroscience today suggests that bodily cleansing affects inner disposition, creating the felt sense of a clean slate. Baptism, too, speaks this truth, an outer washing that signifies inner renewal. Green notes that physical cleansing can symbolically and psychologically remove not only contaminants but also "moral taints and mental residues."

This is where Scripture as mirror and window expands. As a mirror, James exposes our tendency toward duplicity: professing faith while living otherwise. As a window, he opens us to the integrative vision of heart and hands aligned in love, mercy, and compassion. The woman at the well embodies that shift. She begins concerned with correct worship—on the mountain or in the temple—but Jesus redirects her to spirit and truth. Eternal life, he tells her, is not about the quantity of years but about the quality of love now. She imagines heaven as a destination; Jesus imagines heaven alive within her.

When we read James through this integrative lens, theology, sacrament, and even science converge. Baptism becomes more than ritual, cleansing becomes more than hygiene, and life in God becomes more than waiting for heaven. It becomes a psychological wholeness and spiritual soundness where inner disposition and outer action reflect the same reality—God's life at work in, with, and through us.

To humble ourselves, then, is to discover that exaltation is not self-made but Spirit-breathed. It is to discover the living water flowing within, washing mind and heart, until our lives are mirrors of God's mercy and windows of God's truth.

Symbolic Reading

- *Submit:* to humble oneself before mystery
- *Resist:* to turn from false stories of God, self, and the world
- *Draw near:* to live relationally, drinking deeply of God's life
- *Cleanse:* to allow the outer washing to mirror inner renewal
- *Purify:* to bring heart and hands into harmony so love shapes both being and doing

The mirror reveals our duplicity: professing faith while clinging to distorted narratives. The window opens to a life where mercy, compassion, and truth flow outward like living water.

Prayer

Holy One,
Wash us with living water.
Cleanse not only our hands,
but the hidden corners of our hearts.
Reshape our thoughts where they distort,
and humble us until we find freedom in You.

Draw near to us as we draw near to You,
that our lives may reflect Your mercy
and open as windows of Your truth.
Amen.

Reflection Questions

- Where do you sense false narratives about God, self, or reality distorting your vision?
- What does "drawing near to God" look like in the rhythms of your daily life?
- How might the practices of cleansing and purifying, both bodily and spiritually, reshape your inner disposition?
- In what ways is your faith more about "where" you worship than "how" you live?
- How do James' imperatives invite you into a congruence of heart and action?

When Jesus goes through Samaria, He also goes through the borderlands of our souls. He steps into the contested ground of our inner life—the place where our faith and our fear wrestle, where our dignity and our shame clash, where our hopes and our failures live side by side.

A Spiritual Narrative of Jesus

I never planned to walk through Samaria. It was easier to take the long way around, like everyone else did. It was safer too. Why risk the stares, the hostility, the feeling of not belonging? The road east along the Jordan might add a few days to the journey, but at least it kept me far from those old wounds, those people I was taught not to trust.

And yet on this day, something inside me shifted. I could feel it before the first step was taken. I had to go through Samaria. I didn't know why, not at first. All I knew was that avoiding it was no longer possible. It wasn't about geography; it was about something deeper, something in me that could no longer take the detour.

The Land I Carry Inside

Samaria was more than a strip of earth between Galilee and Judea. It was a borderland in my own soul. I had built walls around certain memories, buried certain shames, avoided certain truths. Walking into Samaria felt like walking into the very heart of my fears.

As the sun rose higher, each step grew heavier. I wasn't just crossing into someone else's land; I was crossing into the unspoken parts of myself.

The Well at Noon

By the time I reached Jacob's well outside Sychar, the heat was unbearable. Noon was not the hour for drawing water. The women of the village came at dawn or at dusk when the sun was kinder, when they could chatter and laugh together. Noon was for the solitary, the outcast, the one who wanted no eyes upon her.

And that's when I saw her, a woman with a jar, moving slowly toward the well. She was weary, not just from the heat but from carrying something heavier—the weight of stories no one else cared to hear.

I sat down, thirsty, and waited.

The Necessity of This Road

Looking back now, I understand why I had to go through Samaria. If I hadn't, our paths would never have crossed.

Her story would never have met mine. My thirst would never have called out to her.

Samaria wasn't just a place between two cities. It was the meeting ground of need and grace, of shame and truth, of a woman's hidden life and God's unrelenting love.

My Reflection

We all carry our own Samaria, the places we would rather avoid, the people we would rather not face, the truths we would rather not name. I know I do. And yet there comes a day when the detours end, when the Spirit says, "You must go through there. You must face this land inside yourself."

Walking Through the Places I Wanted to Avoid

It was my first church. I found myself in a kind of Samaria that I would have avoided, a place on the margins, a place filled with struggle where people carried stories I did not fully understand. Yet this was where I was called, and this was where my faith was tested.

There are places in life I never wanted to go, valleys filled with shadows, roads marked by fear, situations I would have gladly passed by if given the choice. Yet it is often in those very places—the ones we would avoid—that God does His deepest work in us and through us.

I remember one day vividly. I found myself with fifteen young people, barely adults, some still children in many ways, ages fifteen to eighteen. Their lives had been tangled in drugs, and the weight of it showed in their eyes. I didn't understand their world, not really, but I could see the desperation, the danger. A distributor was using fear and coercion, pressing them into acts they didn't choose. Their lives were on the line.

With the help of two men, we had to act. Together we had made plans to get them out of town, to give them a chance at something better. Every step felt like walking into fire, but we pressed on. When the task was finished, when they were finally safe, I thought I might breathe more easily. But that's when I realized I was being followed.

Fear set in quickly, not for myself alone but for my family. The thought that my wife and my children could be touched by this darkness shook me to my core. Everything in me wanted to retreat, to hide. Yet I knew that stepping back would mean leaving those young people and perhaps countless others at the mercy of destruction.

So I pressed on—through fear, through the uncertainty, through the gnawing awareness of my own inadequacy. I discovered something in that season: Courage is not the absence of fear; it is the decision to keep walking even when fear has its grip around your heart.

Looking back, I see it more clearly. That experience was not just about helping others find a better life; it was also about God showing me the truth of my own heart. My fear revealed my weakness, yes, but it also revealed how deeply I cared, how far I was willing to go to protect life and hope.

Scripture says, "Even though I walk through the valley of the shadow of death, I will fear no evil, for You are with me." (Ps. 23:4 NASB). I understand those words differently now. The valley is not a place to avoid but a place we are sometimes called to walk through for others and for the transformation of our own souls.

And so I testify: The places we most want to avoid are often the very places where God is waiting, ready to reveal His power in our weakness, His courage in our trembling, His redemption in our fear.

Prayer

Lord, give me courage to walk into my Samaria.
Not to skirt around it, not to bury it,
but to sit beside the well until You meet me there.
Amen.

Reflection Questions

- Where is your Samaria? Is it a broken relationship, a long-held resentment, a truth you have buried?
- What detours do you take to avoid facing it?
- Can you hear Christ saying, "I must go through there with you"?

Prayer

Lord Jesus, you crossed into Samaria because love compelled You.
Cross also into my hidden places,
into the wells I draw from in shame,
into the lands I avoid out of fear.
Sit with me there at noon,
and let living water begin to flow.
Amen.

A Theological Understanding

The Literal Route

The quickest way from Judea (in the south) to Galilee (in the north) was straight through Samaria.

But Jews in Jesus's day typically avoided Samaria because of centuries-old hostility. They would take the longer Jordan Valley route, deliberately bypassing Samaritan soil to avoid contamination.

So when John writes that Jesus "had to go," he signals that this is not a matter of efficiency; it is a matter of divine purpose.

The Divine Must

In Greek, the word "must" is *dei*, which means "it is necessary" or "it must be."

This word appears throughout John's Gospel when Jesus acts under divine compulsion:

- "So must the Son of Man be lifted up" (John 3:14).
- "He must increase, but I must decrease" (John 3:30).

So here, Jesus must go through Samaria, not because of roads but because of mission.

Breaking Barriers

Samaria symbolized division—religious, ethnic, gender, and moral.

It was Jews versus Samaritans, men versus women, the righteous versus the shamed.

Jesus had to go there because the gospel is incomplete until the walls come down.

His presence at the well declares that God's love crosses boundaries human beings have erected.

Meeting the Wounded Place

Samaria represents the wounded places of humanity that are despised, avoided, and shunned.

By having to go, Jesus shows us that grace does not bypass woundedness. It goes straight into it.

The well is precisely where a woman, carrying her shame, meets the One who offers dignity, truth, and living water.

The Inner Geography

We all have "Samaritan places" we avoid—memories, failures, prejudices, wounds.

Jesus must go there because only by entering those avoided places can healing come.

The living water of the Spirit doesn't flow around our wounds; it flows through them.

At first glance, this verse reads like a travel note, a small detail on the way from Judea to Galilee. But John never wastes words. His Gospel is a tapestry where every thread carries deeper meaning. When he says Jesus had to go through Samaria, he is not simply pointing to a shortcut on the map. He is naming a divine necessity.

The Geography of Avoidance

The road through Samaria was, in fact, the shortest route north. But most Jews in Jesus's day would not take it. Centuries of hostility separated Jews and Samaritans—disagreements over worship, over ancestry, over what was holy and what was defiled. To walk through Samaria was to risk contamination, insult, or worse.

So the pious detoured. They added days to their journey, following the Jordan Valley just to avoid stepping onto enemy soil. The safe way was the long way around.

Yet John tells us that Jesus had to go through Samaria.

Crossing Barriers

Why must Jesus go? He had to go because love will not be kept out by prejudice, because the kingdom cannot remain locked in old hostilities.

Samaria stood as a symbol of division: Jew versus Samaritan, man versus woman, and righteous versus shamed. By going through Samaria, Jesus declares that the gospel cannot bypass anyone. Salvation is not tribal, national, or limited to geography. It crosses every border human beings erect.

The disciples might have preferred to avoid it. Religion might have chosen the longer, safer road. But Jesus had to go because healing requires going through the places we resist.

The Inner Samaria

It's a story of religious trauma, wounds we would rather detour around, truths we would rather not face.

But Christ "had tot go" there. Grace does not flow around our brokenness; it flows through it. Living water is not found in the temples of comfort but at the wells of our need.

Jesus Sits by the Well

So Jesus comes to Jacob's well at Sychar, tired and thirsty, sitting in the heat of the day. There He waits for a woman who also carries her Samaria within her, a past marked by broken relationships and a present marked by isolation. She comes to the well at noon when others will not see her. And there, in that avoided place, her life changes forever.

Reflection Questions

- Where is your Samaria? A broken relationship? An old wound? A prejudice you carry?
- What detours do you take to avoid facing it?
- Can you hear Christ saying, "I must go through there with you"?

Prayer

Lord Jesus, You did not bypass Samaria.
You walked straight into the land of division
and sat beside the well of shame.
Come also into the avoided places of my life
where I hide, where I hurt, where I fear to go.
Meet me there with living water.
Amen.

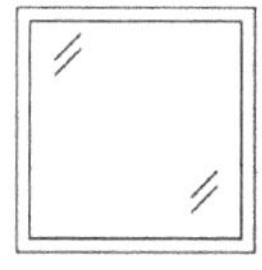

CHAPTER 2

A Prophet Who Sees Me

The Samaritan Woman's Voice

I came to the well at noon because it was easier that way. No whispers. No cutting remarks. No men reminding me I belonged at the margins. I carried my jar, and with it the weight of a story others had written for me.

He was there—a Jewish man, weary and thirsty. I thought he would ignore me, or worse, look at me the way all men did, with suspicion or contempt. But instead, he asked me for a drink.

I was startled. "How is it that you, a Jew, ask a drink of me, a woman of Samaria?" My words held both shock and defiance. I had lived too long under rules that declared me less than human.

Then he spoke of living water, of a gift from God that would never run dry. I wanted it—oh, how I wanted it—a life where I would no longer thirst for dignity, for belonging, for love that did not wound.

But then came the words I dreaded: "Go, call your husband."

My stomach tightened. I said simply, "I have no husband."

And then he named the truth: "You are right. You have had five husbands, and the one you have now is not your husband."

Most men would have spoken those words to shame me. But his voice carried no scorn, no blame. Instead, it was as though he was lifting the burden from my shoulders, showing me that the failures were not mine alone. I had been passed from man to man, each one claiming me, discarding me, breaking me down. And the one I lived with now? He was no husband. He was harsh, controlling, the kind who reminded me every day that I was less than he was.

Jesus saw through it all. He named the injustice. He spoke into the wound men had inflicted on me—the sexism, the abuse, the prejudice. He was telling me, "You are not the problem. The problem is the way you have been treated. The problem is not your worth but their blindness."

For the first time, I felt seen—not as an object, not as a sinner to be despised, but as a woman of dignity. My voice mattered. My story mattered.

And so I said the only words I could find: "Sir, I see you are a prophet."

The Disciple's Voice

We had gone into the city to buy food, and when we returned, I could hardly believe my eyes. He was talking to her—a woman, and not just any woman but a Samaritan. It was unthinkable. No rabbi did such a thing.

We thought she was the problem. Her kind. Her story. Her status. But as I listened, I began to realize He was not exposing her sin; He was exposing ours—the sin of men who had taken her life apart piece by piece.

He was restoring her voice. The same woman we thought had no worth would soon run back to the city and proclaim, "Come and see a man who told me everything I have ever done!" And they would listen to her because her voice carried a truth that could not be silenced.

Jesus had not come to shame her; He had come to unmask the shameful systems that oppressed her. He had not come to strip her down but to lift her up.

And as I stood there, holding bread in my hands, I realized I was witnessing something greater than food, greater than custom, greater than law. I was watching dignity reborn in the voice of a woman.

Reflection Questions – Self-Image and Liberation

- What if her story is not about "a sinful woman" but about a broken system that diminished her?
- What if Jesus's words "you have no husband" were not condemnation but compassion—an unveiling of abuse, sexism, and racism?
- What if the miracle here is not that He shamed her into silence but that He gave her the courage to speak—and the whole city listened?

This reframing makes the story not about her shame but about her liberation. Jesus is not the accuser but the advocate. He restores her self-image and reveals that the sin lies in the oppressive structures around her.

Two Lenses

From the woman's voice we hear the ache of being known and not condemned.

From our voice as disciples, we wrestle with the shock of our categories collapsing.

Together, we begin to glimpse what it means to worship God in spirit and truth, to worship a God who meets us at the wells of our avoidance and sees us as more than our past.

Reflection Questions

- What happens when I allow God to see me fully?
- How do I respond when truth about my life is revealed?

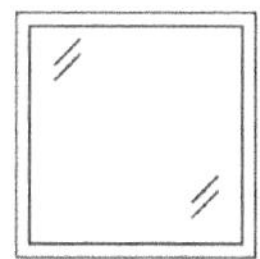

CHAPTER 3
A Messiah Who Knows Me

The Samaritan Woman's Voice

I had learned to expect disappointment. Men made promises, and then they left. Teachers spoke with authority, but none of them saw me. Religion spoke of holy places, but I was never allowed near them.

So I tried to change the subject. When he named the truth of my life, I felt exposed and strangely safe. But still, I wanted to move the conversation away from my pain. "Sir," I said, "our ancestors worshiped on this mountain, but you Jews say the place to worship is in Jerusalem."

It was the old debate, one that divided our people for centuries: Who was right, the Samaritans or the Jews? Which mountain? Which temple? Which God?

I expected him to argue, to take a side, to tell me again why I was wrong. But instead, he said something I had never heard before: "The hour is coming, and is now here, when true worshipers will worship the Father in spirit and truth. God is spirit, and those who worship must worship in spirit and truth."

Spirit and truth. Not mountains and temples. Not Jew and Samaritan. Not men above women or insiders above outsiders. Spirit and truth—that meant I had a place too.

And then, almost without thinking, I said aloud the hope I had carried for years: "I know that Messiah is coming. When he comes, he will proclaim all things to us."

I wanted to believe there was someone greater than our divisions. Someone who could see through our hatred and give us something whole. Someone who could tell me, once and for all, who I really was.

And then he looked straight into me and said the words that shattered every wall: "I am he, the one who is speaking to you."

The Messiah. To me. Not to priests in Jerusalem. Not to elders on the mountain. To me, a Samaritan woman, standing with my water jar in the heat of the day.

In that moment, I knew I was not forgotten. I was not invisible. The Messiah had come, and he had chosen to reveal himself to me.

The Disciple's Voice

We had spent our lives waiting for Messiah. Every rabbi we studied with spoke of him. Every prayer we prayed longed for him. And in our minds, we knew exactly how it would happen: in Jerusalem, among the righteous, to the leaders of our people.

Never here. Never in Samaria. Never to a woman with a story like hers.

When I returned and saw them speaking, I did not dare ask what he had said to her. But later, when I heard her words echo through the city, I understood he had given her what he had not yet spoken so clearly to us. He told her, "I am he."

I confess, it shook me. Why would he choose her? Why would the Messiah entrust his identity to an outsider, an enemy, a woman most men ignored?

And then it struck me: That is exactly who he came for. Not the powerful, not the certain, not the ones who think they own God. He came for the thirsty, for the excluded, for the ones whose self-image had been shattered by others' cruelty.

He came to reveal that the kingdom was not for the few but for the world.

We had expected Messiah to tell us what we already believed. But he revealed himself in a way that undid everything we thought we knew. And as I watched her leave her jar behind, running with joy toward the very people who had scorned her, I began to realize that the Messiah not only reveals himself; he restores us to ourselves.

Reflection – Knowing and Being Known

- For the woman, the Messiah's revelation healed her fractured self-image. She was not defined by the men who hurt her but by the God who chose her.
- For the disciples, the revelation broke their narrow world-view. Messiah was not property of a chosen few but a gift for the world.
- To know Christ is also to be known by Him—fully, truly, and without shame.

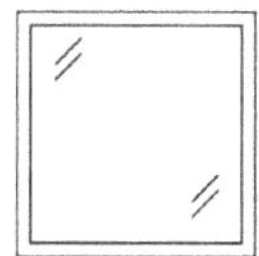

CHAPTER 4

In the Meanwhile: Food for the Soul

The Samaritan Woman's Voice

When I left my jar behind at the well, I knew I could never go back to who I was. That jar had carried more than water; it had carried the weight of my shame, the burden of being unseen, the silence I had chosen to protect myself.

But now, something inside me had shifted. I was no longer hiding. I was running back into the village, into the very streets where the whispers used to follow me. My feet pounded the dust, and with each step, I felt the chains of secrecy loosening.

The words spilled out of me: "Come and see a man who told me everything I have ever done! Could this be the Messiah?"

Once, I would have hidden everything I had ever done. I would have built walls, woven excuses, slipped away quietly at noon. But now I named it openly, not with shame but with hope. My self-image was changing. My past was no longer a prison. My voice—once silenced—had become a testimony.

And yet I was still in the middle of the road—between shame and freedom, between fear and courage. I could not see how the village would respond. But I knew I could not go back.

The "meanwhile" for me was this: I was no longer hidden but not yet fully embraced. And in that space of risk and trembling, I found a strange peace. The Messiah had seen me. That was enough to make me transparent at last.

The Disciple's Voice

We had come back with food, our arms full, thinking that was what mattered. But he would not eat. He said, "I have food to eat that you do not know about."

We argued among ourselves, confused. Who had fed him? What could he mean? And then he told us: "My food is to do the will of the one who sent me and to complete his work."

We did not understand it then, but we were being drawn into the same "meanwhile" the woman had entered. We had left Judea; Galilee still lay ahead. We were between the old life and the new kingdom.

The "meanwhile" is hard. It feels anxious, restless, unresolved—like being caught in the glare of light with no way forward. But he was teaching us that the meanwhile is not empty. It is filled with the presence of God. It is food for the soul.

And as I looked past him into the distance, I saw her. She was no longer walking alone in the heat of noon, avoiding the stares of others. She was running, shouting, beckoning her people with courage I never thought possible. She had entered her meanwhile too—between her old shame and her new freedom. And already, I could see that the fields were ripe for harvest.

Reflection – Transparency in the Meanwhile

- For the woman, the "meanwhile" is the risk of transparency—no longer hiding, not yet fully accepted. Her healed self-image gives her courage to speak.

- For the disciples, the "meanwhile" is the restlessness of not understanding, caught between certainty and revelation and learning to feed on trust.
- For us, the "meanwhile" is wherever we stand between what was and what will be, and the discipline is to practice God's presence right there.

Closing Image

At the well, jars are left behind. In the village, voices rise. Between hunger and harvest, disciples begin to see. The meanwhile is no longer just waiting. It becomes the space where transparency, trust, and God's presence meet.

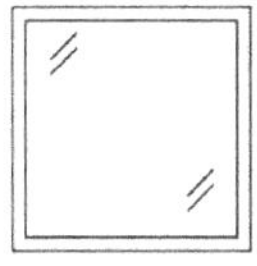

CHAPTER 5

Connecting Our Stories

The Samaritan Woman's Voice

I never thought they would listen to me. For so long, I had been the shadow at the edge of the crowd, the one who spoke only in whispers, the one others avoided. But now I found myself in the center of the marketplace, breathless, my words tumbling out like water from a jar too full to carry.

"Come and see a man who told me everything I have ever done! Could this be the Messiah?"

Some laughed, some frowned, but others leaned in, curious. They could hear it in my voice. This was no longer shame speaking, but hope. I was no longer hiding. My past, once my prison, had become my testimony.

And to my amazement, they followed me—the men who had once dismissed me, the women who had once shunned me, the children who had never heard me speak aloud in public. They came with me, back to the well, back to him.

For the first time in my life, my story was not just mine. It was becoming part of something larger. My healing was weaving into the healing of the village. My voice was no longer an echo in the dark. It was a call that others could follow.

The Disciple's Voice

We watched in silence as the villagers streamed toward him. They were not coming because of us. They were not coming because of our teaching, our reputation, or our signs. They were coming because of her.

It stunned me. We had thought of her as a problem, a woman with a past, a distraction to our rabbi's mission. But she was becoming the very bridge to her people. Her testimony—fragile, unpolished, filled with questions—was strong enough to open the doors of her city.

And then we saw something even greater. They invited him to stay, not for a conversation at the well, not for a passing miracle, but to abide with them. And he said yes. We were two days in Samaria—two days in the place we had always avoided.

By the end of those days, many said to the woman, "It is no longer because of what you said that we believe, for we have heard for ourselves, and we know that this is truly the Savior of the world."

Her story had led them to his story. Her voice had given them the courage to listen for themselves. And we, the disciples, had to admit a hard truth: The kingdom was not coming through our pride or privilege. It was coming through the testimony of a woman we almost dismissed.

Reflection – The Ripple of Transparency

- The woman's healing of self-image led to her transparency. Transparency led to testimony. Testimony led to communal healing.
- The disciples discovered that their role was not to control the story but to witness its surprising expansion.
- True connection happens when our wounds, once healed, become bridges for others.

Closing Image

At first, the woman came to the well alone, in silence. Now she returned with a crowd, her voice echoing throughout the streets. What had been her shame became her witness. What had been her silence became their salvation. And in that connection—her story woven into theirs—an entire city discovered living water.

> *Scripture:* John 4:39–42
>
> *Theme:* The woman becomes a witness: "Come and see!"
>
> *Narrative spirituality:* Sharing our story connects us to others. Healing multiplies when stories ripple outward into community.

Reflection Questions

- Who has been changed because I shared my story?
- What testimony do I carry that could bring hope to others?

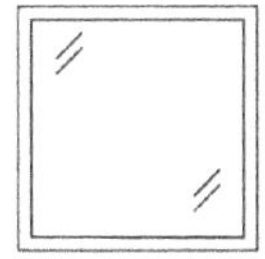

CHAPTER 6

Theology Without Spirituality

The Samaritan Woman's Voice

I tried to change the subject. He had just spoken truth into my life, and I felt both exposed and healed. But I wasn't ready to linger there, so I pointed to an old debate: "Our ancestors worshiped on this mountain, but you Jews say the place where people must worship is in Jerusalem."

It was the argument everyone knew: Gerizim versus Zion, Samaritans versus Jews. I thought he would take a side, perhaps defend Jerusalem as the only holy place. That's what men always did when they wanted to win.

But he didn't. Instead, he looked at me with a gentleness that went deeper than any argument. "Woman, believe me, the hour is coming when you will worship the Father neither on this mountain nor in Jerusalem. The true worshipers will worship the Father in spirit and truth."

In spirit and truth.

His words sank into me like living water. Spirit meant it wasn't about location or ritual or who was "in" and who was "out." Truth meant it wasn't about pretending, hiding, or following rules out of fear. Worship wasn't about a mountain or a temple. It was about presence—the God who saw me, here at the well, in the middle of the day, and called me beloved.

I realized then that I had always thought worship was for others. For the men. For the holy places. For the voices louder than mine. But he was telling me that worship was for me too. My spirit, my truth, my voice—they mattered.

The Disciple's Voice

We had grown up on debates about worship—where to sacrifice, how to keep purity, who could draw near. We thought theology was about answers—fixed, precise, defended at all costs.

But when we saw him speak with her, we realized something we hadn't wanted to admit. Theology without spirituality is empty. Arguments about mountains and temples meant nothing if people were still thirsty.

He was moving us beyond categories, beyond places, beyond the pride of being "right." He was showing us that God was not confined to the walls we built. God was spirit—free, moving, uncontainable. And God was truth—unmasking lies, dismantling prejudice, calling even the least likely into worship.

It unsettled me. For if God could be worshiped here, in Samaria, by this woman, then everything we thought we controlled about God was undone.

And maybe that was the point.

Reflection – Spirit and Truth

- Theology without spirituality becomes an argument about places, laws, and control.
- Spirituality without theology can drift into sentiment without grounding.

- But worship "in spirit and truth" holds them together. It is both rooted and alive, both honest and transcendent.
- True worship is not about geography or power; it is about presence.

Closing Image

At the well, no mountain loomed, no temple towered. Yet in that ordinary place, worship was born—not of law but of spirit; not of division, but of truth. And the woman realized that the God who could be worshiped anywhere could also be worshiped in her own life, in her own voice, in her own truth.

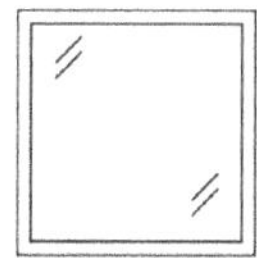

CHAPTER 7
Healing Diminished Mindsets

The Samaritan Woman's Voice

For years, my life felt like a verdict.

Five husbands: That's what they whispered. "The one she has now is not her husband"—that's what they said. They thought they knew me, and I began to believe them. My self-image shrank under their words until I no longer saw myself as a person, only a shadow of mistakes.

I carried that shame like a heavy jar every day, trudging to the well at noon when no one else was near. Alone was safer. Alone meant fewer eyes, fewer accusations.

But then he looked at me and spoke the truth of my story, not to condemn me but to free me. "You are right. You have had five husbands, and the one you have now is not your husband."

For the first time, I heard my story without judgment. He named it, but he did not weaponize it. Instead, he lifted it from my shoulders as if to say, "This is not the sum of who you are. You are more than the failures of others. You are more than the pain of the past. You are more than the names they have called you."

And suddenly, the jar of shame felt lighter. My self-image began to stretch again, like lungs filling with air after too long under water. I was not defined by diminishment. I was defined by being seen.

The Disciple's Voice

We thought we knew who she was. We assumed her life was proof of sin, of failure, of why we kept away from Samaritans in the first place. Our minds were fixed, diminished by prejudice, rigid with shame-based theology.

But as I listened, I saw him do what I could not. He reframed her. He told her story differently. He did not deny her past, but he refused to let her be imprisoned by it.

It struck me hard. How often do we let our mindsets diminish others? How often do we assume their failures define them? How often do we shrink our own selves, trapped in guilt or fear, convinced that God sees us only as broken?

A diminished mindset cannot hold the expansiveness of God's grace. Jesus was showing us a different way: an integrative mindset—one that could see brokenness and possibility together, sin and grace in the same breath.

He was teaching us that healing begins when our minds are no longer locked in shame but opened in truth and compassion.

Reflection – Fixed vs. Healing Mindsets

Fixed/Diminished Mindset: Shame says "I am what I've done." Prejudice says, "They are what their past reveals." Fear says, "There is no way forward."

Healing/Integrative Mindset: Christ says, "You are more than your past. You are more than what others have done to you. You are seen, known, and called."

To heal is to allow our minds to expand, to hold pain honestly but also to trust that grace is larger.

Closing Image

At the well, shame began to lose its grip. The woman who once hid began to stand tall. The disciples who once judged began to learn compassion. And in that desert place, minds once diminished began to open like fields ready for harvest.

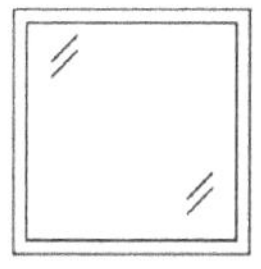

CHAPTER 8
Forgiveness: The Open Door

The Samaritan Woman's Voice

Forgiveness was not a word I trusted. Too often it had been used against me. "Forgive and forget," they said after the wounds had already been carved into me. "Forgive," they whispered while never once asking men to change their ways.

So I learned to live hardened, carrying my bitterness like a shield. It felt safer to close the door than to risk being hurt again.

But then he spoke to me, not with accusation, not with dismissal, but with truth wrapped in compassion. He named my past without defining me by it. And in that moment, something inside me shifted. The door I had kept locked so long began to creak open.

I realized forgiveness wasn't about excusing those who had harmed me. It was about stepping out of the prison of shame they had built around me. It was about reclaiming my voice, my dignity, and my freedom.

When I ran back to the village, I was no longer the woman who hid at noon. I was no longer the one they whispered about. I was the one who invited them to meet the Messiah. Forgiveness had opened a door, not back into the past but forward into a new community, a new future.

The Disciple's Voice

Forgiveness was not easy for us either. We had carried generations of prejudice against Samaritans. We had believed them to be half-breeds, heretics, and outsiders. And suddenly, we were watching our Teacher sit among them, receive their hospitality, and call them into the kingdom.

It unsettled me. To forgive meant letting go of the superiority I had been taught to carry. It meant admitting that the barriers we had built were not God's barriers but ours.

But then I saw her. The woman whose story we dismissed had become a witness to her whole village. The very people we avoided were now gathering around him in joy. And I realized that forgiveness is not just about pardoning wrongs. It is about entering reconciliation with people we thought unworthy, with wounds we thought unhealable, with God's presence we thought was ours alone.

Forgiveness is the open door into the new creation.

Reflection – Forgiveness as Release

- Forgiveness is not excusing or minimizing harm. It is refusing to let harm have the final word.
- Forgiveness is releasing the prison of shame, bitterness, and superiority so that reconciliation can become possible.
- Forgiveness is the doorway—not the destination but the threshold into freedom, healing, and community.

Closing Image

At the well, forgiveness cracked open the hardened places of a woman's heart. In the village, forgiveness stretched open the narrow walls of the disciples' minds. Together, they stepped through the door of grace into a larger room—one filled with living water, open tables, and voices once silenced now singing.

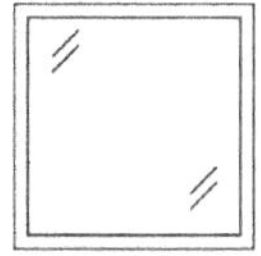

CHAPTER 9
The Narrative of Sin and Grace

The Samaritan Woman's Voice

I set the jar down.

It seemed a small thing, but for me it was everything. That jar had been my daily burden—heavy, ordinary, necessary. It carried not just water but the weight of my routine, the symbol of my thirsts that were never satisfied.

When I left it behind, I was leaving more than clay and rope. I was leaving the story that said I was defined by lack, by failure, and by shame. I was leaving the narrative that had chained me to the past.

I ran without it, empty-handed but freer than I had ever been. Grace had rewritten my story. My sin was not that I was unworthy. My sin was that I had believed the lie of unworthiness. Grace shattered that lie and replaced it with truth: I was seen, known, and chosen.

The jar remained at the well, but I no longer needed it. I carried something better: living water welling up within me, flowing into words that spilled onto the streets—"Come and see a man who told me everything I have ever done!"

The Disciple's Voice

I noticed the jar too. When she ran past us, her hands were empty. That clay vessel sat by the well, forgotten.

It struck me later how symbolic it was. She had come for water but found something deeper. She had carried her life in that jar—thirst that never ended, effort that never satisfied, shame she could never escape. But when she met him, she no longer needed the jar.

That is sin, I realized—the endless cycle of disconnection. Sin is not just breaking rules; it is carrying emptiness as though it could sustain us. And that is grace—when the emptiness is no longer necessary, when the jar can be left behind, when we learn that true life comes not from what we carry but from what God gives.

Her story became the living parable of sin and grace. She left behind what was broken and carried forward what was eternal.

Reflection – Leaving the Jar Behind

Sin is not just moral failure but disconnection from God, from others, from our own dignity.

Grace is not abstract pardon but restored flow, the living water within us that renews life.

Leaving the jar is the act of trust: choosing to let go of the old narrative and run into the new one.

Closing Image

By the well, the jar sat heavy, forgotten in the dust. But in the streets, her voice rang with joy, carrying living water to all who would listen. The story of sin had ended. The story of grace had begun.

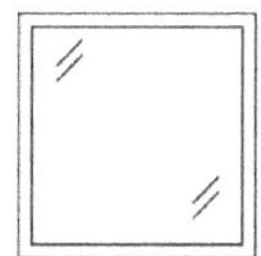

CHAPTER 10

Baptism and Eucharist: Sacramental Presence

The Samaritan Woman's Voice

They asked him to stay.

For two days, the man who had met me at the well, the one who told me everything I had ever done, dwelled among us—in our homes, at our tables, in ordinary places we never thought holy.

And something remarkable happened. The people listened. They believed it. At first, they came because of my voice, my testimony. But soon, they said, "It is no longer because of what you said that we believe, for we have heard for ourselves, and we know that this is truly the Savior of the world."

Their words did not silence me; they completed me. My story had been the doorway. But the living water had filled them too. Together, we were baptized into a new belonging—no longer Jew or Samaritan, man or woman, outsider or insider. Just children of God, drinking from the same well.

I thought of the jar I left behind. That was my baptism. Going into the village empty-handed, I emerged with a new identity, a new community. And every time I remembered his words, "The water I give will become in you a spring gushing up to eternal life," I knew that water was alive in me still.

When he broke bread at our tables, I tasted something deeper than food. It was as though heaven itself had sat down with us, blessing what was ordinary until it became holy. That was my Eucharist.

The well had been the place of shame. But now it had become the font of my baptism, the table of my communion, the sanctuary of my new life.

The Disciple's Voice

We never thought we would stay in Samaria. We imagined it as a place to pass through quickly, if at all. But he lingered there. He ate their bread, drank their water, and received their welcome. And we had to do the same.

At first, it was awkward. Their tables were not our tables. Their prayers were not our prayers. Their stories were not our stories. But slowly, we began to see in him that it was all one story.

We saw entire families gather to listen, to believe, to rejoice. It felt like baptism—not just individuals washed clean but a whole community reborn. And as we sat at their tables, sharing food as if we had always belonged, I realized this was Eucharist: his presence transforming strangers into family, enemies into kin.

When they finally said, "This is truly the Savior of the world," I knew we had reached a new horizon. Not the Savior of the Jews only. Not the Savior of men only. Not the Savior of the righteous only. The Savior of the world.

And the world began right here, in Samaria.

Reflection – Sacramental Presence

- Baptism is leaving the jar behind, dying to the old story and rising into new belonging.

- Eucharist is dwelling with Christ in the ordinary—bread, water, table, presence—and discovering that all of life can be holy communion.
- The sacraments remind us that salvation is not just personal healing but communal transformation. The well becomes the font, the table becomes the altar, and the village becomes the body of Christ.

Closing Image

The story began with avoidance—Jews detouring around Samaria, a woman hiding from her village. It ends with presence—the Messiah dwelling in Samaria, a woman leading her people to him, a whole city confessing: "Truly, he is the Savior of the world."

The well is no longer a place of shame. It is a sacrament of living water overflowing into eternity.

Epilogue – The Wells of the World

The story does not end in Samaria. It continues wherever living water flows into thirsty places.

The woman left her jar behind, but her story carried forward, flowing from her voice into her village, from her village into the Gospel, from the Gospel into your hands today. Every generation has its wells—places of division, shame, avoidance, and silence. And every generation hears again the words of Jesus: "The water that I give will become in them a spring of water gushing up to eternal life" (John 4:14).

The well is not a ruin of the past; it is a fountain of the present.

In every community divided by prejudice, Christ waits at the well.

In every life weighed down by shame, Christ waits at the well.

In every heart caught in the "meanwhile," restless and afraid, Christ waits at the well.

And when He meets us there, He gives us what the world cannot: living water, Spirit and truth, food for the soul, presence in the in-between. He gives us Himself.

So leave your jar behind. Let your story become testimony. Drink deeply and then invite others to come and see.

And this is the story's final word: "We have heard for ourselves, and we know that this is truly the Savior of the world" (John 4:42).

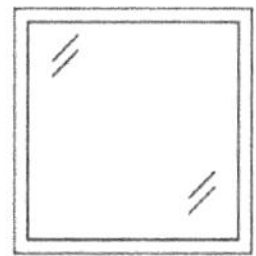

APPENDIX PART ONE:

Why Samaria Mattered

When John tells us that Jesus "had to go through Samaria" (John 4:4), he is not simply giving directions on a map. He is locating the story within centuries of history, conflict, and wounded identity. To understand why Jews and Samaritans avoided one another, we must go back to the days of Israel's divided kingdom.

The Fall of the Northern Kingdom

After King Solomon, Israel split into two kingdoms:

- The Northern Kingdom of Israel with its capital at Samaria
- The Southern Kingdom of Judah with its capital at Jerusalem

In 722 BCE, the Assyrian Empire invaded the north. The elites, leaders, and much of the population were exiled. But not everyone was carried away. A remnant of peasants and farmers was left behind in the land. Over time, these survivors intermarried with foreign settlers whom the Assyrians brought in to occupy the region.

This blending produced what later Jews considered a "hybrid" people—neither fully Israelite nor fully Gentile. Their religion retained echoes of the Torah but was mixed with other influences.

They built their own temple on Mount Gerizim and claimed it as the true place of worship.

The Southern View of the North

For centuries, the Jews of Judah looked down on the Samaritans. They saw them as ethnically compromised, religiously impure, and politically suspect. The Samaritans returned the resentment, pointing to their own history and sacred mountain as proof that they, not the Judeans, were the faithful heirs of Israel.

This hostility became so deep that by Jesus's day, Jews and Samaritans avoided sharing food, cups, or fellowship.

Most Jews traveling between Judea (south) and Galilee (north) took the long road—crossing the Jordan River to the east, walking up the valley, and crossing back again—simply to avoid Samaritan soil.

Walking through Samaria was not only unusual; it was provocative. It risked insult, hostility, or worse.

Why This Matters for the Woman at the Well

Against this backdrop, Jesus's choice to sit by Jacob's well in Samaria is astonishing. He not only passes through the land; He lingers there. He not only speaks to a Samaritan; He speaks to a Samaritan woman. And not only does He speak, but He reveals Himself as Messiah, the "I AM," more openly than He had yet revealed it to anyone else.

For John's first readers, this would have been shocking. Jesus was crossing every boundary:

- Ethnic – a Jew speaking to a Samaritan
- Gendered – a man conversing publicly with a woman
- Religious – a rabbi declaring true worship beyond mountains and temples
- Social – elevating the testimony of a woman whose voice had been silenced

A Spiritual Reflection

The history of Samaria is the history of a wound—a wound of exile, invasion, suspicion, and rejection. For centuries, that wound hardened into prejudice and avoidance. The road east of the Jordan became a metaphor for what people do with pain: walk around it rather than through it.

But Jesus "had to go through Samaria." He had to face the wound, not bypass it. He had to sit at the well of division and transform it into a fountain of reconciliation.

In the woman's story, we see the reversal of centuries of hostility. Her healing becomes her village's healing. Her voice, once diminished, becomes the invitation that draws others into faith. And her encounter with Christ shows us that the very places we call unclean, unworthy, or "less than" are the places where living water springs up.

Why This Matters for Us

The Samaritans remind us of those we are tempted to see as outsiders, compromised, or "less than." Every age has its Samarias. Every community has its avoided places. And every soul carries a Samaria within, a part of ourselves we deem unworthy of love.

The gospel insists that Christ goes there—not around it, not past it, but through it.

Healing cannot come to what we refuse to face.

Timeline of Samaria: From Kingdom to Outsider

- 922 BCE – Division of the Kingdom
- After Solomon's reign, Israel splits
- North: Kingdom of Israel (capital: Samaria)
- South: Kingdom of Judah (capital: Jerusalem)
- 722 BCE – Assyrian invasion

- Assyria conquers the Northern Kingdom
- Many Israelites are exiled
- A remnant remains in the land
- 722–600 BCE – Intermarriage and "hybrid identity"
- Assyria imports foreign settlers into Samaria
- Survivors intermarry with them
- Religion blends: Torah traditions + outside influences
- c. 400 BCE – Mount Gerizim temple
- Samaritans build their own temple on Mount Gerizim
- They claim it as the true place of worship
- Tensions with Jerusalem deepen
- Second Century BCE – Jewish hostility hardens
- Jewish rulers destroy the Gerizim temple (c. 128 BCE)
- Samaritans viewed as impure, outsiders, less than Jewish
- First Century CE – Avoidance in Jesus's day
- Jews routinely bypass Samaria, traveling the long way on the east side of the Jordan when moving between Galilee and Judea
- Shared food, water, or fellowship is taboo
- John 4:4 – Jesus had to go through Samaria
- Jesus breaks the pattern, walking into the avoided land
- At Jacob's well, he reveals himself as Messiah, not to priests or kings but to a Samaritan woman

Quick Takeaway

Samaria = wound of history (exile, invasion, rejection).
Jews saw Samaritans as compromised outsiders.
Jesus enters that wound, transforming shame into testimony, division into belonging.

Appendix Part One Study Questions – The History of Samaria and Our Avoided Places

Exile and Loss

The Assyrian invasion left the Northern Kingdom fractured, with many carried into exile and a vulnerable remnant left behind.

Where in your life have you experienced "exile"—a place where you felt displaced, powerless, or forgotten?

How might Christ be present even in those places of loss?

Hybrid Identity

The Samaritans were seen as impure because of intermarriage with foreign settlers.

Who today is labeled "less than" because of race, culture, gender, or social status?

In what ways have you felt the sting of being seen as "less than"?

The Long Road Around

Most Jews in Jesus's time avoided Samaria altogether, walking on the east side of the Jordan to bypass it.

What "detours" do you take in your spiritual life to avoid places of pain, shame, or conflict?

What would it mean for you to stop going around and let Christ walk with you through?

The Well as a Meeting Place

Jesus chose to sit at a well, a place of daily need, not a temple or a throne.

Where are the "ordinary wells" in your own life—workplaces, kitchens, conversations—where Christ might be waiting to meet you?

Healing the Wound of Division

The history of Samaria is a story of division that hardened into prejudice.

Where in your community, church, or world do you see "Samarian divides"?

How could your story—like the woman's—become a testimony that bridges wounds and opens doors for healing?

Book 'Graphe' Two

The Woman at the Well: A Spiritual Narrative of Healing and Living Water

Preface

Why This Story Matters

I shared how John 4 shaped my life as both theologian and pilgrim, a story not of condemnation but of healing, not of avoidance but of encounter. This book is written as a narrative, weaving the woman's voice and the disciple's voice to help readers face their own Samaria with courage and grace.

Prologue

The Well We Carry

Every one of us carries a "well" inside—the place of shame, longing, or silence we would rather avoid. John says Jesus had to go through Samaria, not because of geography but because grace always enters our avoided places.

Part One – The Encounter

Where Christ meets us at the well

Chapter One – Samaria: The Place I Avoid

Theme: Jesus goes through the land others avoid
Psychological: Facing the places of denial, shame, and fear
Theological: Grace must meet us where we least want to go

Chapter Two – A Prophet Who Sees Me

Theme: Jesus reveals the woman's truth with compassion

Psychological: Healing of distorted self-image; naming abuse without shame

Theological: Prophecy uncovers truth to restore, not condemn

Chapter Three – A Messiah Who Knows Me

Theme: "I am he, the one speaking to you."

Psychological: Moving from doubt and diminished worth to dignity and trust

Theological: Messiah reveals Himself first to an outsider, a Samaritan woman

Chapter Four – In the Meanwhile: Food for the Soul

Theme: Practicing presence in the in-between

Psychological: Anxiety of liminality—no longer who we were, not yet who we are becoming

Theological: Christ nourishes us not with bread but with presence and purpose

Narrative: The woman runs transparent into the village; the disciples wrestle with confusion

Part Two – The Transformation

Where stories become healing

Chapter Five – Connecting Our Stories

Theme: Transparency becomes testimony; testimony transforms community

Psychological: Her healed self-image allows her voice to be heard

Theological: Narrative spirituality—our stories ripple outward to others

Chapter Six – Theology Without Spirituality

Theme: Worship not on mountains or temples but in spirit and truth

Psychological: Moving beyond arguments that diminish the soul

Theological: Worship as presence, not control; truth as liberation, not division

Chapter Seven – Healing Diminished Mindsets

Theme: From shame and guilt to wholeness

Psychological: Breaking free from the prison of self-condemnation

Theological: An integrative worldview: sin and grace held together in Christ

Chapter Eight – Forgiveness: The Open Door

Theme: Forgiveness is not excusing harm but releasing shame and bitterness

Psychological: Forgiveness frees the self to belong again

Theological: Forgiveness is reconciliation with God, self, and neighbor

Chapter Nine – The Narrative of Sin and Grace

Theme: Leaving the water jar behind

Psychological: Sin as disconnection; grace as restored flow of selfhood

Theological: Grace as story, not doctrine—a narrative of liberation

Part Three – The Abiding Presence

Where the well becomes a font and a table

Chapter Ten – Baptism and Eucharist: Sacramental Presence

Theme: The well becomes baptismal font; shared meals become Eucharist

Psychological: Sacraments heal belonging and identity

Theological: Christ dwells in bread, water, table, and presence

Narrative: Samaritans confess: "This is truly the Savior of the world."

Epilogue – The Wells of the World

The story of John 4 is not finished. Every generation has its Samaria, its avoided places, its silenced voices. Christ still waits at the wells of the world, offering living water. The invitation remains: Leave your jar behind, let your story become testimony, and say with the Samaritans, "We have heard for ourselves, and we know that this is truly the Savior of the world" (John 4:42).

Appendix – Why Samaria Mattered

Historical Context:

- Division of the kingdoms (922 BCE)
- Assyrian invasion of the north (722 BCE)
- Intermarriage and hybrid identity
- Mount Gerizim temple and rival worship
- Jewish hostility toward Samaritans
- Travel detours along the Jordan to avoid Samaritan soil

Timeline Sidebar: Samaria briefly

Quick bullet points from Solomon's division ? Assyrian conquest ? Gerizim temple ? Jewish avoidance ? Jesus' entry.

Spiritual Reflection

Samaria is both a historical region and a spiritual metaphor. It represents wounds of prejudice, shame, and avoidance. Jesus "had to go" there because grace does not bypass our wounds; it walks straight into them.

Study Questions

- Where do you feel "exiled" or displaced?
- Who in your community is treated as "less than"?
- What detours do you take to avoid pain?
- Where are the "ordinary wells" in your life?
- How could your story become testimony in a divided world?

Book 'Graphe' Three

Who Is My Neighbor?
A Spiritual Narrative of Luke 10:25–37

Overview

This story invites readers into a transformative journey of Scripture as both mirror and window. Scripture is not a static text but a living conversation, a mirror that reflects who we are in our present condition and a window that opens us into the wideness of God's kingdom.

Drawing on the parable of the Good Samaritan (Luke 10:25–37) and related passages, this third graphe explores how spiritual reading moves beyond literalism into symbolic, metaphorical, and integrative ways of seeing. It guides readers through a rhythm of construction, deconstruction, and reconstruction, leading ultimately to Jesus's invitation: "Go and do likewise" (Luke 10:37).

This part of the book blends narrative, meditation, practical exercises, and reflective prayer, making it both a spiritual reading companion and a guide for personal transformation.

Preface

From Signs to Spirit

When we open the Bible, we do not just open a book; we open a world of signs, symbols, and metaphors. To read Scripture only literally is like stopping at the surface of a river without ever entering its current. The words on the page are real, but they are meant to carry us into deeper realities.

A sign is only as good as the message it points toward. Imagine arriving in a frontier town in 1842. At the edge of the road, you see a curious wooden post with a red octagon nailed to it. You stare at the strange shape and color, but it has no meaning to you. The sign works only when you know its message. So it is with Scripture. The words point beyond themselves toward meaning, toward Spirit, and toward God.

Symbols go even further. They not only point to meaning but participate in it. To say "9/11" in our own time is not to speak of two numbers but to enter a shared memory, a wound, and a story that reshaped history. A symbol, once awakened, carries us inside its power.

Metaphor draws us still deeper. When Jesus says, "I am the door," He does not ask us to imagine hinges or a handle. He asks us to see how He functions as the threshold, the passageway, the opening into God's new world. Metaphor is not less real than literal language is more. It presses us to see with the eyes of the heart.

This is where Samaria enters the story.

Samaria as Sign

Samaria first appears as a geographical reality. It is the stretch of land that pious Jews once crossed over the Jordan to avoid, lest they be contaminated by those they considered impure. It is the place where Jesus "had to go," though others went around.

Samaria as Symbol

Samaria is more than dirt and borders. It becomes a symbol of all that divides us—religion from religion, neighbor from neighbor, even heart from heart. Samaria is the fault line of human history where Babel still speaks confusion and fear. And yet precisely there, the gospel story breaks in. What once was Babel becomes the place of Pentecost where the Spirit unites what division had torn apart.

Samaria as Metaphor

Finally, Samaria becomes a metaphor for the places within us we would rather avoid:

- The wounds we keep hidden
- The prejudices we pretend not to carry
- The addictions and attachments that rob us of freedom

Samaria is the spiritual crossroads where Christ waits for us, not to condemn but to meet us with living water.

Jesus knew this truth. There was no room for Him at his birth, no place to lay His head in His ministry, and no fire from heaven to destroy His opponents (though His disciples once begged for it). Instead, there was only the quiet insistence of the Kingdom of God: love God, love your neighbor. Freedom and love are the twin ethics of a life worth living.

Samaria, then, is not just ancient geography. It is our own threshold, our own mirror and window. Where is your Samaria? What place in your soul do you avoid crossing? What part of your neighbor do you refuse to see? What fire would you rather call down than reconcile?

Invitation to the Reader

This book is about learning to read Scripture not only as text but as mirror and window, sign and symbol, metaphor and mystery. Literal words open the door, but it is symbolic and spiritual language that teaches us how to walk through.

Jesus went to Samaria, and so must we. For it is there—in the place we resist most—that Christ waits with living water.

What you are is God's gift to you; what you become is your gift to God.

Bridge into Chapter 1

And so we begin. If Samaria is a symbol of where we avoid going, then Scripture itself is the mirror that shows us why we avoid it and the window that reveals who we can become when we walk through it.

This is why Jesus's question matters so deeply: "What do you read there?" (Luke 10:26). Reading Scripture is never just about words; it is about the reader. We do not see the Bible as it is; we see it as we are.

That is where our journey opens.

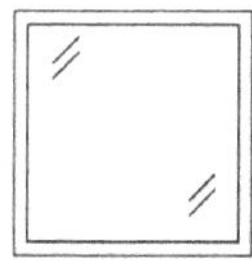

CHAPTER 1

Seeing as We Are

Meditation

As author Anaïs Nin wrote, "We do not see the world as it is; we see it as we are." The same is true for Scripture. We do not read the Bible as it is in its raw and infinite fullness but as we are, with our histories, our wounds, our hopes, and our worldviews.

Every reading is a mirror. When we open the sacred text, something of ourselves looks back at us. The way we see God's Word is never neutral. It is shaped by the cracks in our lenses and the healing in our souls.

It has been said, "If a donkey looks in the mirror, you can't expect an apostle to be reflected back out." In other words, the fruit of Scripture in our lives depends not just on the words on the page but on the spirit in which we receive them. A diminished mindset will often see only rules, threats, or boundaries. A fixed mindset will cling tightly to its single story, blind to the wider horizon. But an open, integrative mindset will find in Scripture not only itself but a window into God's larger, more spacious world.

Narrative

Luke tells of a lawyer who once stood before Jesus, looking for certainty: "Teacher, . . . what must I do to inherit eternal life?" (Luke 10:25). He wanted an answer he could frame, contain, and master. Jesus answered with another question: "What is written in the law? What do you read there?" (Luke 10:26). Notice carefully. Jesus did not simply ask, "What does the text say?" He asked, "What do you read there?"

That question is still asked of us. We are not passive vessels waiting to be filled with words. We are active readers, interpreters, bringers of ourselves into the dialogue. We never approach the Bible empty-handed. We bring our traditions, our stories, our griefs, and our joys. Some of us come carrying wounds that ache for healing. Others come armored with certainty, afraid of mystery. Still others come curious, longing for a love that expands beyond the familiar.

And so Jesus's question echoes: What do you read there?

The lawyer replied with the Shema: "You shall love the Lord your God with all your heart and with all your soul and with all your strength and with all your mind and your neighbor as yourself" (Luke 10:27). He had the right words but perhaps not yet the right posture. For when pressed, his heart narrowed: "And who is my neighbor?" (Luke 10:29). His lens was still cracked with self-justification.

In response, Jesus gave not a rule but a story—the parable of the Good Samaritan. And in that story, a mirror became a window.

Practice: A Spiritual Reading Exercise

Take Luke 10:25–37 and read it slowly three times.

First, in a mirror: Who am I in this story? The lawyer? The wounded traveler? The priest or Levite who walks by? The Samaritan?

Second, as a window: Where does this story open into God's larger world? What new horizon does it show?

Third, as a call: What action or posture is the Spirit inviting me to embody today?

Journal a short reflection after each reading.

Close with silence, asking God to show you how you are reading and how God is inviting you to see differently.

Reflection Questions

- What assumptions, experiences, or fears do I bring when I open the Bible?
- When have I read Scripture only as a mirror, only seeing myself?
- When have I read it as a window, seeing God's wider world?
- How is Jesus asking me, even today, "What do you read there?"

Closing Prayer

God of truth and mercy,
You know the lenses I carry and the stories I bring.
When I open Your Word, let it be both mirror and window—
a mirror that shows me who I am and a window that shows me
who I can become in You.
Amen.

Theme: "We do not see the world as it is; we see it as we are."
Scripture: Luke 10:25–37 (introduction to Good Samaritan)
Meditation: How our worldview, mindset, and wounds color the way we see Scripture

Reflection Question

In what ways do I read my assumptions into the text?

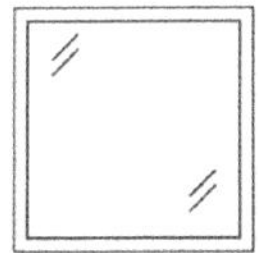

CHAPTER 2

Mirror Reading

Meditation

The first movement of spiritual reading is mirror-reading. Scripture, before it opens as a window to God's world, first reflects the state of our own soul. The text meets us where we are, revealing our hidden motives, our fears, and our hopes.

The truth is sobering. We often find in Scripture what we bring to it. A fixed mindset will see only what confirms its certainties. A wounded spirit will see mostly judgment. But an open, seeking heart will find, in the same words, a mirror of grace.

When we read the Bible, we are never simply reading it; it is reading us.

Narrative

In Luke's story, the lawyer stands before Jesus with the question: "What must I do to inherit eternal life?" (Luke 10:25). His words are religious, but beneath them is fear of not being enough, fear of being wrong. He is not seeking God so much as he is seeking to justify himself.

Jesus listens and then turns the question back: "What do you read there?" (Luke 10:26). It is as though Jesus is holding up a mirror. The law is not just text on a scroll; it reflects the reader's own posture. The lawyer answers correctly—love God, love your neighbor—but the mirror shows his hesitation. He cannot yet see himself in that love. His next question exposes the crack: "And who is my neighbor?" (Luke 10:29).

So it is with us. Scripture holds up a mirror, showing both our faith and our resistance, our desire and our limits. In that mirror, God does not shame us but invites us to honesty.

Practice: Mirror Reading

Choose a passage: Begin again with Luke 10:25–29

Hold it like a mirror: Read it slowly and ask:

- What does this reveal about me?
- What fears or desires do I bring into this story?
- Where do I see my need to justify myself?

Notice your reactions. Do you want to argue? To excuse yourself? To turn away? Write these down in a journal.

Receive the truth gently. Remember, God does not use the mirror to condemn but to invite.

Reflection Questions

- When I read Scripture, do I notice myself rushing to defend or justify my position?
- Where does the mirror of Scripture show me resistance?
- Can I allow God to meet me there with mercy rather than judgment?

Closing Prayer

Mirror of my soul,
You see me more clearly than I see myself.
When I look into Your Word, do not let me turn away quickly.
Show me my fear, my self-justification, my longing to be loved.
And let Your mercy be the truest reflection in which I rest.
Amen.

Theme: Scripture first reflects us before it transforms us.
Image: "If a donkey looks into a mirror, you can't expect an apostle to look back"
Practice: Journaling with Scripture as self-disclosure
Reflection: What do I see in myself when I encounter this story?

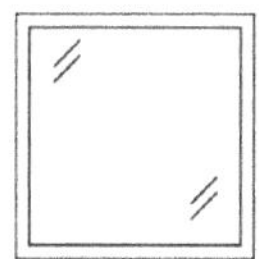

CHAPTER 3
Window Reading

Meditation

If mirror-reading shows us who we are, then window-reading shows us who God is and what God is doing in the world. The mirror turns us inward, but the window opens us outward.

The Bible is never only a private book of reflection. It is also a window into God's reign, a view into a reality wider than our own. Through it we glimpse a kingdom where mercy triumphs over judgment, where outsiders become neighbors, and where love breaks every boundary.

A mirror tells the truth of my present condition; a window invites me into God's future possibility.

Narrative

In Luke 10, Jesus answers the lawyer's narrow question: "Who is my neighbor?" (v. 29), not with a definition but with a story—a traveler, beaten and left for dead; a priest and a Levite, both passing by; and finally, a Samaritan—despised, distrusted, and dismissed—who becomes the very face of mercy.

This is more than a moral tale. It is a window into God's new world where the labels we cling to collapse under the weight of compassion. For Jesus's hearers, the Samaritan was not supposed to be the hero. Yet throughout this story, a window opened onto a kingdom where neighborliness is defined not by blood or tribe but by mercy.

When we read the Bible only as mirror, we risk circling endlessly around ourselves. When we read it as a window, we are drawn beyond ourselves into the horizon of God's love.

Practice: Window Reading

Read Luke 10:30–37 slowly.

Imagine yourself looking through a window into the story:

- What world do you see on the other side?
- What surprises you about the way Jesus reorders expectations?
- Where do you glimpse mercy at work?

Step back from the window. Ask, "What does this vision of God's reign ask of me here and now?"

Reflection Questions

- When I read Scripture, do I stop at the mirror, or do I let it open into a window?
- What new world does this passage reveal to me?
- Who in my life is "the Samaritan"—the one I would least expect to be the face of God's mercy?

Closing Prayer

God of mercy and surprise,
Open the windows of Your Word to me.
Let me see beyond my narrow definitions,
beyond my familiar boundaries,
into the wide world of Your love.
Through Christ, who is both mirror and window,
Amen.

Theme: Scripture opens onto God's larger reality
Practice: Lectio Divina with the Good Samaritan

Reflection Question

What new horizon is revealed when I read not just for me but for the world?

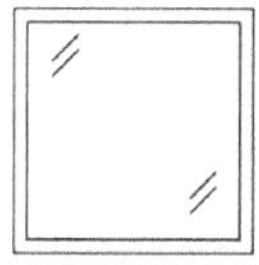

CHAPTER 4

The Danger of a Single Story

Meditation

Stories shape us. They are the lenses through which we see ourselves, others, and even God. But a single story can be dangerous. When we cling to only one version of reality—one interpretation, one cultural lens, one fixed mindset—we shrink the spaciousness of God into the narrowness of our fears.

Chimamanda Ngozi Adichie once said, "The single story creates stereotypes. And the problem with stereotypes is not that they are untrue, but that they are incomplete." The Bible, too, suffers when we reduce it to one story: a rule book, a weapon, or a private escape hatch. Scripture resists such reduction. It is not one story but many-layered narratives woven together, opening us to the many ways God meets us.

When we live inside a single story, we risk missing the surprising ways grace appears, often from the very people or places we least expect.

Narrative

Consider again the Samaritan. In Luke 10, he is the stranger who becomes a neighbor through mercy. But that is not the only Samaritan story.

Later, in Luke 17:11–19, Jesus heals ten lepers. All are cleansed, but only one returns to give thanks, and Luke makes sure we notice: "He prostrated himself at Jesus's feet and thanked him, giving thanks to him. And he was a Samaritan" (Luke 17:16).

First, the Samaritan is the merciful neighbor; now the Samaritan is the grateful worshiper. Together, these stories shatter the single story of "enemy." To the Jewish imagination of the time, Samaritans were heretics, outsiders, and untouchables. But in Jesus's storytelling, they become vessels of mercy and faith.

The mirror shows us our prejudices; the window shows us God's wider kingdom. And both warn us to beware of the single story.

Practice: Breaking the Single Story

Choose a group of people in your life or community whom you find hard to understand or trust.

Write down the "single story" you tend to believe about them.

Now reread Luke 17:16. Ask, "What if grace, gratitude, or mercy were to appear from this very place I dismiss?"

Spend time in prayer asking God to show you the "second story"—the hidden gift that might come from where you least expect it.

Reflection Questions

- Where in my life do I reduce people or situations to a single story?
- What "second story" of grace or mercy have I overlooked?
- How does the Samaritan in Luke 17 invite me to see beyond stereotypes into gratitude?

Closing Prayer

God of many stories,
Save me from the danger of a single story
where I am tempted to dismiss.
Open my eyes to mercy
where I am tempted to reduce.
Open my heart to gratitude.
Let me see in every neighbor,
even the unexpected Samaritan,
the reflection of Your kingdom.
Amen.

Theme: Fixed mindsets, diminished imagination, and broken lenses
Meditation: Scarcity versus abundance mindsets in reading
Reflection: Where am I tempted to narrow God's story into one single thread?

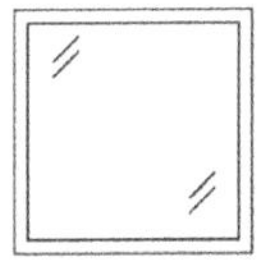

CHAPTER 5
An Integrative Mindset

Meditation

A fixed mindset clings to certainty, to one interpretation, to a single story. But an integrative mindset holds many threads at once. It knows that truth is not diminished by being seen from different angles. Rather, it is revealed more fully.

To read Scripture with an integrative mindset is to read with humility and openness. It is to listen for voices other than our own, to welcome perspectives from different cultures, and to allow the Spirit to weave together meaning in community. The gospel itself is integrative: Jew and Gentile, slave and free, male and female, Samaritan and Jew. When these voices converge, the kingdom is revealed in its fullness.

Narrative

Imagine standing at a stained-glass window. From outside, it looks dull, a collage of dark fragments. But step inside, and light floods through. Suddenly the fragments are revealed as a radiant image.

So it is with Scripture. Each cultural voice, each interpretive tradition, is like a fragment of colored glass. Alone it may look incomplete. But when the light of the Spirit shines through the whole, it becomes beauty and truth.

Jesus modeled this integrative way of seeing. When He asked the lawyer in Luke 10, "What do you read there?" He invited him to consider not just the words of the law but the broader reality of love. And when He lifted the Samaritan as the neighbor or the Samaritan leper as the grateful one, He integrated voices long excluded. The kingdom of God is not built on one narrow lens but on the gathering of many.

Practice: Reading with Many Voices

Choose a passage (again, Luke 10 or 17).

Read it through three lenses:

- Your own immediate reading
- How someone from another culture or tradition might hear it
- How someone on the margins of society today might receive it

Notice what shifts. Write down insights that emerge only when multiple voices are honored.

Pray with the image of stained glass—fragments becoming whole when lit by God's Spirit.

Reflection Questions

- Do I tend to cling to one interpretation of Scripture, or am I open to many voices?
- How does hearing Scripture through another culture or tradition expand my understanding?
- What does it mean for me personally to practice "integrative seeing"?

Closing Prayer

God of many colors and many voices,
Break my attachment to a single story.
Shine Your Spirit through the fragments of Scripture,
through the voices of my neighbors,
until the whole becomes radiant with Your light.
Make me an integrative reader
so that I may see not just myself
but the wideness of Your kingdom.
Amen.

Theme: Multicultural, many-layered, open reading
Practice: Reading a passage through multiple voices (historical, theological, cultural)
Reflection: How does my neighbor's lens open the Scripture in a way mine cannot?

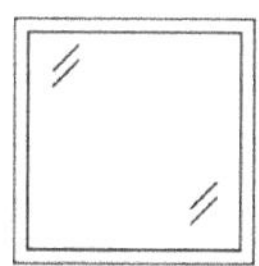

CHAPTER 6

Construction

Meditation

Every spiritual journey begins with construction. We are handed stories, traditions, and foundations from which we build a sense of meaning. These early frameworks shape how we first encounter Scripture and God.

For some, this foundation is solid and nurturing. For others, it is rigid or even harmful. But construction is necessary. It gives us something to stand on. And Jesus Himself begins here: with the great commandments.

"You shall love the Lord your God with all your heart and with all your soul and with all your strength and with all your mind and your neighbor as yourself" (Luke 10:27).

This is the bedrock on which the rest of our journey stands. Without love of God and neighbor, the house of faith has no foundation.

Narrative

The lawyer, when asked by Jesus, quotes the Shema—the central prayer of Jewish faith: love of God. Then he adds the command from Leviticus: love of neighbor. Together, these form the cornerstone of Jesus's own teaching.

This is construction. Before we wrestle with difficult questions, before we dismantle or reconstruct, we must know the foundation: love—not as sentiment but as ethic; not as feeling but as practice.

Think of a child learning to build with blocks. The base must be firm; otherwise, the tower will topple. In the same way, our spiritual reading must begin with a grounding truth: God is love, and we are called to live in that love toward others.

Practice: Naming Your Foundations

Reflect on your own story of faith. What "building blocks" were handed to you in your early years (Scripture, hymns, prayers, traditions)?

Which of these blocks remain firm in your life today? Which has shifted or crumbled?

Write down your own "foundation statement" of faith, a few sentences that express your grounding in love of God and neighbor.

Pray over this statement, asking God to strengthen what is life-giving and to heal what is cracked.

Reflection Questions

- What foundations of love were laid for me in my spiritual upbringing?
- Where have those foundations been life-giving, and where have they been limiting?
- How might I return to the great commandments as the grounding center of my faith?

Closing Prayer

God of love,
You are the foundation of my life.
Where my blocks are steady, bless them.
Where they are cracked, heal them.
Where they are missing, restore them.
Let the house of my faith be built on love of You
and love of neighbor,
for without these, I cannot stand.
Amen.

Theme: Building foundations: Love God and love your neighbor.

Practice: Naming the building blocks of faith that first shaped me

Reflection: What foundation is already present in my story?

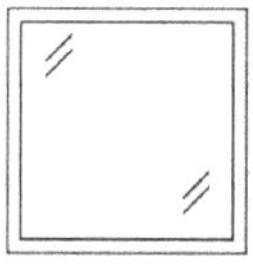

CHAPTER 7

Deconstruction

Meditation

Deconstruction is not destruction. It is the necessary work of asking questions, taking apart what no longer holds, and allowing faith to breathe again. Every building, no matter how strong its foundation, must be inspected. When cracks appear, when walls no longer shelter but suffocate, we need the courage to take them down.

Scripture itself invites this process. In Luke 10:29, the lawyer, having affirmed the foundation of love, cannot resist asking, "And who is my neighbor?" Behind that question is both fear and hope—fear that love may demand too much and hope that love might still be possible.

Deconstruction is the holy work of exposing our limits, doubts, and blind spots so God's larger truth can break in.

Narrative

The lawyer's question is our own: Who belongs? Who counts? How far does love stretch?

For him, the cracks showed in his boundary lines. Surely "neighbor" could not mean everyone. Surely it must mean those like him—safe, familiar, manageable. His construction was too narrow to contain the wideness of God's mercy.

So Jesus tells a story that dismantles his categories. The priest and Levite, religious insiders, fail to embody love. The Samaritan, despised outsider, becomes the neighbor. The story collapses the lawyer's walls, deconstructing his single story of who deserves compassion.

In that moment, the lawyer's faith is not destroyed. It is open.

Practice: Holy Questioning

Choose a teaching of Scripture you once accepted easily but now find difficult or limiting.

Write down the honest questions that rise in you. (What troubles me? What seems too narrow? What doesn't fit anymore?)

Pray with these questions, not demanding answers but allowing them to be held in God's presence.

Imagine Jesus saying to you, as He did to the lawyer, "What do you read there?" Listen for where your interpretation needs to be stretched.

Reflection Questions

- What parts of my inherited faith no longer hold for me?
- Where do I feel the need to justify myself, as the lawyer did?
- Can I trust that my questions are not threats to God but invitations into deeper truth?

Closing Prayer

God of truth,
Give me courage to ask hard questions.
Where my walls are too narrow,
break them open.
Where my love is too small,
stretch it wider.
Meet me in my doubt,
and show me that deconstruction
is not the end of faith
but the doorway into Your mercy.
Amen.

Theme: Honest question: "Who is my neighbor?"
Meditation: Wrestling with doubt and critique as sacred work
Reflection: What parts of my story or tradition need questioning?

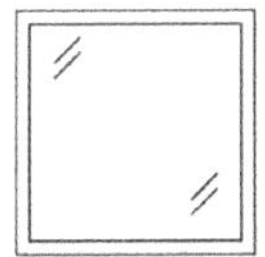

CHAPTER 8
Reconstruction

Meditation

Deconstruction clears the ground, but it cannot be the final word. If all we do is dismantle, we are left with rubble. Reconstruction is the Spirit's gift of renewal, rebuilding faith not as it once was but as it can become.

This is not a return to old certainties but a reweaving of truth, love, and mystery into a larger whole. The Bible itself models this rhythm: exile followed by return, crucifixion followed by resurrection, tearing down followed by new creation.

Reconstruction is where faith breathes again, where the fragments of our story are joined with God's story in a way that is more honest, more merciful, and more spacious than before.

Narrative

The lawyer's world has been dismantled. His categories of "neighbor" have collapsed under the weight of Jesus's parable. Now comes the invitation to rebuild.

"Which of these three, do you think, was a neighbor to the man who fell into the hands of robbers?" (Luke 10:36).

The lawyer answers, "The one who showed him mercy" (Luke 10:37).

Notice the shift. The lawyer does not even say the word *Samaritan*. Perhaps the word still sticks in his throat. But he has seen enough to know the truth, that mercy is the new foundation. The story he once resisted has become the story he cannot escape.

This is reconstruction. The law of love, once narrow, now stretches wide enough to include even an enemy. The walls are rebuilt, but this time with windows and doors open to grace.

Practice: Rebuilding with Mercy

Return to a part of your faith you once deconstructed.

Ask, "What truth remains, even after my old certainty has crumbled?"

Write down how mercy might be the new foundation for this part of your faith.

Pray for courage to live from this reconstructed space, not with arrogance but with humility and openness.

Reflection Questions

- Where has deconstruction left me with rubble?
- What does mercy teach me about rebuilding?
- How can my reconstructed faith be more open, compassionate, and honest than before?

Closing Prayer

God of resurrection,
You never leave me among the ruins.
Where my walls have fallen,
raise up a dwelling place of mercy.
Where my faith has been dismantled,
rebuild it in love.
Let my story be joined to Your story,
not as it once was,
but as it is becoming in Christ.
Amen.

Theme: Reconnecting story and Scripture after disruption
Meditation: From rubble to renewal—discovering a new way of seeing
Reflection: Where have I found God in surprising reconstructions of my faith?

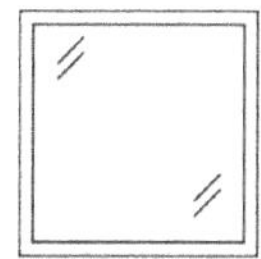

CHAPTER 9

From Mirror to Window

Meditation

Spiritual reading begins with the mirror. We see ourselves—our fears, hopes, questions, and limits—reflected in Scripture. But the mirror is not the destination. It is the starting point.

The Spirit does not leave us staring only at ourselves. The mirror must open into a window, a wider horizon where God's love reshapes not only how we see ourselves but how we see the world.

Mirror-reading asks, "Who am I right now?"

Window-reading asks, "Who am I becoming in Christ?"

Narrative

In the parable of the good Samaritan, the lawyer begins by looking into the mirror of the law. "Love God, love your neighbor." He sees the reflection of duty but also the cracks of self-justification.

Then Jesus holds up a window. "A man was going down from Jerusalem to Jericho" (Luke 10:30). A new world opens. In that world, boundaries collapse. Neighbors are redefined. Mercy becomes the measure of life.

Finally, Jesus asks, "Which of these three . . . was a neighbor?" (Luke 10:36). The mirror of self-examination has become a window into transformation. The lawyer's heart is nudged from "Who is my neighbor?" to "Go and do likewise."

This is the shift: from reflection to vocation, from insight to action, from mirror to window.

Practice: Moving Through the Glass

Mirror: Choose a passage of Scripture (Luke 10:36–37 works beautifully). Ask, "What does this show me about myself right now?"

Window: Ask, "What vision of God's kingdom does this passage reveal?"

Step Through: Ask, "What is one concrete way I can act today so my story reflects this kingdom vision?"

Write down your commitment, no matter how small. Carry it with you into your day.

Reflection Questions

- Where have I lingered too long at the mirror without letting it open into a window?
- How does Scripture's vision of mercy stretch my understanding of who I can become?
- What small action today could move me from reflection to transformation?

Closing Prayer

God of transformation,
Do not let me stop at the mirror.
Open windows where I see only walls.
Give me courage to step through the glass,
to live not only in reflection
but in the wideness of Your love.
Shape me into the person I am becoming in Christ
for the sake of my neighbor and Your kingdom.
Amen.

Theme: Moving from "how I am" to "how I can become"
Practice: Rereading Luke 10 with this lens
Reflection: How is the Spirit inviting me to shift from self-reflection to outward compassion?

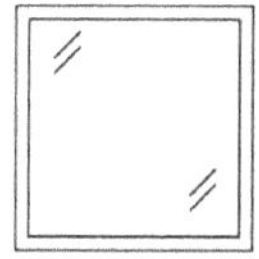

CHAPTER 10

Go and Do Likewise

Meditation

The journey of spiritual reading is never complete until it bears fruit in action. Reflection without movement is unfinished; vision without embodiment is incomplete. The Bible does not simply call us to think differently; it calls us to live differently.

At the end of the good Samaritan story, Jesus does not offer applause for the lawyer's correct answer. He simply says, "Go and do likewise" (Luke 10:37).

The point of Scripture is not only to inform us but to transform us into people of mercy.

Narrative

The lawyer asked, "Who is my neighbor?"

Jesus answered with a story that turned the question around: "To whom will you be a neighbor?"

That shift changes everything. The lawyer had hoped for a limit, a boundary that would let him measure who deserved his compassion. Jesus gave him a calling, a boundless invitation to become mercy in the flesh.

The Samaritan, the outsider, shows us what this looks like:

- He saw the wounded man.
- He was moved with pity.
- He acted with care.

Seeing, feeling, acting—that is the rhythm of mercy. It is the rhythm of God's own love.

And it is the rhythm into which Jesus invites us: Go and do likewise.

Practice: Embodying Mercy

Look Around: Take one day to practice awareness. Who is on the roadside of your life—overlooked, wounded, or ignored?

Be Moved: Let yourself feel compassion rather than avoidance. Pause and notice what stirs in you.

Take One Step: Do something tangible—a word of kindness, an act of generosity, a willingness to stop and listen.

At the end of the day, reflect: Where did I meet Christ in the neighbor I chose to love?

Reflection Questions

- Who is lying on the roadside of my life today?
- What keeps me from stopping—fear, busyness, prejudice, indifference?
- What small act of mercy can I embody this week that reflects Christ's love?

Closing Prayer

Christ of the roadside,
You meet me in every neighbor I am tempted to ignore.
You call me not to pass by
but to see, to feel, to act with mercy.
Give me eyes that notice,
a heart that is moved,
and hands willing to serve.
Let my reading of Scripture
become the living of Scripture
until my life itself says,
"Go and do likewise."
Amen.

Theme: The fruit of integrative reading is embodied mercy
Meditation: Becoming the neighbor

Reflection Questions

- Who is on the roadside in my life today?
- How can my reading of Scripture move into merciful action?

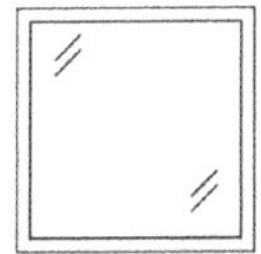

EPILOGUE:

The Journey of Mirror and Window

We began with a mirror. Scripture first reflects who we are—our questions, our fears, our hidden desires. In its pages we glimpse ourselves more honestly than we might like. A lawyer justifying himself, a priest passing by, a Levite distracted, a Samaritan surprising us with compassion—these are not only their stories; they are ours.

But the mirror was never meant to hold us forever. Slowly it became a window, opening onto God's larger world. Through Scripture, we glimpsed a kingdom where mercy triumphs over boundaries, where outsiders become neighbors, and where gratitude rises from unexpected places—even the lips of a Samaritan who falls at Jesus's feet.

Along the way, we discovered the danger of a single story and the gift of an integrative mindset. We saw how faith moves through the rhythm of construction, deconstruction, and reconstruction—not as loss but as renewal. We learned that the Bible is not just a book of words to be analyzed but a living conversation, a stained-glass window shining with light when many voices are welcomed.

And then we reached the threshold: from mirror to window, from reflection to transformation. Jesus's final word was not a doctrine but an invitation: "Go and do likewise."

This is where all spiritual reading leads us—to lives of mercy, to neighbors who notice, to hearts that are moved to hands that bind wounds, to faith that is not only believed but embodied.

A Final Reflection

- Where is your Samaria, the place you avoid but where Christ waits with living water?
- What mirrors has Scripture held before you on this journey?
- What windows has the Spirit opened, calling you into a wider love?
- And what will it mean for you, in your own time and place, to "go and do likewise"?

A Blessing for the Reader

May the Word you have read become the Word you live.
May your eyes see both the mirror of truth and the window of mercy.
May your heart be spacious enough to hold many stories yet anchored enough to rest in God's love.
May your questions lead you not to fear but to wisdom.
And may your life become a parable, a story of mercy in which Christ Himself is revealed.
Go now and do likewise.

Book 'Graphe' Four

A Spiritual Reading of John 3 From Night to New Birth: Narrative Spirituality

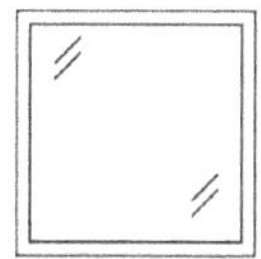

CHAPTER 1

Nightfall: Nicodemus Comes in the Dark

Now there was a Pharisee named Nicodemus, a leader of the Jews. He came to Jesus by night and said to him, "Rabbi, we know that you are a teacher who has come from God, for no one can do these signs that you do unless God is with that person."

—John 3:1–2

Meditation

Night is not just a time of day; it is a condition of the soul. It is the hour of secrecy, of hidden questions, of fear mixed with longing. Nicodemus comes to Jesus under the cover of darkness. He is curious but cautious, hungry but hesitant.

We know this night well. It is the night of unanswered questions. The night when our faith feels fragile. The night when we cannot yet risk being seen in the light of truth.

And yet night is also holy. It is in the night that Nicodemus begins his journey. It is in the night that many of us first dare to approach God honestly. The darkness is not our enemy. It is the place where questions are born and where we can see the first glimmer of dawn.

Narrative

Imagine Nicodemus walking through the quiet streets of Jerusalem. The lamps are dim; the city is asleep. He pulls his cloak tighter, hoping not to be noticed. He is respected—a teacher, a leader of the Jews. To be seen with Jesus would raise eyebrows, perhaps even endanger his reputation.

And yet something in him cannot stay away. The signs Jesus has performed, the authority in His voice, the unsettling hope that perhaps God is closer than he thought—these have drawn him out of hiding.

At last, he arrives and finds Jesus awake. Their conversation begins not with confrontation but with a confession: "Rabbi, we know you are a teacher who has come from God" (John 3:2). It is a timid beginning, but a beginning nonetheless.

So it is for us. Our first steps toward deeper faith are often small, uncertain, and half-hidden. We will come at night, but we will come.

Practice: Naming Your Night

Find a quiet place and sit in stillness. Dim the lights if possible.
Ask yourself, "What is the 'night' I am living in right now?"
Is it a night of questions I am afraid to ask?
A night of doubt I don't want to admit?
A night of longing I can't yet speak aloud?
Write down one sentence that names your night honestly.
Offer that sentence to God in prayer, just as Nicodemus brought his hesitant words to Jesus.

Reflection Questions

- Why do you think Nicodemus came at night? What fears or risks kept him hidden?
- What does "night" symbolize in your own life right now?
- How might you see your night not only as darkness but as a holy beginning?

Closing Prayer

Christ of the night,
You meet me in the shadows where I hide.
You do not despise my fear
but welcome me as I am.
As I come with questions,
as I come with hesitations,
meet me in the dark and give me courage.
Let this night become the doorway to dawn
until I see Your light with new eyes.
Amen.

Meditation: Why Nicodemus approaches Jesus at night—fear, secrecy, longing
Narrative: A reimagining of that midnight meeting
Theme: Night as the space of questions, uncertainty, and spiritual hunger

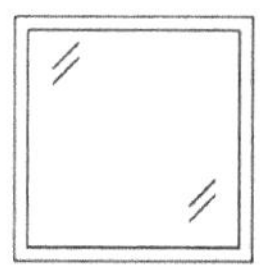

CHAPTER 2

The Teacher of Israel and the Teacher from God

"Rabbi, we know that you are a teacher who has come from God; for no one can do these signs that you do apart from the presence of God." . . . Jesus answered him, "Are you a teacher of Israel, and yet you do not understand these things?"

—John 3:2, 10

Meditation

Nicodemus comes as a teacher, a man respected for his knowledge, authority, and mastery of Scripture. He addresses Jesus as Rabbi, acknowledging Him as a fellow teacher, perhaps even as more than a teacher.

Yet Jesus gently exposes a gap: Knowledge is not the same as understanding. Nicodemus knows the texts, but he has not yet entered their depths. He clings to literal categories when Jesus invites him into symbolic truth.

This is often our struggle. We made mistakes in the information for transformation. We equate knowing about God with knowing God. But the Spirit cannot be mastered like a textbook. The Spirit must be entered, experienced, and lived.

Narrative

Picture the two of them in conversation. Nicodemus, the elder teacher, leans forward with careful words: "Rabbi, we know that you are a teacher who has come from God" (John 3:2). He speaks with authority and knowledge as though offering a conclusion.

Jesus listens but then turns the ground beneath him: "Are you the teacher of Israel, and yet you do not understand these things?" (John 3:10). It is not a rebuke as much as an invitation. Jesus does not shame Nicodemus, but He does call him beyond the limits of literal thinking.

Nicodemus has spent his life teaching others, but tonight he must learn again. He must become a student in the school of Spirit.

Practice: From Knowing to Understanding

Take a passage of Scripture that you "know" well (John 3:16, the Lord's Prayer, Psalm 23).

Write down everything you already know about it—what you've been taught and how it has been explained.

Now pause. Ask God, "What do you want me to understand differently today?"

Read the passage again, slowly this time, not to confirm your knowledge but to receive something new.

Journal one insight that moves from the head into the heart.

Reflection Questions

- Where in my faith do I confuse knowledge with understanding?
- How does Jesus's invitation challenge me to read beyond the literal?
- What does it mean for me to become a student again, even in areas where I feel like a teacher?

Closing Prayer

Teacher of teachers,
You are patient with my knowledge
and gentle with my limits.
Where I cling to information,
draw me into transformation.
Where I am proud of what I know,
teach me what I do not yet understand.
Make me Your student again
so that my learning leads to love
and my knowing leads to life.
Amen.

Meditation

Nicodemus knows the Law but senses something deeper.

Theme: The limits of literal knowledge versus the openness of spiritual wisdom

Practice: Reflection on what I "know" versus what I am still afraid to ask

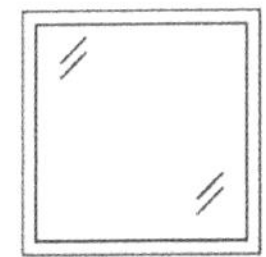

CHAPTER 3

Born Again / Born from Above

Meditation

We often hear this passage through the filter of modern religious language: "How do I get born again?" But notice that Nicodemus never asks that question. He doesn't come seeking a formula for salvation. He comes with an affirmation: "Rabbi, we know that you are a teacher who has come from God" (John 3:2).

That statement itself is faith. It is not fully understood, but it is recognition. Nicodemus, a respected leader, risks his reputation to acknowledge that God is present in Jesus.

It is Jesus who brings up the language of new birth, and perhaps not as a challenge—"you must do this"—but as a recognition: Nicodemus, seeing me as from God is already the evidence that Spirit is moving in you.

To be "born from above" is not about mastering a ritual or reciting the right words. It is about awakening to the life of God already stirring and moving us from knowing about God to experiencing God's presence in Jesus.

Narrative

Nicodemus begins in the only way he knows how: carefully, respectfully, affirming what is safe to say. "We know that you are from God." It may sound small, but for him it is bold. It is the confession of a man whose heart is opening, whose night is not as dark as it once was.

Jesus hears this affirmation and names it for what it is: birth pangs of the Spirit. "No one can see the kingdom of God without being born from above" (John 3:3). Nicodemus' words show that he already sees, even if dimly. He recognizes God's presence where others see only a threat.

When Nicodemus stumbles over the literal, Jesus pushes him gently toward the symbolic. He tells Nicodemus that this is not about reentering the womb. It is about entering into life. He told him that what he felt stirring is Spirit, and that is birth from above.

Practice: Receiving Faith as a Gift

Reread John 3:1–7. Pay attention: Nicodemus never asks a question about being born again. He begins with affirmation.

Ask yourself: Where in my life am I already affirming God's presence, even without full understanding?

Write one sentence of affirmation: "I know you are from God because . . ." Fill in the blank with a place you have glimpsed God's presence.

Pray with gratitude, receiving your affirmation not as your achievement but as Spirit's gift.

Reflection Questions

- Have I misread this passage as a demand for a how-to rather than hearing it as Jesus's recognition of Spirit already at work?
- What is the difference between knowing about God and experiencing God?
- How might my affirmations of who Jesus is already be signs of new birth in me?

Closing Prayer

Jesus, Teacher from God,
You receive my hesitant affirmations as seeds of faith.
You show me that even in my questions,
Spirit is already moving.
Let me not reduce Your words to a formula,
but hear them as recognition:
new life is stirring,
and I am being born from above.
Amen.

Meditation: Literal misunderstanding (physical birth) versus symbolic invitation (spiritual rebirth)
Theme: How symbolic language shifts us from control to mystery
Reflection: Where do I cling to literal answers instead of symbolic truth?

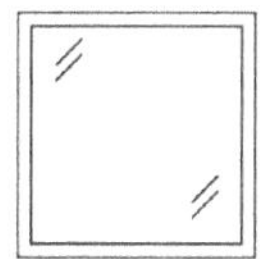

CHAPTER 4

Water and Spirit

Very truly, I tell you, no one can enter the kingdom of God without being born of water and Spirit. What is born of the flesh is flesh, and what is born of the Spirit is spirit.

—John 3:5–6

Meditation

Nicodemus was a teacher of Israel. He knew the Scriptures. He knew the symbols. Water, for him, was purification, cleansing before worship, and ritual for holiness. Spirit was breath, the life of God hovering over creation, the wind that filled the prophets.

But Jesus is saying something more. These are not just religious symbols to be known. They are realities to be experienced. Water must wash the heart, not just the hands. Spirit must move the soul, not just the imagination.

Religion teaches us about water and Spirit. Faith allows us to be born of water and Spirit. The difference is as vast as reading about the ocean and being swept into its waves.

Narrative

Nicodemus shifts uneasily as Jesus speaks. He knows the rituals of water well. He has taught them to others. He knows the stories of Spirit—the prophets, the wind, and the fire. But what Jesus is describing feels less like teaching and more like transformation.

It is as if Jesus is saying, "Nicodemus, you already see me as from God; that is Spirit at work. But you cannot just explain these things; you must live them. You must let the water of renewal and the wind of Spirit carry you into new life."

Nicodemus came at night to affirm what he knew. Jesus invites him to awaken to what he can only experience.

Practice: From Symbol to Experience

Water: Fill a small bowl or glass with water. Hold it in your hands. Notice its coolness, clarity, and life. Ask, "Where in my life do I long to be cleansed, renewed, and refreshed?"

Spirit: Sit quietly. Breathe slowly and deeply. Feel the rise and fall of your breath. Ask, "Where in my life do I need the wind of Spirit to move freely?"

Pray: "God, let me not only know these symbols but live them. Wash me. Breathe in me."

Reflection Questions

- What is the difference between knowing the symbols of faith and experiencing them?
- Where do I need to let water (renewal) and Spirit (freedom) move in me, not just as ideas but as realities?
- How does this passage invite me to trust Spirit more than my own understanding?

Closing Prayer

Living Water,
Breath of God,
I know your symbols, but I long for Your life.
Wash me where I am weary.
Breathe in me where I am dry.
Let your Spirit be more than words on a page.
Let it be new birth within me
so that I live not only by knowledge
but by Your renewing grace.
Amen.

Meditation: The dual imagery of cleansing and renewal
Theme: Water and Spirit as the elements of transformation
Practice: Prayer with water as symbol of both cleansing and birth

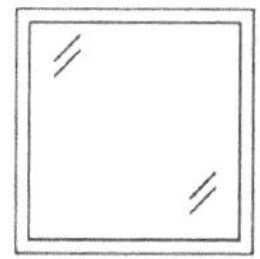

CHAPTER 5

The Wind Blows Where It Chooses

The wind blows where it chooses, and you hear the sound of it, but you do not know where it comes from or where it goes. So it is with everyone born of the Spirit.

—John 3:8

Meditation

The Spirit cannot be pinned down. Like the wind, it is free—uncontained, untamed, and unmeasured. We cannot predict it, control it, or manage it. We can only open ourselves to it.

Nicodemus wants understanding. He wants clarity, categories, and a framework he can teach. But Jesus offers mystery instead. The Spirit will not fit into neat theological boxes. It blows where it wills.

And yet we know when it is present. We hear it rustle in our souls. We see its effects in compassion, in courage, in mercy. The Spirit is unpredictable, but it is never absent.

Narrative

Nicodemus furrows his brow. He wants to nail this down. "How can these things be?" he will soon ask. Jesus smiles, perhaps even with a trace of tenderness, and gestures toward the night air.

"Listen," he says. "The wind stirs through the olive trees, a sound felt more than explained. You hear the wind, but you do not know where it comes from or where it goes. So it is with the Spirit."

Nicodemus feels the breeze on his skin. He cannot trace its origin and cannot predict its destination. But he cannot deny its reality. It is present, moving, and undeniable.

This is what Jesus is offering him—not certainty, but Spirit. Not control, but freedom.

Practice: Listening to the Wind

Go outside or open a window. Sit quietly and listen for the sound of the wind or simply feel your breath moving in and out.

As you listen, reflect: Where in my life am I trying to control what can only be received?

Pray: "Spirit, blow where you will in me. Even if I do not understand, let me feel your movement."

Write a short prayer or poem beginning with these words: "I hear the wind . . ."

Reflection Questions

- Where in my faith do I try to control, predict, or contain God?
- How do I know when the Spirit is moving in me, even if I cannot explain it?
- What might it look like to trust mystery more than certainty?

Closing Prayer

Spirit of the wind,
You are free, and You are near.
I cannot see where You begin
nor where You will carry me.
But I feel Your presence
rustling through my soul.
Unbind me from my need to control,
and let me live with freedom in Your breath.
Amen.

Meditation: Spirit as breath, wind, freedom
Narrative: How unpredictability challenges Nicodemus (and us)
Reflection: Where do I resist the Spirit's freedom?

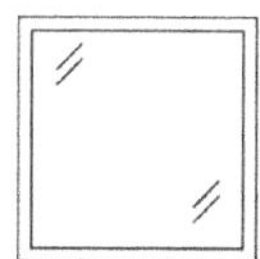

CHAPTER 6

Night Vision: Seeing Beyond the Literal

Nicodemus said to him, "How can these things be?" Jesus answered him, "Are you the teacher of Israel, and yet you do not understand these things? Very truly, I tell you, we speak of what we know and testify to what we have seen, yet you do not receive our testimony. If I have told you about earthly things and you do not believe, how can you believe if I tell you about heavenly things?"

—John 3:9–12

Meditation

Nicodemus has the same struggle we often do: He hears the words, but he cannot yet see the meaning. He wants the kingdom explained in earthly terms, but Jesus is pointing to heavenly realities.

Literal sight is limited. It keeps us bound to what we can measure and prove. Symbolic sight—"night vision"—allows us to see beyond the literal into the deeper truth that Spirit reveals.

We do not fault Nicodemus for stumbling. He is, in truth, no different from us. Faith requires a shift in vision, a way of seeing with the eyes of the heart.

Narrative

Nicodemus shakes his head, bewildered. "How can these things be?" (John 3:9).

Jesus does not dismiss the question, but he names the struggle. "Are you the teacher of Israel, and yet you do not understand these things?" (John 3:10). It is not an insult; it is a reminder. Nicodemus has built his whole life on knowledge, but now he must learn to see differently.

Jesus speaks of water, Spirit, and wind—images that point beyond the literal. But Nicodemus clings to concrete: wombs and rules, beginnings and endings. His sight is sharp, but it is daylight sight. What he needs is night vision, the ability to see the unseen, to trust the Spirit's light even in the dark.

This is the turning point for all of us, to admit that faith is not about control but about seeing through the symbolic in the Spirit.

Practice: Training the Eyes of the Heart

Choose a familiar verse of Scripture (e.g., "The Lord is my shepherd").

First, read it literally. What does it mean on the surface?

Next, read it symbolically. What does "shepherd" mean as a metaphor for God's care in your life today?

Journal what shifts in your understanding when you move from literal sight to symbolic sight.

End by praying, "God, give me eyes of the heart to see beyond the surface into Your Spirit."

Reflection Questions

- Where do I struggle with taking Scripture too literally?
- What symbols or metaphors of faith have helped me see God more deeply?
- How might Jesus be inviting me, like Nicodemus, to expand from earthly categories into heavenly vision?

Closing Prayer

Jesus, Light in the night,
I confess that I cling to what I can measure and explain.
Teach me to see with night vision,
to trust the symbols and metaphors that carry Your truth.
Where I stumble over the literal,
let Your Spirit guide me into deeper sight.
Open the eyes of my heart
that I may see You as You are.
Amen.

This chapter deepens Nicodemus's tension. His literal sight keeps failing, but Jesus is gently training him to see symbolically—with "night vision."

Meditation: Nicodemus's literal lens keeps him from seeing.
Theme: The spiritual life requires symbolic imagination.
Practice: Lectio Divina exercise on "seeing with the eyes of the heart."

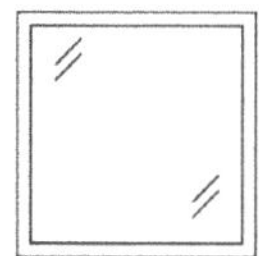

CHAPTER 7

The Serpent Lifted Up

And just as Moses lifted up the serpent in the wilderness, so must the Son of Man be lifted up, that whoever believes in him may have eternal life.

—John 3:14–15

Meditation

This moment must have startled Nicodemus. Jesus reaches back to a troubling story from Israel's past: the bronze serpent lifted in the wilderness (Num. 21:4–9). The people, plagued by venomous snakes, were healed by gazing at a symbol of death transformed into a sign of life.

Why would Jesus invoke such a strange, unsettling image? Because symbols often disturb before they heal. The serpent is not comfortable to look upon; it confronts the people with their fear. And yet it becomes the very channel of God's healing.

So it will be with the Son of Man. Lifted on the cross, He will become for the world both confrontation and healing, both death and life. Literal sight will stumble at the scandal. Symbolic sights will see salvation.

Narrative

Nicodemus listens intently. He knows the story well. His ancestors had murmured against God, and snakes brought death into the camp. Yet the cure was not to kill the serpents but to face the very thing that terrified them. To look upon the lifted serpent was to live.

Now Jesus dares to say, "So the Son of Man must be lifted up" (John 3:14). The image unsettles Nicodemus. To look upon a crucified one as salvation? To see life in what appears to be defeat?

And yet something stirs. Could it be that God works not by avoiding death but by transforming it? Could it be that what we most fear becomes the place of God's healing?

Nicodemus feels the shift. The literal story of serpents becomes a symbol of salvation.

Practice: Facing What Heals

Reflect on a difficult or painful experience in your life. Write it down briefly in a journal.

Ask, "What did I fear most in that moment?"

Now ask, "What healing or growth has come through facing it rather than avoiding it?"

Pray, "Christ lifted up, help me see how you transform even what I fear into a channel of life."

Reflection Questions

- Why do you think Jesus chose such an unsettling image to explain eternal life?
- Where in my life am I being asked to face what I fear rather than turn away?
- How does the cross become for me not just a symbol of suffering but also of healing and hope?

Closing Prayer

Christ lifted up,
You transform what terrifies into what heals.
You take death and turn it into life,
fear and turn it into courage,
shame and turn it into grace.
Lift my eyes to You
that I may live,
and let my gaze be healed by Your love.
Amen.

With this chapter, the conversation between Jesus and Nicodemus turns toward the cross—unsettling at first but symbolic of transformation.

Meditation: Jesus uses a strange Old Testament image (Numbers 21).
Theme: Symbols that disturb us can also heal us.
Reflection: What images in Scripture unsettle me but carry hidden healing?

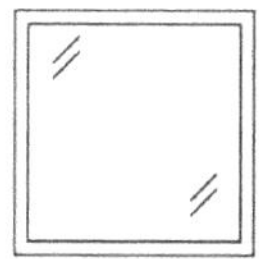

CHAPTER 8

For God So Loved the World

For God so loved the world that he gave his only Son, so that everyone who believes in him may not perish but may have eternal life. Indeed, God did not send the Son into the world to condemn the world, but in order that the world might be saved through him.

—John 3:16–17

Meditation

If there is a heartbeat to John's Gospel, it is here: God so loved the world. Not God condemned, not God despised, not God abandoned, but God loved.

This is the truth Nicodemus most needed to hear and perhaps the truth we most resist. We expect judgment, but we are met with mercy. We fear rejection, but we are embraced with love.

And notice the scope: not just God so loved Israel or the righteous or the religious, but God so loved the world. The love that births new life is not narrow but expansive; it is not conditional but abundant.

To be born from above is to step into this love, to let it flow through us as a gift, a healing, and a calling.

Narrative

Nicodemus listens in silence. The images of water, Spirit, wind, and serpent all swirl in his mind. But then Jesus speaks words that pierce through the confusion: "For God so loved the world . . ."

The words land with power. For years Nicodemus has known a God of covenant and law. He has feared a God of judgment and exile. But here is a God who loves without limit, who sends not to condemn but to save.

Nicodemus feels his night opening to dawn. He came seeking knowledge. He finds love.

Practice: Receiving Love Without Condition

Sit quietly and repeat this phrase slowly: "For God so loved the world."

Replace "the world" with your own name: "For God so loved [your name] . . ."

Let the words rest in you, not as a requirement but as a gift.

Write a short prayer of gratitude beginning with "For God so loved me that . . ."

Reflection Questions

- Have I truly believed that God's love is expansive—for the whole world and for me?
- How has my faith sometimes been shaped more by fear of condemnation than by trust in love?
- What difference does it make that God's love comes first, before my understanding, my worthiness, or my response?

Closing Prayer

God of love,
You so loved the world that You gave,
not to condemn but to save.
Help me to trust Your love,
not as an idea but as my foundation.
Let me live as one who is loved,
and let that love flow through me
into the world You hold so dear.
Amen.

This chapter shifts the tone from mystery and symbol to love and gift—the climax of Jesus's words to Nicodemus.

Meditation: The heart of John's Gospel in one verse
Theme: Love not as abstraction but as embodied gift
Practice: Writing a prayer of gratitude that begins "For God so loved me that . . ."

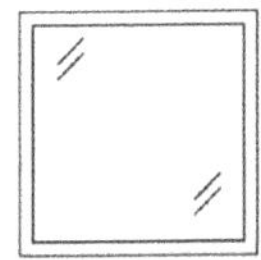

CHAPTER 9

Light Has Come into the World

And this is the judgment, that the light has come into the world, and people loved darkness rather than light because their deeds were evil. For all who do evil hate the light and do not come to the light, so that their deeds may not be exposed. But those who do what is true come to the light, so that it may be clearly seen that their deeds have been done in God.

—John 3:19–21

Meditation

John's Gospel is a Gospel of contrast: night and day, flesh and Spirit, death and life, darkness and light. Nicodemus began his journey at night—literally and symbolically. But the conversation with Jesus presses him toward the dawn.

The judgment is not that God condemns but that we resist light. We hid, afraid of being seen. Yet the invitation remains: Come into the light, not to be shamed but to be revealed as God's beloved.

The shift from night to day is not about becoming flawless. It is about stepping out of fear and secrecy into the radiance of love.

Narrative

Nicodemus feels the weight of the words. He came under cover of night, afraid of being seen. And now Jesus speaks of light. He describes a choice that is less about punishment and more about presence—to remain in darkness or to step into light.

The light reveals. It exposes, but not to humiliate. It uncovers so that healing can begin, so that life can be lived openly in God.

Nicodemus' heart wrestles. Can he risk being seen? Can he let the dawn break over his hidden questions? Jesus's words linger: "Those who do what is true come to the light" (John 3:21).

Perhaps for Nicodemus the dawn has already begun.

Practice: Stepping into Light

Find a quiet space and light a single candle (or sit near a window where sunlight enters).

Reflect: Where am I still hiding in fear, secrecy, or shame?

Hold that part of yourself before the light. Whisper a prayer: "God, let Your light reveal not to condemn me but to heal me."

Sit for a few minutes simply receiving the warmth and clarity of the light.

Reflection Questions

- What parts of my life do I keep hidden in "night"?
- What fears keep me from stepping fully into God's light?
- How do I hear Jesus's invitation, not as a threat but as mercy calling me into freedom?

Closing Prayer

Light of the world,
You enter my night with mercy.
Where I hide, You call me out.
Where I fear exposure,
You shine with healing.
Draw me into Your light,
not to shame me but to free me,
that my life may be lived openly in You.
Amen.

With this chapter, Nicodemus' night journey is poised for resolution. He begins in secrecy, but Jesus is calling him toward light, freedom, and openness.

Meditation: The shift from night to day, secrecy to openness
Narrative: Contrast between those who cling to darkness and those who step into light
Reflection: Where am I still hiding in the night? Where is God calling me into day?

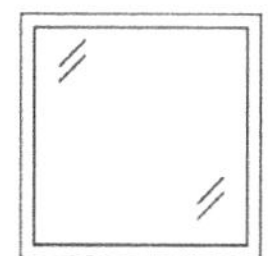

CHAPTER 10

Walking into the Day

Nicodemus, who had gone to Jesus before, and who was one of them, asked, "Our law does not judge people without first giving them a hearing to find out what they are doing, does it?" . . . Nicodemus, who had at first come to Jesus by night, also came, bringing a mixture of myrrh and aloes, weighing about a hundred pounds.

—John 7:50–51; 19:39

Meditation

Nicodemus begins at night, cautious and hidden. But his story does not end there. Slowly, step by step, he walks into the light of day.

In John 7, he speaks timidly among the Pharisees, urging fairness in how Jesus is treated.

In John 19, after Jesus's crucifixion, he comes boldly in daylight, carrying burial spices and honoring Jesus with costly devotion.

Nicodemus' journey shows us that transformation is often gradual. The night gives way to dawn, then to morning, and then to the full light of day. Faith is not a single leap but a series of steps: small acts of courage growing into public witness.

Narrative

Picture Nicodemus, once a secret seeker and now standing in the open. He bends over the lifeless body of Jesus, the same teacher he once visited at night. With Joseph of Arimathea, he wraps Jesus's body in linen, anoints Him with fragrant spices, and lays Him in the tomb.

It is no longer night. It is no longer hidden. He is seen, identified, and remembered: "Nicodemus, who had at first come by night." His night has become day. His questions have become devotion. His secrecy has become witness.

Nicodemus embodies what Jesus promised: to be born from above, to step into light, and to live not in fear but in love.

Practice: Taking One Step Toward the Light

Reflect: Where am I still living in "night"—cautious, hidden, afraid of being seen?

Ask: What is one small step I can take this week into "daylight faith" (a word of kindness, a public act of compassion, a prayer spoken aloud)?

Write it down and commit to it.

End with thanksgiving: "God, thank You for the steps already taken and for the courage to take the next one."

Reflection Questions

- What do Nicodemus' later appearances show me about faith as a process?
- Where do I see my own growth—from secrecy to openness, from night to day?
- What step is the Spirit inviting me to take now, however small, into fuller light?

Closing Prayer

God of dawn and day,
You are patient with my beginnings.
You do not rush me from night to noon
but walk with me step by step.
Thank You for Nicodemus
who shows me that transformation is gradual
and that every step into the light is sacred.
Give me courage to carry my faith into the open
until my life, too, becomes a witness to Your love.
Amen.

With this chapter, Graphe Three is complete. Nicodemus' story begins in the shadows and ends in the daylight, moving from knowledge to experience, from secrecy to witness, from literal to symbolic faith.

Meditation: Nicodemus' journey continues (appearing later in John 7 and John 19).
Theme: Transformation is gradual, moving from questions in the night to public witness at the cross.
Practice: Naming one step of courage I can take today toward the light.
Closing Prayer: A blessing for walking from night into day.

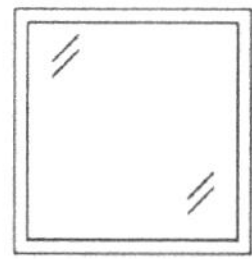

EPILOGUE

From Night to Light

Nicodemus's story is our story. He comes in the night carrying questions, fears, and uncertainties. He listens to words that stretch him beyond religion into Spirit, beyond knowledge into love, and beyond secrecy into courage.

He does not change all at once. Neither do we. Faith rarely bursts like lightning. More often, it dawns like sunrise. Slowly, gradually, the shadows retreat, and the light grows.

By the end, Nicodemus is no longer a night disciple. He is one who walks in the open day, carrying the fragrance of devotion, honoring the One who gave him words of eternal life.

So it is with us. The invitation is not simply to believe once but to keep stepping into the light, to let our questions turn into prayer, our seeking into trust, and our secrecy into witness.

The journey of faith is not about perfection but about direction. It's not about eliminating all shadows but about walking toward the light until our lives reflect the love of God revealed in Jesus.

This epilogue closes the circle. The story that began in secrecy ends in openness, a metaphor for every reader's journey.

A Final Blessing

Beloved of God,
may your nights be met with mercy,
your questions with wisdom,
your fears with gentleness,
your searching with presence.
And may the light of Christ
grow brighter in you each day,
until all shadows flee,
and you walk in the full dawn
of God's eternal love.
Amen.

Book 'Graphe' Five

Echoes of the Innocents

Matthew 2:16–18; Mark 4:35–41; John 11; Mark 8:22–26; Mark 10

Preface

Echoes That Do Not Die

The gospel is not afraid of tears. From the cries of Bethlehem's mothers to the disciples' shouts in the storm, Scripture gives voice to the extremity of the human condition. It does not sanitize the story of God into neat, triumphant endings. Instead, it holds the rawness of grief, the terror of danger, the blur of half-seeing, and the silence of unanswered questions.

These cries are not forgotten. They are echoes—reverberations of innocence, lament, and longing—that reach into eternity. The God of Jesus Christ does not erase them but gathers them. The voice in Ramah, the cry on the sea, the wail at Lazarus' tomb, even the laughter of children in the streets—all are preserved, all are sanctified, all are folded into the story of redemption.

This book listens to those echoes. In each story, the pain of human life is set alongside the mercy of God. We see innocence violated, storms that terrify, grief that feels unbearable, blindness that only slowly becomes sight, and children who embody a kingdom the powerful can neither control nor define.

At the center stands Christ, the One who weeps with us, calms the storm around us, calls us out of our tombs, and opens our eyes to see again. He does not silence the cries of the innocents. He transforms them into songs of resurrection.

May these chapters invite you to listen for the echoes in your own life—the laments you have carried, the fears you have faced, the prayers you have whispered in storms, and the childlike trust you may have buried but not lost. Each echo is sacred. Each echo belongs to God.

Opening Prayer

O God who hears the cries of the innocent,
who gathers every tear and whispers peace into every storm,
open my heart as I read these stories.
Let me hear the echoes of grief, fear, and hope,
not only in the pages of Scripture but in my own life.
Give me ears to listen, eyes to see,
and courage to believe that no cry is lost in You.
Through Christ, the One who weeps with us and lifts us into life.
Amen.

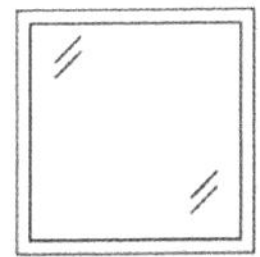

CHAPTER 1

The Cry in Ramah
Matthew 2:16–18

Meditation

The night was torn by screams. No lullabies could soothe them, no comforting embrace could undo what had been done. Rachel wept for her children, and would not be consoled because they were no more. Her cry became a wound in history—the sound of innocence crushed under the weight of power.

We often read this story at Christmastime, although we rarely linger there. We prefer shepherds and angels, magi and gifts. But Matthew does not let us escape. He places joy beside terror, birth beside massacre, salvation beside bloodshed. The echo of Ramah belongs in the nativity story because incarnation does not come into an untouched world. It comes into our violence, our betrayals, and our fragile cries.

Narrative Reflection

Herod is threatened by a child. That is the absurdity of evil: fear of innocence, fear of vulnerability, fear of the possibility that another story might be told. Herod orders the slaughter not because the children had done anything but because their very existence reminded him that his reign was not absolute.

Ramah is not just a village in Judea. Ramah is every place where the innocent suffer because the powerful are insecure. Ramah is Aleppo. Ramah is Columbine. Ramah is a refugee camp in Gaza. Ramah is the street where children play under the shadow of guns.

And yet Matthew anchors this horror in the words of Jeremiah: "A voice was heard in Ramah, weeping and loud lamentation" (Matt. 2:18). The cry is not forgotten. It is written in Scripture, carried into liturgy, and prayed by generations. God does not erase the lament; He remembers it.

This is the beginning of hope, that no cry is lost in the silence of history. God's memory is deeper than forgetfulness. The tears of Rachel and the tears of every mother are gathered into the divine heart.

Metaphorical Shift

When we read this story literally, it shocks us. But when we read it symbolically, it begins to speak to our own inner life. Herod is not only a king; he is the part of us that clings to control, that fears losing power. The innocents are not only children; they are the tender places in us, the unguarded dreams, the fragile hopes. And Ramah is not only a place on the map; it is the geography of our soul where grief has left its mark.

To pray with this story is to let Rachel's cry become our own. Where are the places in my life where innocence has been lost? Where has fear silenced joy? Where do I need to trust that God has remembered, even when others have forgotten?

Invitation to Prayer

Sit quietly. Imagine Rachel's cry echoing across time. Hear it not only in the text but in your own heart. Do not rush to silence it. Let it speak. Then imagine Christ cradling that cry, holding it with tenderness.

Pray

O Christ, you entered our world of grief,
not to erase the lament
but to carry it with us.
Hold the places in me where
innocence has been wounded.
Remember the cries I cannot even voice.
Gather them into Your heart
and transfigure them into hope.
Amen.

Reflection Questions

- Where in your life do you most feel the "echoes of Ramah"—grief that will not be consoled?
- How does remembering that God remembers change the way you carry sorrow?
- What "Herods" in your world threaten the vulnerable, and how might you resist their violence with the gentleness of Christ?

Narrative

Herod's rage thunders into Bethlehem, and the cries of mothers rise to heaven. Innocence suffers because of fear, power, and insecurity. Scripture does not hide this grief; it preserves it. "A voice was heard in Ramah, . . . Rachel weeping for her children" (Matt. 2:18).

Meditation

The gospel begins not with sentimentality but with lament. God is born into a world of violence.

Reflection

Where do you hear echoes of Rachel's weeping in our world today? How do you hold space for lament in your faith?

The Silence of God and the Cry of the Vulnerable

Meditation

The storm came suddenly. The waves rose high, the wind howled, the small boat tossed like a leaf. Experienced fishermen—men who knew the sea—panicked. Their voices cracked with fear: "Teacher, do you not care that we are perishing?" (Mark 4:38).

And there He was—asleep, His silence louder than the storm. His rest was a scandal to their terror, His calm almost unbearable when chaos raged.

We know this story well, but perhaps we know it too quickly. We leap to the ending—the stillness, the miracle, and the awe. But before that, there is silence. Before the calm, there is the cry. Before faith, there is the question: Do You care?

Narrative Reflection

The sea in Scripture often represents chaos, the deep, uncontrollable forces of life. Crossing it is always a risk. And here, the disciples discover not only the power of the sea but the vulnerability of their own hearts.

We have all prayed their prayer, maybe not with words but with groans, with sighs, and with tears in the night. Do You care that I am perishing? Do You see this storm? Can You feel my fear?

It is not a polite prayer. It is not theologically precise. It is desperate, raw, and real. And perhaps that is why it belongs in Matthew's Gospel. This, too, is prayer— not only praise and thanksgiving but the unfiltered cry of the vulnerable.

Jesus does not scold them for their words. He rises, rebukes the wind, and calms the sea. And then He asks, "Why are you afraid? Have you still no faith?" Faith, it seems, does not mean never crying out. Faith means trusting that our cry is heard, even when He appears asleep.

Metaphorical Shift

Read symbolically, the storm is not only weather; it is the turbulence within us. The sea is not only Galilee; it is the chaos of our fears, our griefs, and our anxieties. The silence of Jesus is not only His nap; it is the unsettling seasons when God seems absent, unresponsive, or hidden.

And yet to see symbolically is to glimpse more. The silence is not absence; it is presence in another form. Christ is in the boat. That is enough. His very being there means the storm will not have the last word.

Sometimes God stills the storm around us. Sometimes He stills the storm within us. But always, He is present.

Invitation to Prayer

Sit with this story. Picture your own storm. See the waves, feel the wind, name the fear. Then imagine Christ present in your boat—not far away but with you. What does His presence change, even before the waves calm?

Pray:

O Christ, in the chaos of my fears,
in the turbulence of my heart,
be present.
When You seem silent,
remind me You are still with me.
Calm the storm within me,
even if the sea around me rages on.
Amen.

Reflection Questions

- What storm in your life feels overwhelming right now?
- When have you felt the silence of God most strongly, and what did that silence teach you?
- How does knowing that Christ is in the boat change your perspective, even before the storm is stilled?

Narrative

Innocent lives end, and no angel swoops down. The holy family flees. God seems absent yet is hidden in exile, bearing suffering with us.

Meditation

God is not indifferent but present in hidden ways, walking the road of the refugee, the parent, the wounded.

Reflection Questions

- When God seems silent, do you lose heart, or do you dare to trust that presence is deeper than appearances?
- What storms in your life have forced you to ask, "God, do You not care?"

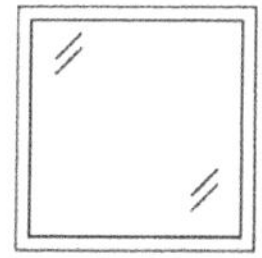

CHAPTER 2

Once I Was Blind, But Now I See
John 9:1–41

Meditation

As Jesus walked along, He saw a man blind from birth. His disciples asked Him, "Rabbi, who sinned, this man or his parents, that he was born blind?" (John 9:2).

Jesus answered, "Neither this man nor his parents sinned; he was born blind so that God's works might be revealed in him" (John 9:3).

Jesus spat on the ground, made mud with the saliva, and spread the mud on the man's eyes, saying to him, "Go, wash in the pool of Siloam" (John 9:7).

So he went and washed—and came back able to see.

The neighbors and those who had seen him before as a beggar began to ask, "Is this not the man who used to sit and beg?" (John 9:8). Some said, "It is he" (John 9:9). Others said, "No, but it is someone like him" (John 9:9). He kept saying, "I am he" (John 9:9).

Later, when questioned by the Pharisees, he testified: "One thing I do know, that though I was blind, now I see" (John 9:25).

Narrative Reflection

The disciples want a simple answer: Whose fault is this? They assume blindness must be punishment. Jesus refuses their categories. He shifts the focus from blame to possibility: "so that God's works might be revealed" (John 9:3).

The healing itself is earthy, messy, and deeply human—mud, spit, water. God does not hover above human need but presses divinity into the dust of our lives. Healing is not magic; it is incarnation.

But the real drama unfolds, not in the healing but in the man's testimony. His neighbors doubt him. The Pharisees interrogate him. His parents, fearing exclusion, keep silent. But he persists. Each time he tells his story, his voice grows stronger. From saying "the man called Jesus" to "a prophet" to "a man from God," finally he kneels before Christ and says, "Lord, I believe."

In the end, it is not the once-blind man who is exposed as unseeing, but those who claim perfect vision yet cannot recognize God at work.

Metaphorical Shift

Blindness in this story is not only physical; it is spiritual. It is the refusal to see beyond categories of sin, blame, and fear. True sight comes not just from healed eyes but from a heart open to transformation.

The blind man becomes a mirror for us: Where am I clinging to explanations that blind me to God's presence? Where am I more invested in being right than in being healed?

And the man becomes a widow. His boldness shows us how testimony grows—at first uncertain, then steady, and then radiant. "One thing I do know: I was blind, but now I see" (John 9:25).

Invitation to Prayer

Close your eyes for a moment. Feel the darkness. Imagine Christ drawing near, touching your eyes with healing mud. Hear Him whisper, "Go, wash, and see."

Pray:

Lord of Light,
heal my blindness.
Where I cannot see Your presence,
open my eyes.
Where I cling to blame,
release me into grace.
Give me the courage to tell my story,
not with certainty but with honesty:
I was blind, but now I see.
Amen.

Reflection Questions

- Where do you recognize spiritual blindness in yourself or your community?
- How might Jesus be inviting you to move from blame to possibility?
- What is your "one thing I know" testimony of God's work in your life?

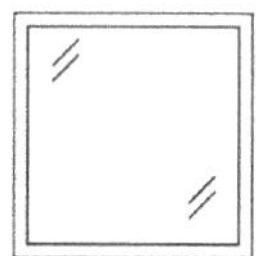

CHAPTER 3

I See People as Trees
Mark 8:22–26

Meditation

They brought a blind man to Jesus and begged Him to touch him. Jesus led him outside the village, spat on his eyes, and laid His hands on him.

Jesus asked, "Can you see anything?" (Mark 8:23).

The man looked up and said, "I can see people, but they look like trees, walking" (Mark 8:24).

Again, Jesus laid His hands on his eyes, and this time he saw clearly.

Narrative Reflection

Most miracles of Jesus happen instantly—sight restored, lepers cleansed, demons cast out. But here, healing comes in stages: first, blurred vision; then clarity—first an impression of reality; then reality itself.

This is the story of discipleship. We do not move from blindness to perfect sight in a single moment. We move through stages: confusion, distortion, partial insight, growing clarity. We begin to see, but often what we see is fuzzy and incomplete, like trees walking.

How comforting this is for us who struggle! The blind man's partial sight was not a failure; it was the beginning of healing. Jesus did not rebuke him for seeing dimly. He touched him again. Grace is patient; healing takes time.

Metaphorical Shift

Symbolically, this story speaks of spiritual perception. To be human is to see through veils, filters, and perspectives shaped by culture, wounds, and experience. Our first sight of God's truth is rarely clear. We glimpse shapes, and we feel movement, but we do not see the fullness.

The blind man's journey is ours. We, too, begin by seeing trees walking—metaphors, fragments, impressions. And then as grace touches us again, our sight clears.

This story reminds us that faith is not about instant clarity but about progressive transformation. God works in us gradually, persistently, patiently. We are always moving from dim vision to clearer sight.

Invitation to Prayer

Close your eyes. Imagine your life as a series of blurred images. What feels unclear right now in faith, in love, in calling? Picture Jesus laying His hands on you once, and you begin to see shapes, movement, and impressions. Then imagine Him touching you again, and clarity begins to dawn.

Pray:

Lord Jesus,
I confess that my sight is partial,
my vision dim.
But I trust Your patient grace.

Touch me again and again
until I see clearly.
Teach me to trust the process
of slow healing,
and to walk by faith
even when my vision is blurred.
Amen.

Reflection Questions

- What areas of your life feel like "trees walking" where you see something but not clearly?
- How does this story encourage you to trust God's patience in your process of growth?
- Who in your life might need a second touch of grace, and how might you help them wait for clarity?

Narrative

The man's first sight is distorted: people as trees walking. He names what he sees honestly, and that honesty opens the way to full vision.

Meditation

There is no shame in partial sight. God works with honesty, not pretense.

Reflection

What is your "people as trees" moment when you saw only in part yet learned to wait for more?

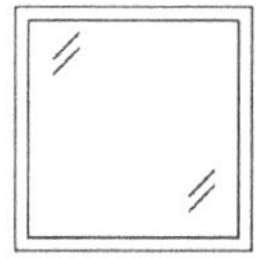

CHAPTER 4

The Blind Man of Bethsaida Mark 10:46–52

Meditation

Jesus was leaving Jericho with His disciples when a blind beggar named Bartimaeus sat by the roadside. Hearing that it was Jesus of Nazareth, he began to shout, "Jesus, Son of David, have mercy on me!" (Mark 10:47).

Many tried to silence him, but he cried out even louder.

Jesus stopped. He called him forward and asked, "What do you want me to do for you?" (Mark 10:51).

"My teacher, let me see again" (Mark 10:51).

And immediately he regained his sight and followed Jesus on the way.

Narrative Reflection

Bartimaeus' cry is the voice of desperate faith. He had no wealth, no status, and no reason to think the crowd or the Master would notice him. Yet he dared to name Jesus as "Son of David"—a messianic title, a recognition of kingship.

Bartimaeus refused to be silenced. The crowd tried to shush him, to push his voice into the margins. But desperation makes prophets of beggars. Bartimaeus knew what he wanted, and he knew where to direct his cry.

Unlike the disciples who often misunderstood, Bartimaeus saw with spiritual eyes before he saw with physical ones. His faith gave him vision before his eyes were opened.

Metaphorical Shift

Symbolically, Bartimaeus represents the human condition at its most raw—marginalized, silenced, begging for mercy. His story teaches us that the first step toward clarity is desire.

Notice Jesus's question: "What do you want me to do for you?" (Mark 10:51). It is not rhetorical. God invites us to name our deepest longing. Bartimaeus did not ask for riches, safety, or revenge on those who silenced him. He asked for sight.

This is the heart of prayer—not eloquence but honesty; not complexity but clarity; to cry out, "Let me see again" (Mark 10:51).

And when the eyes of our hearts are opened, sight leads to following. Bartimaeus did not merely regain his vision; he joined the way of discipleship.

Invitation to Prayer

Sit quietly and recall the cries you often silence in yourself—the desires you push down, the prayers you feel too small to voice. Imagine yourself on the roadside, crying out to Jesus. Hear Him stop, notice you, and ask, "What do you want me to do for you?"

Pray:

Jesus, Son of David,
have mercy on me.
Give me the courage
to name my deepest need.
Heal my blindness.
Open my eyes
that I may see You more clearly
and follow You more nearly.
Amen.

Reflection Questions

- What is your deepest cry right now, the prayer that rises up from the roadside of your life?
- How does the persistence of Bartimaeus challenge you in your own prayer life?
- What would it mean for you not only to "see" but also to "follow on the way" after Christ?

Narrative

A man receives sight in stages: first blur, then clarity. Healing is not instant but progressive.

Meditation

Faith, too, is often partial at first. God honors the slow opening of our eyes.

Reflection

Where do you still see only dimly, and where has God already sharpened your vision?

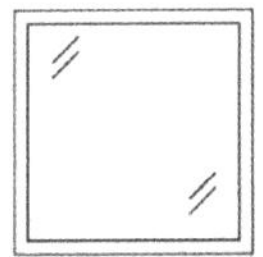

CHAPTER 5

The Extremity of the Human Condition Mark 5:1–20

Meditation

They arrived in the country of Gerasene. Out of the tombs came a man—wild, broken, and possessed by a legion of demons. No chains could hold him. Day and night he cried out among the graves, cutting himself with stones.

When he saw Jesus from afar, he ran and fell before Him, shouting, "What have you to do with me, Jesus, Son of the Most High God?" (Mark 5:7).

Jesus commanded the unclean spirits to leave. They begged to enter a herd of pigs, which rushed down the steep bank into the sea and were drowned.

When the townspeople came, they saw the man clothed, sitting quietly, restored to his right mind.

Jesus told him, "Go home to your own people and tell them how much the Lord has done for you and what mercy He has shown you" (Mark 5:19).

Narrative Reflection

This man represents the extremity of the human condition:

- isolated from community
- chained and abandoned
- crying out in pain
- self-destructive
- dwelling among the dead

He is humanity at its farthest edge, stripped of dignity and consumed by forces beyond his control. Yet even here in the most desolate place, Jesus comes. The gospel does not avoid the tombs. Grace does not shrink back from chaos.

The contrast is striking: a legion of torment within the man versus the calm authority of Jesus's word. The wildness of the tombs gives way to the quiet image of the man sitting, clothed, and restored.

The townspeople were afraid, not because of the chaos but because of the healing. Sometimes healing disrupts economies, traditions, and power structures—pigs drowned, profit lost, normalcy shaken. Restoration is more unsettling than brokenness.

Metaphorical Shift

The Gerasene demoniac is more than one man's story. He is a mirror of us all. He embodies:

- addictions we cannot chain
- the wounds that drive us into isolation
- the violence we turn upon ourselves
- the shame that makes us dwell among the dead

Spiritually, we all have our tombs. We all have our legions. Yet the story is not about how deep the darkness is but how far grace will go to reach it.

Jesus crosses the sea for one broken soul. He steps into unclean territory, confronts chaos, and restores what seemed beyond restoration.

And then, rather than allowing the man to follow Him physically, Jesus sends him back into his community, healed not only for himself but as a witness to mercy.

Invitation to Prayer

Close your eyes and picture your own "tombs"—the places of shame, isolation, or fear that feel beyond hope. Imagine Jesus stepping into that place without hesitation, calling your name, speaking authority over the chaos.

> **Pray:**
>
> *Jesus, Son of the Most High God,*
> *enter the tombs of my life.*
> *Break the chains that bind me.*
> *Quiet voices that torment me.*
> *Restore me to my right mind,*
> *clothe me in mercy,*
> *and send me to bear witness*
> *to Your healing love.*
> *Amen.*

Reflection Questions

- What "legions" (voices, fears, addictions, ideologies) feel overwhelming in your life or in our world?
- Why do you think healing can feel more frightening than brokenness, both for individuals and communities?
- Where might Jesus be sending you as a witness to mercy after an experience of restoration?

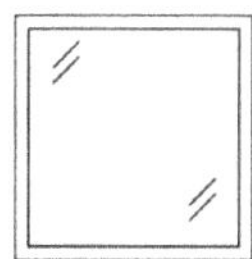

CHAPTER 6
The Child at the Center
Mark 9:33–37; 10:13–16

Meditation

On the road, the disciples argued about who was the greatest. Jesus sat down, called the twelve, and said, "Whoever wants to be first must be last of all and servant of all" (Mark 9:35).

Then He took a little child, placed the child among them, and said, "Whoever welcomes one such child in my name welcomes me, and whoever welcomes me welcomes not me but the one who sent me" (Mark 9:37).

Later, when people were bringing children to Jesus, the disciples tried to stop them. But Jesus was indignant and said, "Let the children come to me; do not stop them, for it is to such as these that the kingdom of God belongs. Truly I tell you, whoever does not receive the kingdom of God as a little child will never enter it" (Mark 10:14–15).

He took them in His arms, laid His hands on them, and blessed them.

Narrative Reflection

The disciples' argument reveals the human obsession with greatness. They want to know who ranks highest in God's kingdom. But Jesus interrupts their logic with a gesture, not a lecture. He places a child at the very center.

In their world—and in ours—children represent vulnerability, dependence, and lack of status. They had no voice, no power, no authority. Yet Jesus insisted that they are the measure of the kingdom.

The child in the center unsettles the adult world. It dismantles the myth that God's kingdom is about control, hierarchy, or prestige. Instead, the kingdom is about welcome, tenderness, and blessing.

Putting a child at the center is also to put innocence, trust, and openness at the center of discipleship. It is to unlearn cynicism and relearn wonder.

Metaphorical Shift

The "child at the center" is more than an image of age. It is a symbol for the vulnerable—those society deems insignificant, those pushed to the margins. To welcome them is to welcome Christ Himself.

Spiritually, the child also represents the part of us that is unguarded, tender, and still capable of awe. To receive the kingdom "like a child" is not about naivety but about openness. It is the courage to trust beyond control.

The disciples try to keep the children away, much as our adult minds push aside vulnerability. Yet Jesus insists on blessing what we would rather overlook.

Invitation to Prayer

Hold an image of a child—perhaps a memory of yourself, a child you know, or even the fragile child within. Imagine Jesus placing that child at the center of your life, blessing them with His hands, and holding them in His arms.

Pray:

Jesus,
let me welcome the child
You place at the center.
Teach me to honor innocence,
to protect the vulnerable,
and to receive Your kingdom
with open hands.
Heal the cynicism
that clouds my heart,
and restore to me
the wonder of a child.
Amen.

Reflection Questions

- Where in your life do you still argue about "greatness"—status, success, or recognition?
- Who are the "children at the center" in our world today—those most vulnerable, overlooked, or marginalized?
- What would it mean for you to receive the kingdom with the openness of a child?

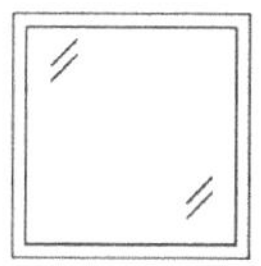

CHAPTER 7

The Widow's Cry
Luke 18:1–8

Meditation

Jesus told them a parable about their need to pray always and not lose heart.

> *In a certain city there was a judge who neither feared God nor had respect for people. In that city there was a widow who kept coming to him and saying, "Grant me justice against my accuser." For a while he refused, but later he said to himself, "Though I have no fear of God and no respect for anyone, yet because this widow keeps bothering me, I will grant her justice, so that she may not wear me out by continually coming." And the Lord said, "Listen to what the unjust judge says. And will not God grant justice to His chosen ones who cry to Him day and night? Will he delay long in helping them? I tell you, he will quickly grant justice to them. And yet, when the Son of Man comes, will He find faith on earth?"*
>
> —Luke 18:2–8

Narrative Reflection

The widow is one of Scripture's most enduring figures of vulnerability. She has no husband to speak for her, no wealth to leverage, and no status to protect her. All she has is her voice—her persistence and her refusal to be silent.

The judge, by contrast, is powerful, insulated, and indifferent. He does not fear God and does not care for people. He embodies the systems that exploit, dismiss, and delay justice.

Yet the widow keeps crying out. Her cry becomes a force stronger than the judge's apathy. She refuses to disappear into silence. She insists on her dignity.

Jesus elevates her not just as an image of persistence in prayer but as a mirror of God's own justice. If even an unjust judge will relent in the face of her cry, how much more will God respond with compassion to those who call on Him?

The challenge comes in Jesus's haunting question: "When the Son of Man comes, will He find faith on earth?" Faith here is not quiet resignation but courageous persistence, a trust that keeps crying out even when silence lingers.

Metaphorical Shift

The widow's cry is more than an ancient parable. It echoes in every oppressed person, every silenced victim, and every forgotten community. Her voice is the voice of all who still believe justice is possible, even when the world resists.

Spiritually, the widow represents the part of us that refuses to surrender hope. She is our own soul crying out against despair, demanding that God's promises are not to be forgotten.

The judge lives in us too—the part that grows cynical, weary, or dismissive. Jesus invites us to recognize both voices: the widow who will not give up and the judge who has ceased to care. Faith is choosing which voice will define us.

Invitation to Prayer

Listen to the cries within and around you. Where do you hear the voice of the widow—in your own longings, in your community, in the world?

Pray:

God of justice,
give me the faith of the widow—
a faith that does not lose heart,
a faith that keeps crying out,
a faith that trusts
You will not delay forever.
Help me to resist the apathy
of the judge
and to live with the persistence of prayer
and the courage of hope.
Amen.

Reflection Questions

- Where in your life do you most feel the temptation to "lose heart"?
- Who are the widows of our world today—those without protection or voice— whose cries we must hear?
- How can you embody the persistence of prayer and hope, even when justice feels delayed?

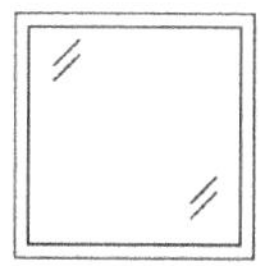

CHAPTER 8

Unbind Him and Let Him Go John 11:1–44

Meditation

When Jesus arrived, He found that Lazarus had already been in the tomb for four days. Martha met Him and said, "Lord, if you had been here, my brother would not have died" (John 11:21).

Jesus replied, "I am the resurrection and the life. Those who believe in me, even though they die, will live, and everyone who lives and believes in me will never die" (John 11:25–26).

He asked, "Do you believe this?" (John 11:26).

Later, He came to the tomb. He wept. Then He cried with a loud voice, "Lazarus, come out!" (John 11:43).

And the dead man came out, his hands and feet bound with strips of cloth, and his face wrapped in a cloth. Jesus said to them, "Unbind him, and let him go" (John 11:44).

Narrative Reflection

This story is filled with layers of human experience—grief, delay, hope, disbelief, and astonishment. Martha and Mary both confront Jesus with their lament: "If you had been here . . ." Their words echo the human cry in the face of absence and loss.

Jesus does not dismiss their grief. He enters into it, weeping with them. His tears reveal a God who does not stand apart from human sorrow but participates in it fully.

Then comes the moment of power—not only the raising of Lazarus but the command: "Unbind him, and let him go" (John 11:44). Resurrection is not just about life after death. It is about freedom from the graveclothes that still bind us such as fear, shame, despair, addiction, bitterness, and all that stifles life.

This is a resurrection story, but it is also a liberation story. Jesus does not simply give life back; He calls Lazarus—and us—into unbound life.

Metaphorical Shift

Lazarus represents all that is bound, silenced, and sealed away. He is every part of us that feels buried before its time. The tomb is the place of despair where hope seems impossible.

But Jesus calls us out. The voice that spoke creation into being now speaks our names in the darkness. He calls us not just to survive but to be unbound.

The community also has a role: "Unbind him." Resurrection is not private. It requires others to help peel away the layers that imprison us. Healing, freedom, and new beginnings always come through relationships.

Invitation to Prayer

Imagine yourself standing at the mouth of Lazarus' tomb. Hear Jesus calling your name. Feel the graveclothes loosen as the Spirit of life breathes into you.

Pray:

Jesus, Resurrection and Life,
call me out of every tomb
where I have been bound.
Free me from the wrappings
of fear and despair.
Teach me to hear Your voice
in the darkness
and give me courage
to live unbound.
Amen.

Reflection Questions

- What are the "graveclothes" in your life—habits, fears, or wounds—that still bind you?
- Who has helped "unbind" you, and how can you help unbind others?
- Where in your life is Jesus calling you out of despair into hope, out of death into life?

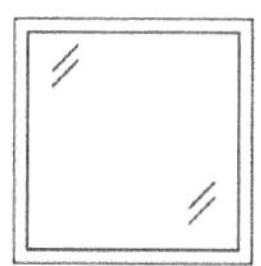

CHAPTER 9

The Cross and the Cry of Abandonment Mark 15:33–39; John 19:30

Narrative Reflection

The Gospel of Mark records Jesus's cry of abandonment: "My God, my God, why have You forsaken me?" (Mark 15:34). It is a haunting sound—the Son of God echoing the lament of the human heart. But John records another cry as Jesus breathes His last: "It is finished" (John 19:30).

To the casual listener, those words sound like surrender, like the end of a dream. Yet in the mystery of God, "finished" does not mean over. It means fulfilled. It means that the work Jesus was sent to do—to reveal the love of God in its fullest depth—has reached its climax on the cross.

But here is the paradox: While Jesus says "It is finished," God is not finished with you. The story does not end with the cry, with the silence, or even with the tomb. God's story is still unfolding in your life, in your community, and in creation itself.

The cross is not only the end of Jesus's earthly ministry; it is the beginning of resurrection life in us. It is the place where the worst of human cruelty meets the depth of divine love, and love refuses to give the last word to death.

When Jesus cries "It is finished," He closes one chapter, but He opens another. The torn curtain reveals that God's presence is now woven into every place of human suffering and every act of mercy. The centurion sees it: "Truly this man was God's Son" (Mark 15:39). What had seemed like an ending becomes a revelation.

Metaphorical Shift

The cry of "It is finished" is not the end of hope but the completion of love. Think of a master painter who lays down the brush and whispers, "It is finished." The canvas is complete, but the beauty of it has just begun to touch the lives of those who see it.

So too with the cross. Jesus's work is fulfilled, but God's Spirit continues to write new chapters through us. The echoes of that final cry reverberate into our unfinished lives, calling us into resurrection, healing, and hope.

Invitation to Prayer

Stand before the cross in silence. Hear the cry of abandonment. Hear the final words: "It is finished." Then listen for the whisper of the Spirit: "But I am not finished with you."

Pray

God of Resurrection,
thank You that the cross is not the end.
Where I see endings,
You are making beginnings.
Where I feel abandoned,
You are most nearby.
Teach me to trust that my unfinished life
is still in Your hands
and that in Christ,
Your love will have the last word.
Amen.

Reflection Questions

- How do you hear the words "It is finished" in your own life: as an ending or as a fulfillment?
- Where do you sense that God is not finished with you yet?
- How might you live differently if you believed every ending could be a beginning in God's love?

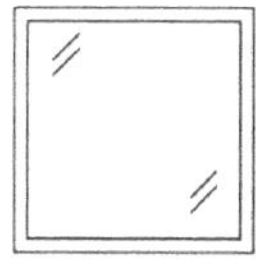

EPILOGUE

Gathered into God's Memory

The cries of Bethlehem are not forgotten. The storm on Galilee's Sea has not ceased. The tears of Mary and Martha at Lazarus' tomb are not overlooked. The blurred vision of a man who first saw people as trees is not dismissed. The laughter and vulnerability of children are not trivial.

All of it—every cry, every fear, every tear, every half-seeing, every small hand reaching for blessing—is gathered into God's memory. What echoes in time resounds in eternity.

The story of the innocents is not simply a tragedy; it is a testimony. It reveals that God's reign takes shape not in power but in vulnerability—not in control but in compassion; not in forgetting but in remembering.

Innocence cries out. Jesus responds. And what He begins, He does not abandon. The storm is calmed, but the disciples' faith is awakened. Lazarus is raised, but a community learns to unbind. The blind man sees, but he discovers that truth comes in stages. Children are blessed, but they reveal the doorway to God's kingdom.

Your story, too, echoes—perhaps in lament, perhaps in hope, perhaps in silence still waiting to be heard. But no echo is lost. No voice is too small. No tears are too hidden.

For in Christ, the echoes of the innocents and the echoes of our own lives become part of a greater song—a song of resurrection, of redemption, of life without end.

"He will wipe every tear from their eyes. Death will be no more; . . . for the first things have passed away. . . . See, I am making all things new" (Rev. 21:4–5).

Closing Prayer

Faithful God,
You hold the echoes of history and the cries of my heart.
You do not forget.
You do not abandon.
You gather every fragment and weave it into Your story of love.
As I leave these pages,
teach me to carry the innocence of children,
the courage of the grieving,
the persistence of the blind,
and the hope of resurrection into my daily life.
Let every echo in me
become a song of praise to You,
until the day when all is made new.
Amen.

Book 'Graphe' Six

Faith Seeking Understanding: The Christ Event

Theme: At the center of discipleship lies the question Jesus asks: "Who do you say that I am?"

This is not only about doctrine but about identity, trust, and transformation. Faith seeks understanding by moving through awareness, understanding, knowledge, and perspective.

The Christ event reveals Jesus not just as miracle-worker or teacher but as the great "I AM"—the One in whom all names and symbols converge.

"I AM WHO I AM" (Exod. 3:14).

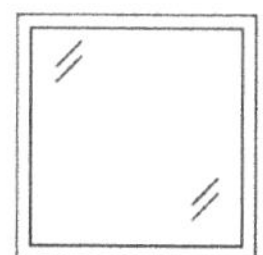

CHAPTER 1

Do You Not Yet Understand? Mark 8:21

Chapter One sets the theological and spiritual tone for all of Book Five, showing how the Christ event isn't only about Peter's confession but about our own ongoing process of discovery. It becomes not a static answer but a living journey—integrative, relational, and transformative.

Meditation

The disciples have seen bread multiplied, storms stilled, bodies healed, and yet Jesus looks at them with compassion and asks, "Do you not yet understand?" (Mark 8:21). The question is not one of intellect but of vision. Can they see beyond the surface of events into the depth of meaning? Can they let go of fixed expectations and enter the new horizon Jesus is unveiling?

Faith does not begin with certainty but with wonder. It is not the possession of answers but the willingness to live in the tension of mystery.

The Christ event is not simply a moment in history but an unveiling of reality itself. It confronts us with a question, not merely of knowledge but of being: Do you not yet understand?

Faith is not blind assent to doctrine. It is the slow awakening of awareness—a shift of mindset, a transformation of worldview. When we meet Jesus in the Gospels, we do not meet only a teacher of religion but the very presence of God drawing us into a new way of perceiving reality.

A diminished, fixed mindset clings to a single story. It reduces Scripture to literal facts or rigid categories. But an integrative mindset sees deeper. It perceives signs, symbols, and metaphors that open into mystery. It knows that Scripture is both mirror and window—revealing who we are and who we may yet become.

Narrative Reflection

Imagine the disciples in the boat with Jesus after the feeding of the multitudes. Bread was broken, abundance was revealed, and yet they argued because they had forgotten to bring bread. Jesus looked at them and asked, "Do you not yet understand?" (Mark 8:21).

In that question lies the heart of discipleship. Understanding Jesus is not about memorizing correct answers; it is about learning to see differently. It is about moving from fear to trust, from scarcity to abundance, from rigid categories to integrative awareness.

The Christ event shatters our narrow frames. In it, God reveals not only who Jesus is but who we are called to be. This is not about escaping the world but about learning to live within it with a new vision—one that integrates heaven and earth, humanity and divinity, the visible and the invisible.

A fixed mindset—or what we might call a diminished mindset—reads the Christ event as though it were locked in a single story: Jesus as miracle-worker, moral teacher, or political liberator. Such reduction flattens the gospel into fragments and leaves us blind to its fullness.

An integrative mindset, however, anchored in a spiritual worldview, reads Jesus's life as a process—a mirror of who we are and a window into who we are becoming. It weaves together the threads of history, symbol, and experience into a tapestry of discovery.

This mindset does not deny the literal story, but it refuses to be trapped there. Like Peter who confessed Jesus as Messiah but resisted the cross, we too must move beyond categories that comfort us. To confess Christ is not to reduce Him but to be drawn into His inexhaustible mystery.

Thus, "Do you not yet understand?" is not a rebuke. It is an invitation to leave behind our cracked lenses, to be healed of partial sight, and to discover anew who Jesus is for us.

Signs, Symbols, and Metaphors

Symbolic Reading

Bread: Not only physical nourishment but the symbol of God's sustaining presence

Boat: Our life together, fragile yet carried by grace

Misunderstanding: The disciples' forgetfulness is not stupidity but a mirror of our own partial seeing.

An integrative mindset anchors itself in a spiritual worldview: Reality is more than what meets the eye. It refuses to be trapped in the literal or reduced to fear. Instead, it allows paradox and mystery to open the heart to God.

The question itself is a sign, pointing at us beyond what we think we know.

The disciples' confusion is a symbol of our own limited vision, always needing enlargement.

The Christ event becomes a metaphor for the journey from awareness, understanding, knowledge, and perspective.

Prayer

O Christ, you are the question and the answer,
the mirror that shows me my blindness
and the window that opens to a larger horizon.
Break the rigidity of my fixed stories.
Heal my partial vision.
Anchor me in a worldview vast enough
to hold Your mystery and my becoming.
Lord of Bread and Storm,
teach me to see beyond appearances.
When I cling to certainty,
open me to mystery.
When I live from fear,
call me into trust.
Let my heart awaken to the Christ event,
not as an answer already given
but as a presence ever unfolding.
Amen.

Reflection Questions

- Where in my life am I tempted to reduce Jesus to a single role or story?
- How might I practice an integrative mindset when I read Scripture, holding both history and mystery together?
- What does it mean for me to confess Jesus not only with words but with my lived perspective and choices?
- In what ways do I still hear the question, "Do you not yet understand?" addressed to me?

- Where in my life do I sense Jesus asking, "Do you not yet understand?"
- How do I read Scripture—through the lens of certainty or through the lens of openness?
- What might an "integrative mindset" look like in my daily faith practice?

This sets the stage for the whole book: discipleship as the movement from a diminished to an integrative reading of Jesus, anchored in a spiritual worldview.

The disciples are blind to Jesus's identity, even after miracles. Spiritual growth begins with awareness of our unknowing.

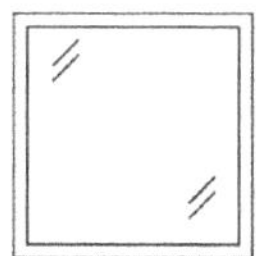

CHAPTER 2

Who Do You Say That I Am? Mark 8:27–33

In this chapter, which naturally deepens the movement of Chapter One, the question sharpens: "Who do you say that I am?" (Mark 8:29). This becomes both Peter's confession and our own mirror. We'll weave in Exodus 3 and the divine name, showing how the Christ event is not only about recognition but about transformation into the mystery of the I AM.

Meditation

Jesus turns to His disciples with a question that reverberates throughout history: "But who do you say that I am?" (Mark 8:29).

It is neither an academic inquiry nor a matter of public opinion. It is intimate, personal, and existential. The question is not about information but about transformation.

On the road to Caesarea Philippi, Jesus asked his disciples a question that echoes throughout the centuries: "Who do you say that I am?"

It is not a question of doctrine but of encounter.

Many voices give answers: John the Baptist and Elijah, one of the prophets. But Jesus presses closer. He does not ask for hearsay; He asks for confession. He asks for the heart's recognition.

Faith is not inherited by rumor. It is discovered in the depths of relationship. To know Jesus is to see with new eyes—eyes that glimpse God's presence woven into human flesh, God's glory hidden in humility, God's power revealed in vulnerability.

Peter answers rightly: "You are the Messiah" (Mark 8:29), yet moments later he resists the way of the cross. His words are true, but his perspective is still limited. His confession is real, but his understanding is partial.

Faith seeks understanding. It is not a static possession but a living journey.

Narrative Reflection

When Moses encountered God in the burning bush, he asked for a name to hold onto, a word to anchor his people. God responded: "I AM WHO I am" (Exod. 3:14). This was not a definition but an opening—a horizon of Being itself. The name revealed presence, not possession, mystery, or mastery.

In Mark 8, Jesus echoes this same mystery. To confess Him as Messiah is not to pin Him down but to be drawn into the unfathomable "I AM."

Yet like Peter, we struggle with the gap between confession and resistance. We want Christ without the cross, glory without suffering, and certainty without paradox. But the Christ event is not one story among others. It is the story in which all stories are gathered and transfigured.

To answer Jesus's question requires more than words. It asks for an integrative mindset anchored in a spiritual worldview. A fixed mindset clings to single narratives—Jesus as prophet, king, miracle-worker—but an integrative mindset opens to the layers of symbol, sign, and metaphor. It is a process of discovery: awareness, understanding, knowledge, perspective.

"Who do you say that I am?" becomes the turning point between literal seeing and symbolic vision.

Imagine the scene: the disciples walking dusty roads, their sandals stirring questions in their minds. They had seen healings, miracles, and teachings. They had broken bread with Jesus, yet they still struggled to see clearly.

Peter speaks boldly: "You are the Messiah" (Mark 8:29).

It is a moment of revelation, a flash of insight breaking through uncertainty. Yet even here, understanding is partial. Peter's confession is true, but his imagination of the Christ is still bound by expectation.

This is the tension of discipleship: We can name Jesus rightly yet misunderstand what His lordship means. To confess Jesus is to step into mystery, not to master it.

Symbolic Reading

Caesarea Philippi: A place of imperial power and pagan shrines. The question of Jesus's identity rises in contrast to worldly identities.

Confession: More than words; a turning of the heart toward the mystery of God revealed in Christ.

Silence: Jesus's command not to tell anyone hints that confession is not for boasting but for transformation.

Here the Christ event is both question and answer: "Who do you say that I am?" becomes a mirror. It reflects our faith back to us—not only what we believe about Jesus but who we are becoming in His presence.

Signs, Symbols, and Metaphors

Sign: Peter's confession is a signpost pointing to truth, though not yet fully grasped.

Symbol: The divine name "I AM" becomes the symbol of God's abiding presence beyond time and beyond category.

Metaphor: The Christ event as both mirror (revealing our partial faith) and window (opening us to greater depth).

Prayer

Living I am,
You are not captured by names,
yet You speak through every name.
You are Messiah, Christ,
and still beyond every title.
Draw me into the depth of Your presence.
When my words are shallow,
give me perspective.
When my faith resists the cross,
give me courage.
When You ask, "Who do you say that I am?"
help me to answer with my life.
Living Christ,
You ask me not for secondhand answers
but for the confession of my heart.
Free me from the temptation to reduce You
to my expectations.
Teach me to follow the mystery of Your presence,
to know You not by rumor
but by the light of encounter.
Amen.

Reflection Questions

- How do I answer Jesus's question, "Who do you say that I am?" today?
- In what ways does my confession sometimes resist the demands of the cross?
- What does the divine name "I am" teach me about God's presence in my life?
- How might an integrative mindset expand my perspective beyond fixed, single stories about Jesus?
- How can confession move beyond words into transformation?

With this, Chapter Two builds the bridge: Peter's confession, Exodus' burning bush, John's I am saying our own process of faith seeking understanding, Peter's confession and resistance, the tension between proclaiming Christ and rejecting the way of the cross.

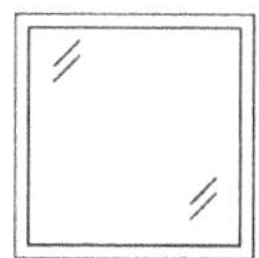

CHAPTER 3

I Am Who I Am (Exodus 3:1–15)

Meditation

Moses stands barefoot before the burning bush, trembling at the mystery of a flame that burns but does not consume. He seeks clarity, a name, a handle for the divine. And God answers in a way that both reveals and conceals.

"I am who I am." Tell them "I am has sent me to you" (Exod. 3:14).

This is not a definition to master but an invitation to trust. God's name is less a label and more a promise of presence. The I am is being itself—alive, dynamic, and uncontainable.

When Jesus asks, "Who do you say that I am?" (Mark 8:29), He echoes this divine mystery. The Christ event is not about shrinking God to our categories but expanding our vision into God's infinite horizon.

Peter has just confessed Jesus as the Christ. But when Jesus begins to reveal what that means—rejection, suffering, death, and resurrection—Peter resists. He takes Jesus aside and rebukes Him.

How quickly insight collapses into fear. How swiftly faith is tangled with expectation.

Peter cannot imagine a Messiah who suffers. He wants the glory without the cross, victory without vulnerability, triumph without sacrifice.

But Jesus turns and rebukes him: "Get behind me, Satan! For you are setting your mind not on divine things but on human things" (Mark 8:33).

The harshness shocks us. Yet it is love's severity, a summons to let go of illusions and embrace the deeper truth that Christ is not a conqueror of others but a redeemer through love.

Narrative Reflection

Every generation tries to define Jesus. Some see Him as prophet, others as healer, teacher, revolutionary, or moral exemplar. All of these signs point to truth, but none exhaust the mystery.

Peter confesses Jesus as Messiah but soon reveals his resistance to the suffering that follows. His mindset is diminished, fixed in a single story. He cannot yet see how the I am unfolds in paradox: life through death, power through weakness, glory through humility.

The integrative mindset invites us to hold symbol and mystery together. Just as Moses had to let go of control at the burning bush, so we must let go of our urge to master Christ with easy answers. Faith seeks understanding not by shrinking the question but by opening us to the vastness of the I am.

Jesus later takes this divine name to His own lips: "I am the bread of life . . . I am the light of the world . . . I am the good shepherd" (John 6, 8, 10). Each metaphor is not literal but revelatory. Each opens a window into divine presence.

I am is not a riddle to solve but a relationship to live.

Picture Peter—fiery, loyal, impulsive. His love for Jesus is fierce, but it is a love still bound by his own imagination of what salvation should look like. He cannot fathom the paradox that God's victory would come through weakness, that life would be born through death.

In rebuking Jesus, Peter voices the very temptation Jesus faced in the wilderness: power without the cross, authority without suffering. It is no wonder Jesus calls it Satan's voice. It is the voice of a shortcut, the whisper of an easier way.

We, too, resist. We want faith without struggle, grace without surrender, discipleship without cost. Like Peter, we confess with our lips but stumble in our living. Yet in this struggle lies the path to transformation. Resistance is the place where our illusions are stripped away and God's truth is born in us.

Symbolic Reading

Peter's rebuke: Symbol of our human attempts to control the shape of God's work.

Jesus's harsh response: A mirror to reveal where our loyalties truly lie—with human desires or divine purposes.

"Get behind me"—not a rejection of Peter, but a repositioning. Discipleship means following, not leading; surrendering, not directing.

Signs, Symbols, and Metaphors

Sign: The burning bush as a sign of God's holiness and nearness.

Symbol: The divine name I AM as symbol of eternal presence—uncontainable yet intimately nearby.

Metaphor: Jesus as the I AM made flesh, the eternal Word embodied in time.

Prayer

Eternal I AM,
flame that burns without consuming,
name that cannot be held yet always holds us—
burn away my illusions of control.
Strip me of shallow answers.
Teach me to live not with certainty
but with holy trust.
Let my confession of Jesus
be more than words on my lips;
let it be a life aflame with Your presence.
Christ of the cross,
Forgive me when I cling to my own visions of glory
and resist the way of surrender.
When fear tempts me to rebuke You,
turn me again to follow You.
Strip me of illusions
so that I may discover the deeper life
that comes only through love laid down.
Amen.

Reflection Questions

- When I think of God as "I AM," what feelings rise within me—fear, awe, comfort, resistance?
- Do I tend to shrink Jesus into roles or titles that are easier for me to accept?
- How does the mystery of the burning bush invite me into a deeper awareness of God's presence?
- In what ways might I live more fully into the I AM as a witness of love, presence, and transformation?

- Where do I resist Jesus's call because it does not match my expectations of God?
- How might my own confession still carry elements of control or fear?
- What does it mean for me to "get behind" Jesus, to follow rather than lead?

Now the thread is clear. Chapter One anchored us in the integrative mindset. Chapter Two brought the question, "Who do you say that I am?" And now Chapter Three widens that question with the mystery of Exodus 3 and the I AM sayings (Exod. 3:13–15). Moses at the burning bush, God's self-revelation as Being—how this divine name opens a horizon for faith.

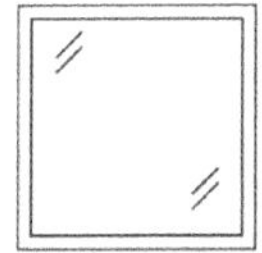

CHAPTER 4

Fear Not, It Is I Mark 6:45–52; John 6:20; John's I AM Sayings

Meditation

The disciples are rowing against the wind, straining in the dark. The sea, ancient symbol of chaos, rises against them. Then across the water Jesus comes walking, not as a ghost, not as a superstition, but as the living presence of God. His words echo like thunder and yet calm like dawn: "It is I. Do not be afraid" (Mark 6:50).

This is more than comfort; it is revelation. The voice from the burning bush now speaks across the storm. The eternal I AM takes flesh and says, I am with you. I am for you. I am here.

The disciples are straining at the oars, battered by the wind. Darkness thickens, waves rise, and fear takes root. Jesus comes walking toward them on the sea, and they cry out in terror, thinking they see a ghost.

But He speaks: "Take heart, it is I; do not be afraid" (Mark 6:50)—literally *ego eimi*, I AM.

The same voice that once thundered from the burning bush now whispers over the waters: I AM with you. I AM here. Fear not.

Narrative Reflection

Fear often narrows our vision. The disciples see a phantom, not a Savior. A diminished mindset hears only the roar of the wind; an integrative mindset hears the deeper word: I AM.

The storm at sea becomes the stage for unveiling Jesus's identity. He is not only teacher, not only miracle worker, but the embodied presence of the God who said to Moses, "I am who I am" (Exod. 3:14).

The storm is not just meteorological; it is existential. The waves represent all that unmoors us—loss, grief, doubt, anxiety, division. The disciples' fear mirrors our own when we cannot recognize God's presence in the chaos.

But the One who walks upon the waters is not a ghost but the living God, the "I am" of Exodus. The I am who I am takes flesh in Jesus who enters our storms, not as an observer but as the Presence itself.

John expands this truth through the great "I am" sayings. And this revelation is not confined to one night on Galilee. It resounds throughout John's Gospel:

- "I am the bread of life" (John 6:35) – I am sustenance in your hunger.
- "I am the light of the world" (John 8:12) – I am clarity in your confusion.
- "I am the good shepherd" (John 10:11) – I am guidance in your wandering.
- "I am the resurrection and the life" (John 11:25) – I am hope when death surrounds you.
- "I am the way and the truth and the life" (John 14:6) – I am the path when you are lost.
- "I am the true vine" (John 15:1) – I am the lifeblood that holds you together.

Each saying is not a doctrine to memorize but a presence to abide in.

Each echoes the same promise: Wherever chaos threatens, God is.

The disciples' terror turns into awe as they realize that the storm is not greater than the One who stands in their midst.

In the storm, Jesus doesn't remove the waves immediately. Instead, He steps into their boat. His "I am" does not cancel chaos; it redefines it. The storm becomes the place where presence is revealed.

Symbolic Reading

The storm: All that shakes us: fear, uncertainty, human limitation

The boat: Our fragile faith communities, straining to hold together against the tide

Jesus walking on the water: The transcendent presence of God entering our vulnerability

Ego eimi: The eternal assurance that God is not far off but here in the thick of the storm

Signs, Symbols, and Metaphors

The storm: The extremity of human fear and chaos

Walking on water: Christ's transcendence of forces that overwhelm us

Ego eimi: God's eternal presence embodied in Jesus

The "I AM" sayings: metaphors that nourish imagination, expand faith, and anchor identity

Prayer

I am,
when the winds rise and my courage falters,
remind me that You are near.
Speak into my fear the words of life:

"It is I; do not be afraid."
Anchor me in Your presence
until my heart learns to rest in You.
Lord of the storm,
When fear blinds me,
when chaos shakes me,
when the waves rise higher than my faith,
speak again Your word: I am.
Bread when I hunger,
Light when I stumble,
Life when I despair—
Be my anchor, my center, my peace.
Amen.

Reflection Questions

- Where in my life do I feel "rowed against the wind"?
- Do I tend to see ghosts or the presence of Christ in my storms?
- Which "I AM" saying speaks to my deepest need right now?
- How might fear itself become the doorway to deeper faith in God's presence?
- What storms in my life feel overwhelming right now?
- How do I recognize God's presence—not after the storm but within it?
- Which "I AM" saying speaks most deeply to me in this season of my journey?

This chapter keeps the storm story as the narrative heart while unfolding the "I am" sayings as echoes of the same divine presence.

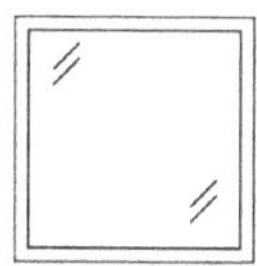

CHAPTER 5

The Cross as Paradox
Mark 8:34–38

Meditation

Jesus turns to the crowd and His disciples and says, "If any wish to come after me, let them deny themselves and take up their cross and follow me. For those who want to save their life will lose it, and those who lose their life for my sake, and for the sake of the gospel, will save it" (Mark 8:34–35).

The cross is not only an instrument of death; it is the paradox of life. It is both an end and a beginning, a loss and a gain, a dying and a rising.

Bread of life, light of the world, resurrection and life—each saying is a window into Christ's identity and our own transformation.

Narrative Reflection

Peter had just confessed, "You are the Messiah." But when Jesus explained what that meant—suffering, rejection, death, and resurrection—Peter resisted. Confession had not yet ripened into comprehension.

This is the human struggle. We want resurrection without the cross, glory without surrender, and certainty without trust. But Jesus names the paradox at the heart of discipleship: to cling is to lose; to release is to receive.

Carrying the cross is not about romanticizing suffering or seeking pain for its own sake. It is about alignment with the self-giving love of Christ—a willingness to let go of false securities, ego-driven identities, and illusions of control.

The paradox is that in surrender, we discover freedom. In dying to self, we awaken to life. In losing, we are found.

This is the Christ event—the collision of human fear and divine love, the moment where faith seeking understanding learns that the path forward is not upward grasping but downward giving.

Symbolic Reading

The cross: Not merely an object of execution, but the symbol of radical self-giving love

Denying self: Releasing the illusions of autonomy and control to discover our true self in God

Losing and saving life: The paradox of grace: We cannot hoard life; we can only receive it as a gift.

Prayer

Christ of the cross,
teach me to let go of what binds me,
to surrender the illusions I cling to,
and to trust that in You,
death is never the last word.
Lead me into the paradox where loss becomes life
and surrender becomes freedom.
Amen.

Reflection Questions

- What "cross" in your life has not chosen suffering but chosen love?
- How have you experienced paradox, where loss led unexpectedly to life?
- What does it mean for you to "lose yourself" in Christ and discover your truest self?

This chapter now sets the stage for the deepening christological identity—Jesus as the One who embodies paradox, and discipleship as learning to walk that paradoxical path.

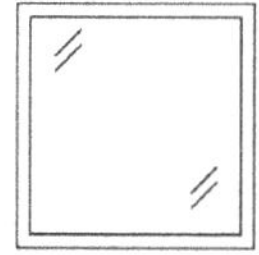

CHAPTER 6

Transfiguration: The Veil Lifted Mark 9:2–9

Meditation

Jesus leads Peter, James, and John up a high mountain. There He is transfigured before them—His clothes dazzling white, His face radiant. Moses and Elijah appear and speak with Him. A cloud overshadows them, and a voice declares, "This is my Son, the Beloved; listen to him!" (Mark 9:7).

Narrative Reflection

Transfiguration is not an escape from the path of suffering. It comes immediately after Jesus has spoken of His coming passion. The mountain light does not erase the valley of shadow; it illuminates it.

For Peter, the temptation was to build booths—to stay on the mountaintop, to capture the glory, and freeze the moment. But discipleship cannot stay in ecstasy. Revelation is given not for escape but for endurance.

The transfiguration is the unveiling of who Jesus truly is: the Christ in whom heaven and earth meet, the I am clothed in light. It is also the unveiling of who we are called to be—children of light, participants in glory, bearers of the divine image.

The paradox of the cross finds its counterpoint here: The same Jesus who will be disfigured on Calvary is first transfigured on the mountain. The veil lifts, and we see that suffering and glory are not opposites but woven into the same mystery.

Symbolic Reading

The mountain: The liminal space where heaven and earth meet, where perspective is widened

The radiance of Christ: The unveiling of His divine identity, the glory hidden within humanity

Moses and Elijah: The Law and the prophets bearing witness to Jesus as their fulfillment

The cloud and the voice: God's presence confirming that listening to Christ is the way to life

Prayer

Radiant Christ,
shine Your light into my shadows,
lift the veil from my eyes,
and grant me courage to descend the mountain
and carry Your glory into the valleys of the world.
When fear clouds my vision,
remind me to listen to You—
the Beloved,
the Word made flesh,
the Light of the world.
Amen.

Reflection Questions

- When have you had a "mountaintop experience" of God's presence?
- How has that moment sustained you when walking through the valleys of suffering?
- What veils might need to be lifted in your life so you can see Christ more clearly?

Faith Seeking Understanding

Anselm's ancient theme renewed: Faith is not static belief but a living journey from awareness to deeper understanding.

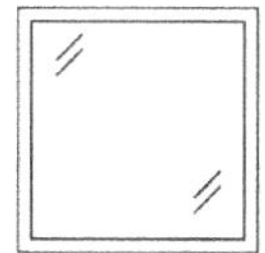

CHAPTER 7

Gethsemane: The Struggle of Surrender and the Gap Between Confession and Resistance Mark 14:32–42

Meditation

In the garden of Gethsemane, Jesus tells His disciples, "My soul is deeply grieved, even to death" (Mark 14:34). He falls to the ground and prays, "Abba, Father, for you all things are possible; remove this cup from me, yet not what I want, but what You want" (Mark 14:36).

The disciples cannot stay awake. Sleep overcomes them while the weight of surrender presses on Jesus.

Gethsemane exposes the truth: Every disciple has a gap between what they confess and how they live. Peter's denial is not unique. It is the human condition. Yet Jesus carries Peter's denial into His prayer, holding even our failures in the embrace of surrender.

The mountain of transfiguration showed us that glory shines through suffering. Gethsemane now shows us how: not through willpower but through letting go; not by eliminating fear but by entrusting fear to the Father.

Our own gaps between belief and practice, confession and action are not healed by effort alone. They are transfigured when we surrender them in prayer.

Narrative

The disciples follow Jesus into the garden, still wrestling with the gap between what they have confessed and what they are willing to live. Peter had said, "You are the Messiah" (Mark 8:29), but in the garden, fear overtakes him. His spirit is willing, but his flesh is weak. He will deny the very One he proclaimed.

Jesus, too, wrestles. But unlike Peter, His struggle does not end in denial but in surrender. He prays, "Not what I want but what you want" (Mark 14:36). In this prayer, we see that the gap between human fear and divine trust can only be bridged through surrender.

If the Transfiguration revealed Jesus's glory, then Gethsemane reveals His humanity. Here we see not radiant light but trembling vulnerability. Here we witness the paradox of the Christ event in its most intimate form: The One who is fully divine is also fully human, capable of anguish, dread, and the longing for escape.

This is not resignation. It is struggle. The will of Jesus wrestles with the will of the Father. His "not what I want" is not instant submission but a costly choice that emerges through prayer, silence, and solitude.

Gethsemane is the place of holy wrestling where faith is tested not by certainty but by surrender. It is where discipleship falters, for even the closest friends fall asleep. And yet it is also where love holds, where Jesus chooses obedience, not because the path is easy but because love demands it.

For us, Gethsemane names the threshold moments of our own lives when we face choices that cannot be evaded, cups that cannot be refused, and loneliness that cannot be explained. It is here that surrender becomes the most profound form of trust.

Symbolic Reading

The garden: A reversal of Eden; where Adam grasped at autonomy, Christ releases in surrender

The cup: The symbol of unavoidable suffering and divine mission

The sleeping disciples: The frailty of human companionship; the loneliness of costly obedience

The prayer of surrender: The hinge of salvation where divine will and human will meet in love

Prayer

Abba, Father,
in my Gethsemane moments,
when fear tightens its grip
and loneliness surrounds me,
teach me to pray with honesty and trust.
Give me courage to say,
"Not what I want but what You want,"
and to discover that surrender is not defeat
but the deepest form of love.
O Christ in the garden,
I bring my confessions and my denials,
my bold words and my trembling heart.
Take the gap between who I say You are
and how I fail to live Your way.
Kneel with me in my Gethsemane.
Pray in me when I cannot pray.
Strengthen me not to erase my fear,
but to entrust it to the Father's love.
Amen.

Modern Echo

A woman stood in church and proclaimed, "Jesus is Lord of my life." But when her workplace demanded that she choose between truth and career advancement, she chose silence. Later in prayer, she confessed her fear. She wept, thinking she had betrayed her confession.

But in that silence of prayer, she heard Christ whisper, "Your fear is safe with me. Surrender it. I will hold you until courage grows."

Like Peter, her gap became the place where Christ's surrender began to live in her.

Reflection Questions

- When have you faced your own "cup"—something you wished could pass but could not?
- What helps you stay awake with Christ in times of struggle?
- How do you hear God's voice in the silence of surrender?

This chapter shows how discipleship is not only about glory but also about holy surrender. The Christ event is as much about the garden as it is about the mountain.

Peter names Jesus as Messiah but refuses the cross. This is a meditation on our own resistance to suffering, paradox, and mystery.

Interlude: The Gap Between Confession and Transformation

Peter's voice rings out at Caesarea Philippi: "You are the Messiah" (Mark 8:29).

It is the high point of recognition, the moment of clarity, the unveiling of truth. And yet almost in the same breath, Peter rebukes Jesus for speaking of suffering, rejection, and death. Jesus responds with words as sharp as a blade: "Get behind me, Satan! For you are setting your mind not on divine things but on human things" (Mark 8:33).

Here lies the gap, the chasm between confessing with our lips and aligning with God's vision. Peter knows who Jesus is, but he cannot yet bear how Jesus will fulfill that calling. He wants glory without the cross, triumph without surrender, a crown without suffering.

And so, six days later on the mountain of Transfiguration, the gap is momentarily healed. Peter, James, and John glimpse the glory hidden within the vulnerability, the light shining through the shadow. The same Jesus who predicts His suffering is revealed as radiant with God's presence. The gap is not erased, but it is held—suspended in mystery, light, and voice: "This is my Son, the Beloved; listen to him" (Mark 9:7).

For us, the challenge is the same. We can confess Jesus as Messiah yet resist the way He chooses to be Messiah. We can say the right words but still act as stumbling blocks when we cling to comfort, control, or our preferred versions of salvation. The gap between confession and transformation is the place of discipleship. It is where we must wrestle with our expectations, our fears, and our resistance.

To investigate this gap in ourselves is to ask, "Do I want a Savior who saves on my terms or on God's terms?"

Am I willing to follow Jesus into both light and shadow, both mountain and garden?

Where in me does resistance still echo the voice of Peter, rebuking the very way of the cross?

The Transfiguration heals this gap, not by erasing it but by reframing it. It assures us that the path of surrender is also the path of glory. The cross does not cancel the radiance; it reveals it.

Spiritual Application

We too live in this tension.

We confess Jesus as Christ yet often resist the implications.

We long for His presence yet recoil from the cost of discipleship.

We want the crown but not the cross.

To investigate this gap within ourselves is the work of spiritual reading. It is the mirror that reveals our fears and the window that opens to grace. The Transfiguration whispers to us that even in our hesitation, glory is present. God is patient with our partial vision, leading us step by step from confession toward transformation.

Prayer

Lord Jesus,
I confess You are the Christ,
yet I stumble in following Your way.
Shine Your light upon my resistance.
Transfigure my fears with Your glory.
Help me walk with You
from mountain to garden,
from confession to surrender,
from partial sight to deeper faith.
Amen.

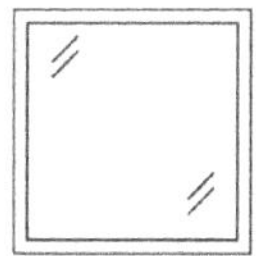

CHAPTER 8

The Cross: God's Vulnerable Glory

Narrative

From Gethsemane's shadows, Jesus walks into the brightness of torches, betrayal, trial, and the way of the cross. The disciples scatter. Peter weeps, his confession shattered by denial. The gap has widened into a chasm, and yet Jesus steps into that chasm carrying not only His own cross but the weight of our broken confessions, our silences, and our betrayals.

At the cross, He cries, "It is finished." Yet in truth, what is finished is not God's work in us but the power of sin to have the last word. God is not finished with Peter. God is not finished with us. The cross exposes human failure and divine faithfulness in one terrible, beautiful intersection.

Reflection

The cross is not the end of the story but rather the place where all our gaps are gathered and redeemed. It is where we confess without understanding, where we proclaim and then resist, where we fear and then deny. Jesus does not abandon us. Instead, He stretches His arms wide, holding together both our faith and our failures.

The vulnerable glory of the cross is that God meets us not where we succeed but where we collapse. It is here that the gap between who we say Jesus is and how we live is healed, not by our effort but by His embrace.

Meditation

O Christ of the cross,
take my broken confessions,
my scattered loyalties,
my fearful denials.
Stretch them upon Your wounded body
and speak over them: "It is finished."
But whisper also in my heart:
"God is not finished with you."
Amen.

Modern Echo

A young man once told his pastor, "I promised God I'd never fail again. But I've already failed. I feel like a fraud."

The pastor looked at him gently and said, "You are exactly the one the cross was meant for. God does not meet us where we are perfect. God meets us where we are broken."

The young man wept. For the first time, he realized that the cross was not a demand for perfection but an embrace of imperfection—and an invitation to begin again.

The Cross as Revelation: "It Is Finished, but God Is Not Finished" (Mark 15:33–39; John 19:30)

So far, we've walked through:

- Peter's confession and resistance
- The Transfiguration
- Gethsemane's surrender

Now let's deepen the Christ event by focusing on the cross itself—not just as death but as revelation.

Narrative Reflection

Darkness falls at noon. The One who healed the blind, raised the dead, and welcomed the outcast now hangs between two criminals. The crowd mocks, the leaders sneer, and even Jesus's disciples have fled. Yet in this place of abandonment, the deepest revelation is unveiled.

Jesus breathes His last and cries out, "It is finished" (John 19:30). To the world, it sounds like failure. But to faith, it is the mystery of completion. What is finished is not the hope of God but the reign of sin and death. What is completed is the offering of love that refuses to retaliate, the surrender of self that trusts entirely in the Father.

And yet even here, God is not finished. For the cross is not the conclusion of Jesus's story but the unveiling of God's faithfulness. The centurion, hardened by execution, beholds the manner of Jesus's dying and declares, "Truly, this man was God's Son!" (Mark 15:39). The one least likely to confess is the first to recognize divinity at the foot of the cross.

Meditation

Lord Jesus,
on the cross You whispered, "It is finished."
Teach me to trust that even in endings,
Your love is still at work.
When I feel abandoned, remind me You are near.
When I feel defeated, open my heart to resurrection hope.
For what You have finished,
God is still completing in me.
Amen.

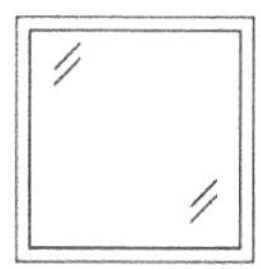

CHAPTER 9
The Christ Event as Mirror and Window

Spiritual Application

The cross reveals that God's way is not domination but love. It unmasks our illusions of power, our reliance on violence, and our desire to save ourselves. It exposes the gap between what we expect of God and what God does.

When Jesus says "It is finished," we might hear resignation. But perhaps we should also hear invitation: God is not finished with you. The story is not over. Resurrection is already stirring beneath the soil of despair.

We are invited to see the cross as both mirror and window:

- *Mirror:* What in me resists surrender? Where do I cling to control or retaliate with violence?
- *Window:* What might God be finishing in me so something new can rise?
- *Resurrection:* Beyond the single story of death

Narrative

Dawn breaks, but the disciples remain in the shadows. They have confessed, resisted, denied, and scattered. Now they sit in silence, convinced that the story has ended. Death, they think, has the final word.

But at the tomb, women come with spices. They expect silence, but instead they find absence. The stone is rolled away. The angel asks, "Why do you look for the living among the dead?" (Luke 24:5). The women become the first witnesses that the gap between confession and denial, between death and life has been crossed—not by them but by God.

The resurrection does not erase their failures; it reframes them. Peter will still carry the memory of his denial. Thomas will still wrestle with doubt. But in the light of resurrection, these wounds become places where grace shines through.

Reflection

Resurrection is not the denial of death but its transformation. It is not pretending the gap never existed but showing that God's love bridges even what seemed unbridgeable.

The disciples are not replaced by better followers; they are renewed as witnesses. Their single story of despair is broken open into a many-layered narrative of hope.

In our lives, resurrection does not mean we never fail again. It means our failures no longer define the end of our story. God's "not finished" becomes our new beginning.

Meditation

O Christ of the morning,
roll away the stones in my life
that keep me sealed in shame.

Let Your light fall into my shadows.
Take my denials, my doubts, my despair
and write resurrection across them.
Teach me to live as one
who knows the end is never the end,
and that love always has another word.
Amen.

Modern Echo

A woman who had battled years of addiction told her recovery group, "I thought my life was over when I lost everything. But that was not the end. The end was where God began again."

Her story did not deny the darkness she had walked through. But it revealed how even death-like seasons can become wombs of new life. She bore witness not to perfection but to resurrection.

With this, the arc is complete:

- Confession and gap (Peter's "You are the Messiah")
- Surrender (Gethsemane)
- Healing embrace (the cross)
- Transformation (resurrection)

Jesus reveals who God is and who we are called to be. Reading His life is both reflection (mirror) and horizon (window).

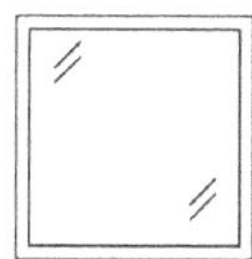

CHAPTER 10

The Cross and the "I AM"

At Golgotha, Jesus's surrender echoes "It is finished" and "I am." The paradox: the One who dies is the One who *is*.

Pentecost: From Fear to Witness

Narrative

The disciples huddle behind locked doors. Their confessions are uncertain; their faith is fragile. They have seen the risen Christ, yet fear still holds them.

Then it happens. A sound like a rushing wind fills the house. Tongues of fire rest upon each one of them. They are not replaced or erased; they are empowered. Their stammering becomes proclamation. Their fear becomes courage. Their single stories of failure and fear are woven into one Spirit-filled narrative of love.

What began as Peter's confession, broken by denial and healed by grace, now becomes Peter's sermon to the crowds. What began as silence becomes song. What began as despair becomes mission.

Reflection

Pentecost is not just the birth of the Church; it is the healing of fractured hearts. The Spirit gathers what was scattered. The disciples' stories remain unique, yet they now speak with one voice—the voice of witness.

The Spirit transforms a gap-filled, wounded community into a living body of Christ. This is not perfection but rather participation—a people learning together to love God and neighbor.

For us, Pentecost means we need not remain locked in fear or trapped in our private stories. The Spirit opens us, lifts us, and sends us into the world with courage to witness.

Meditation

Come, Holy Spirit,
wind of God, breath of life.
Blow through my locked places.
Set fire to my silences.
Turn my fear into witness,
my story into song.
Make me part of a community
where no wound is wasted
and no voice is left unheard.
Amen.

Modern Echo

In a neighborhood torn by violence, a small church began opening its doors each night simply for prayer and song. At first, only a few came. But as voices rose in many languages, neighbors who had once feared each other began to recognize a new story unfolding—not of division but of shared hope.

One young man said, "I used to think I had no place, no voice. But here, I learned my story matters. Here, I found courage to speak."

That is Pentecost: the Spirit turning fear into witnesses, division into community, silence into song.

The journey of Book Five has carried us through one of the deepest questions of the gospel: "Who do you say that I am?" (Mark 8:29).

At first, Peter's confession seems complete: "You are the Messiah." Yet almost immediately, his fear resists the way of the cross. Here lies the gap—between words spoken and life lived, between faith confessed and faith embodied. It is the gap every disciple must face.

Jesus does not condemn Peter for the gap; He walks with him through it. From Caesarea Philippi to the Mount of Transfiguration, from Gethsemane to Golgotha, Peter learns that faith is not a fixed possession but a living process. Confession without transformation risks becoming ideology. But confession held in tension with surrender becomes the soil of growth.

At the cross, Jesus declares, "It is finished." Yet the story is not finished because God's love continues beyond death. Resurrection reframes the gap, not by erasing human failure but by showing that grace can transfigure even denial and despair.

Finally, at Pentecost, the Spirit gathers scattered disciples into communion. Their fractured stories become one living witness. The gap between what they said and what they lived, between fear and courage, is not closed by their strength but healed by God's Spirit.

The Christ Event as Ongoing

The Christ event—confession, cross, resurrection, and Spirit—is not just history; it is the ongoing rhythm of Christian life.

- We confess Christ in faith.
- We struggle with the gap between words and action.
- We are redeemed by love stronger than death.
- And we are empowered by the Spirit to live as witnesses.

This pattern is not a single moment but a lifelong process of faith seeking understanding, of moving from literal certainties into symbolic depth, from fear into freedom, from isolation into communion.

Invitation to the Reader

Your story, too, has gaps—places where your confession falters, where fear holds you back, where silence seems safer than witness. But the Christ event proclaims that these gaps are not endings; they are thresholds where grace waits.

Christ meets you in the confession you can make today. Christ walks with you through the fears you cannot yet release. Christ embraces your wounds and reframes them with resurrection light. And Christ sends you forth in the Spirit, not perfect but empowered, not finished but becoming.

So the question echoes again: “Who do you say that I am?”

The answer is never once and for all but always unfolding until our fragmented stories are gathered into God’s great communion of love.

Epilogue

Benediction of the Christ Event

Beloved,
the journey of confession and cross,
of resurrection and Spirit
is not a story behind us;
it is a rhythm within us.
When you falter,
remember Peter who confessed and denied
yet was still called "rock" upon which love would build.
When you despair,
remember Mary who wept at an empty tomb,
only to hear her name spoken in resurrection light.
When you fear,
remember the disciples locked in an upper room
until Spirit-breath filled them with courage
to walk into the world as witnesses of love.
So go now,
not with answers that end the story
but with faith that seeks and grows.
Go with the courage to face your gaps,
the grace to trust God's unfinished work in you,
and the Spirit's fire that turns confession into communion.
For the One who says "I AM" is with you
in the night and in the dawn,
in your dying and in your rising,
in every broken fragment,
and in the wholeness yet to come.
Amen.

Fivefold 'Graphia': One Story of Love

Scripture, like a mirror and a window, reflects who we are and reveals who we can become. In this book, we have walked through five graphia—five scriptural pathways that are not separate volumes but woven threads in a single garment of grace.

Book One: Samaria (Luke 10; John 4)

Here we learned that Scripture is both mirror and window. In Samaria we saw ourselves—our prejudices, our single stories, our thirst for living water. We learned that the stranger, the Samaritan, the outsider, may carry the very face of God.

Book Two: Echoes of the Innocents (Matthew 2; Mark 4; John 11)

Here we faced the extremity of the human condition: violence, loss, grief, storm, and death. Yet we also heard God's whisper in the silence and the promise that lament and love together form the deepest prayer. "Unbind him and let him go" became both command and invitation for Lazarus and for us.

Book Three: Night Conversations (John 3)

Here we entered Nicodemus' midnight searching, discovering that being "born again" is less about a formula and more about awakening to what is already stirring in us. The movement from night to dawn mirrors our own journey—knowing about God giving way to experiencing God.

Book Four: The Christ Event and the Gap (Mark 8; Exodus 3; John's I AM)

Here we wrestled with the question that defines discipleship: "Who do you say that I am?" Peter's confession revealed the beauty and the fragility of faith. The gap between confession and resistance, between words and transformation, became our mirror. In the transfiguration, the cross, and the resurrection, we saw that God's grace meets us in that gap, healing and reframing it.

Book Five: From Confession to Communion

Here we came to the center: the Christ event itself. Confession leads to the cross; the cross leads to the resurrection; the resurrection leads to the Spirit; and the Spirit leads us into communion. Faith is not static possession but a living process—ever seeking, ever deepening, and ever opening.

One Gospel Story, Many Graphia

Each graphia is its own story, yet together they form a single narrative arc:

- From mirror to window
- From innocence lost to lament voiced
- From night's searching to morning's new birth
- From confession's gap to Spirit's communion

The Bible is not just words on a page. It is the living Word, encountered anew whenever we read not only with our minds but with our hearts, our wounds, and our hopes.

And so, dear reader, this fivefold journey does not end here. It continues in you. For every time you open the Scriptures with an integrative mindset, anchored in love, attuned to symbol, and open to paradox, you are writing the next chapter of this gospel story with your own life.

A Final Blessing

May the Word you have read become the Word you live.
May the mirror show you your truest self.
May the window open onto God's vast horizon.
And may the Spirit, who is always both mirror and wind,
carry you deeper into the mystery of Christ,
who is the Word made flesh,
the I AM who says, even now,
"Do not be afraid. It is I."
Amen.

Litany of the Five Graphia

Book One: Samaria

We look into the mirror and see our thirst;
We open the window and meet the stranger who carries God's face.

Book Two: Echoes of the Innocents

We cry with Rachel, and God weeps with us;
We hear the whisper in the storm: Peace, be still.

Book Three: Night Conversations

We stumble in the dark with Nicodemus;
We awaken to dawn, discovering we were already born from above.

Book Four: The Christ Event and the Gap

We confess with Peter: You are the Christ!
We tremble in the gap yet hear upon the mountain: This is my Beloved; listen to Him.

Book Five: From Confession to Communion

We take up the cross, not as burden but as gift.
We walk into resurrection life where all becomes communion.

Closing Response

- One story, many voices
- One Word, many echoes
- One Christ, many encounters
- All: Mirror and Window, Light and Life, Word made Flesh—be born again in us, now and always

Leader / All Format (for communal use):

Leader (Book One: Samaria)
We look into the mirror and see our thirst.
All:
We open the window and meet the stranger who carries God's face.
Leader (Book Two: Echoes of the Innocents)
We cry with Rachel, and God weeps with us.
All:
We hear the whisper in the storm: Peace, be still.
Leader (Book Three: Night Conversations)
We stumble in the dark with Nicodemus.
All:
We awoke to dawn, discovering we were already born from above.
Leader (Book Four: The Christ Event and the Gap)
We confess with Peter: You are the Christ!
Al\:
We tremble in the gap yet hear upon the mountain: This is my Beloved; listen to Him.
Leader (Book Five: From Confession to Communion)
We take up the cross, not as burden but as gift.
All:

We walk into resurrection life where all becomes communion.
Closing Response (all together)
One story, many voices.
One Word, many echoes.
One Christ, many encounters.
All:
Mirror and window, light and life, Word made flesh—be born again in us, now and always.

Personal Prayer Adaptation

You can pray quietly, pausing after each stanza:

Book One: Lord, quench my thirst, help me see Your face in the stranger.
Book Two: Lord, weep with me, and calm my storms.
Book Three: Lord, awaken me to the dawn of Your Spirit.
Book Four: Lord, steady me in the gap between my confession and my fear.
Book Five: Lord, let the cross become my communion and resurrection my life.

A Blessing for the Reader

Beloved of God,
you have walked through mirrors and windows,
through thirst and storm,
through night and dawn,
through confession and cross.
May the Word you have read
become the Word you live.
When you see only a mirror,
may Christ open for you a window.
When you feel only the storm,
may Christ whisper, Peace, be still.

When you stumble in the night,
may Christ awaken you to morning light.
When you falter in the gap,
may Christ hold you on the mountain.
When you carry the cross,
may Christ turn it into communion.
Go now,
not with answers only,
but with a heart that seeks,
eyes that see,
ears that listen,
and hands that serve.
And may the blessing of the One who is
I AM—Father, Son, and Spirit—
go before you,
walk beside you,
and dwell within you,
now and always.
Amen.

Epilogue: Mirror and Window

Mirror and window,
shadow and light,
the Word has found us
by day and by night.
Storms may surround us,
yet peace will remain;
tears may still flow,
but love bears the pain.
Born in the Spirit,
from night into dawn,
the Christ walks beside us,

our fear is undone.
Cross into communion,
death into song,
the story of Jesus
now carries us on.
So go as a witness,
beloved and free;
for the Word made flesh
is alive in thee.

"The Word you read becomes the life you live."
Poetic:
"Every mirror becomes a window when seen through the eyes of love."
Theological:
"The Word made flesh now seeks to be made flesh again—in you."
Pastoral:
"Go, beloved, and let Scripture be written once more in your life."
Contemplative:
"In every ending, the Word whispers a new beginning."

Part Two

Mirror and Window: Reading Scripture with an Integrative Spiritual Worldview and Social Justice

Introduction: Hermeneutics of the Holy Spirit

When I first encountered the phrase "hermeneutics of the Holy Spirit" in Eastern Orthodox thought, it struck me as both profoundly simple and deeply demanding. Hermeneutics, the art of interpretation, is not just about methods or theories. In this tradition, it is about Spirit. To read Scripture with the Spirit is to read with love.

Love becomes both the safeguard and the guide. True understanding of Scripture is never only intellectual; it is spiritual and transformative. The Spirit does not merely sharpen the mind but reshapes the heart, opening us to the living Word in ways that foster compassion, unity, and communion. If we approach the Bible only as a text to be analyzed, we risk missing its power. But if we read with the Spirit and with love, then Scripture becomes more than words; it becomes a sacred encounter.

This way of reading opens us to layers of meaning. Scripture is not flat; it is rich, textured, and alive. Eastern Christianity has long spoken of four senses of Scripture:

- The literal sense, grounding us in history and story
- The allegorical sense, pointing us to Christ and the Church
- The moral sense, guiding us in how to live with integrity
- The anagogical sense, lifting our eyes to God's promised future

Each layer is revealed through prayer, reflection, and the Spirit's illumination. None cancels the others; together they weave a tapestry of meaning.

In this vision, Scripture is also mirror, window, and icon.

As mirror, the text reflects us back to ourselves. In its stories we see our pride, our fears, our hopes, our resistance, and our longing for God. The mirror calls us to honesty, to repentance, and to growth.

As window, the text opens onto horizons beyond us—the character of God, the mission of Christ, the life of the Spirit, the struggles of the community of faith. Through Scripture we see not only ourselves but the broader story of salvation inviting us into empathy and action.

And as icon, Scripture draws us into the presence of the divine. Just as an icon is not merely an image but a window into mystery, so too the Bible is not simply a book but a living vessel of encounter. To pray with Scripture is to gaze through it into God's reality, allowing the Spirit to transfigure us.

This hermeneutic also carries with it safeguards against false narratives and distortions. The first safeguard is love. Interpretations that harm, divide, or diminish are not of the Spirit. The second is humility. No reader possesses the whole truth, and Scripture is always richer than our grasp. The third is community. Interpretation is not a private possession but a shared journey where diverse voices discern together under the Spirit's guidance.

Theologians speak of Logos and Rhema to describe this interplay. Logos is the eternal Word, the timeless truth of God in Christ. Rhema is the personal, Spirit-given word that speaks into our particular moment. Both are necessary. Logos anchors us, and Rhema animates us. The Spirit holds them together in love.

To read Scripture, then, with an integrative worldview is to allow the Spirit of love to guide us through mirror, window, and icon. It is to embrace many layers of meaning without fear, to listen for both the universal Word and the personal word, to seek truth in ways that heal rather than harm. It is to let love be our hermeneutic so our readings foster justice, compassion, and communion in the world.

That is what it means to read with an integrative spiritual worldview—not simply to interpret texts but to let the Spirit interpret us. It is to be read, reshaped, and renewed in love.

Symbolic Reading

Mirror: Scripture reflects us back to ourselves—our struggles, hopes, fears, and longings.

Window: Scripture opens us to God's broader story—salvation, justice, and communion.

Icon: Scripture invites us into holy encounter—not just knowledge about God but union with God.

Layers of meaning: Literal, allegorical, moral, and anagogical senses weave together a fuller tapestry of truth.

Logos and Rhema: Logos anchors us in God's eternal Word; Rhema awakens us with the Spirit's timely word for our lives.

Prayer

Spirit of truth and love,
Open the Scriptures to us,
that in the mirror we may see ourselves honestly,
in the window we may glimpse Your justice and mercy,
and in the icon we may behold Your presence.
Guard us from false narratives;
guide us into humility and compassion.
Let Your Logos ground us,
let Your Rhema speak to us,
and let all our readings be shaped by love.
Amen.

Reflection Questions

- When have I experienced Scripture as a mirror, showing me myself honestly?
- How has Scripture served as a window, opening me to God's wider story?
- What does it mean to see Scripture as an icon, not just words but presence?
- How do the four senses of Scripture (literal, allegorical, moral, anagogical) shape my engagement with the Word?
- How might a hermeneutic of love safeguard me from misusing Scripture in ways that harm rather than heal?

The hermeneutic of the Holy Spirit is also a hermeneutic of love. It reminds us that reading Scripture is not merely intellectual but transformational. It shows us the many layers of meaning within Scripture and invites us to read with humility, openness, and compassion so our interpretations foster justice, healing, and communion.

Iconography and the Hermeneutics of Love

In Eastern Orthodox spirituality, words are never the only language of theology. Just as Scripture is read, prayed, and sung, it is also seen. Iconography is visual theology, a way of contemplating divine truth that transcends speech and text. Icons are not simply art; they are windows into mystery. In their shapes and colors, in the faces of Christ, the Theotokos, and the saints, they invite us to gaze into the love of God. The image becomes Scripture made visible, a silent sermon that calls us to prayer.

The central mystery of the Christian faith—the incarnation of the Word—lies at the heart of this vision. If God has become flesh, then God can also be seen. The icon proclaims this truth: the invisible made visible, the eternal made tangible, the Word who dwelt among us. To look upon an icon is to confess that Christ is not distant but present, and that love has entered the world in human form.

Yet icons are not meant only for viewing. They are meant for encounter. To sit before an icon is to enter into meditative engagement—a prayer of the eyes. The faithful are not asked to admire or analyze but to dwell, to let the image read them even as Scripture does. Gazing at an icon, you may sense the communion of saints or feel a wordless dialogue stirring in the heart. This contemplative seeing is guided by the Spirit who draws us deeper into the knowledge and love of God.

Icons are also deeply communal. They do not belong to the individual alone but to the Church's shared life. They adorn walls and homes, surround worshipers in liturgy, and accompany prayer in private corners. Through them, believers participate in a tradition that stretches across centuries. The presence of icons fosters a sacred atmosphere, reminding the faithful that interpretation of Scripture and experience of God are not solitary endeavors but journeys of the whole community.

Orthodoxy insists that icons are not merely symbolic. They carry a sacramental quality. Just as Scripture conveys more than ink on a page, icons carry more than paint on wood. They are believed to be infused with grace, vessels of divine presence. To venerate an icon is not to worship an image but to honor the One revealed through it. In this sense, icons stand beside Scripture as holy media of encounter, both word and image becoming avenues of transformation in the Spirit.

That is why iconography is also a teaching tool. Icons tell stories: the annunciation, the baptism of Christ, the raising of Lazarus, the witness of martyrs. In times and places where literacy was rare, icons proclaimed the gospel as clearly as any sermon. Even now, they continue to communicate faith across language and culture, embodying the truth that the message of love is for all people in every form of expression.

This theology of vision, often called visual theology, has its roots in beauty itself. For the Orthodox, beauty is not an ornament but a sign of the divine. The harmony of color, the dignity of form, the stillness of a saint's gaze all point toward the Source of beauty, who is God. To be moved by the beauty of an icon is already to begin to pray, to step into a mystical dialogue where beauty leads to truth and truth to love.

In practice, this interplay of Scripture and image comes alive in Lectio Divina and Visio Divina. Lectio is the slow reading of Scripture where the Word seeps into the soul through repetition, meditation, prayer, and silent resting in God. Visio is the slow gazing upon an icon or sacred image, where seeing becomes prayer and prayer becomes communion. Both practices serve the same end: to bring the believer into deeper relationship with God, one through words and the other through images. Both are guided by the Spirit of love.

In this way, iconography becomes more than decoration. It is interpretation. It enriches the hermeneutics of the Holy Spirit and of love, showing us that divine truth can be heard and seen, read and beheld, spoken and contemplated. Scripture and icons together remind us that faith is not only learned but lived, not only studied but experienced, not only believed but loved.

Lectio and Visio Divina: Pathways of Transformation

In the life of the Church, words and images both serve as doorways into God's presence. Two practices, Lectio Divina and Visio Divina, have long guided believers into deeper communion with the divine. Though they use different mediums—the written word and the sacred image—their goals are the same: to nurture relationship, to foster transformation, and to open the heart to love.

Lectio Divina, or "divine reading," begins with Scripture itself. At its core, it is about deepening your relationship with God through the Word. It is not rushed or analytical but rather slow, prayerful, and attentive. As the words are read and reread, they provide more than knowledge; they offer spiritual nourishment. Insights surface, wisdom emerges, and guidance for daily living begins to take shape.

Over time, Lectio Divina transforms the heart. The reader is not simply informed but reshaped, gently aligned more closely with the will of God. It is a dialogue: Scripture speaks, and the believer responds in prayer. Thoughts, feelings, gratitude, lament—all are brought into conversation with God. Beyond words, the practice opens into silence, cultivating a contemplative awareness in which you can simply rest in the presence of the Holy.

Visio Divina, or "divine seeing," follows a similar path but through sacred images rather than text. An icon or work of sacred art becomes the focus, not as decoration but as a means of encountering the divine. Gazing upon the image is itself a prayer, a way of opening the eyes of the heart.

Icons tell stories in color and form—the face of Christ, the tenderness of the Mother of God, the witness of saints, the mystery of biblical scenes. These images evoke reflection and stir spiritual insights, drawing the viewer into dialogue with God. Like Lectio, Visio leads to prayerful response, but this time born of sight, symbol, and beauty.

Visio Divina also transforms. Beauty itself becomes a teacher, awakening the soul to God's presence. Sacred art fosters aesthetic appreciation that leads to awe and reverence, reminding us that beauty is one of the names of God. Through slow and contemplative seeing, the believer enters into deeper communion, experiencing God's love not only with the mind but with the senses and emotions.

Together, Lectio and Visio Divina reveal the breadth of God's communication. Through the written Word and the painted icon, the Spirit speaks. Both practices aim to cultivate virtues—patience, humility, compassion, love—and to nurture a heart that is open to transformation. Both create space for divine encounter, where the Logos speaks universally and the Rhema whispers personally.

In the end, the purpose of both practices is simple yet profound: to be drawn into intimacy with God, to let His Word and His beauty transform us, and to live lives that reflect the love we have received.

The Virtues of Lectio and Visio Divina

The practice of Lectio Divina is far more than the slow reading of Scripture. It is a school of the Spirit, a way of cultivating virtues that take root in the heart and spill into the rhythms of daily life. As we linger with the Word, faith deepens, nourished by God's promises and presence. In that faith grows patience—the patience to sit quietly with Scripture, to wait for understanding, and to trust the unfolding of God's plan.

Humility, too, is formed in the practice. The reader comes not as master of the text but as disciple, open to what may be revealed in God's time. Love rises naturally from this encounter, for every page of Scripture calls us to love God and neighbor more fully. From love flows compassion: a tender-hearted recognition of the joys and sorrows carried by others. Gratitude follows closely as the Word reminds us of blessings received and mercies renewed each day.

Wisdom comes not as sudden flashes but as steady light, guiding choices and shaping discernment. Hope is rekindled as the promises of God stir expectation for what is yet to come. Joy wells up as the heart encounters grace, and peace settles quietly, a fruit of resting in

God's presence. In these ways, Lectio Divina is not only a practice of reading but of being reshaped—faith, patience, humility, love, compassion, gratitude, wisdom, hope, joy, and peace forming a mosaic of transformation.

Visio Divina, the contemplative seeing of sacred images, nurtures its own constellation of virtues. To stand before an icon is to be invited first into reverence, a posture of awe before the mystery is made visible. Contemplation follows as the eyes linger, learning to slow down, to notice, and to be present. Such seeing requires openness—a willingness to receive whatever insight, emotion, or whisper of the Spirit may arise.

Icons, with their depictions of Christ, the Theotokos, saints, and biblical scenes, stir compassion. They bring to life the struggles and sacrifices of holy figures, inviting us to empathize and extend mercy in our own lives. Gratitude is awakened in the beauty of color, form, and story, reminding us that God's grace is both seen and experienced. Joy, too, springs forth—the kind of joy that beauty bestows when it becomes a doorway to divine presence.

From these encounters, wisdom grows as the symbolism of the image opens into deeper truths. Love is nourished as we behold acts of sacrifice and tenderness depicted in paint and gold. Peace comes through the contemplative stillness of gazing, and hope emerges from images of resurrection, redemption, and the promise of new creation.

Both practices—reading the Word and beholding the image—lead to transformation. They are not ends in themselves but pathways of encounter, shaping virtues that ripple outward into daily interactions. Faith and reverence, patience and contemplation, humility and openness, love and compassion, gratitude and joy, wisdom and peace, hope for what is yet unseen—all are cultivated in the heart of those who linger with God in Scripture and in sacred art.

Through Lectio and Visio Divina, the Spirit invites us to live what we behold, to become what we contemplate. In these practices, virtue is not abstract; it is incarnate, expressed in lives marked by prayer, compassion, and love.

Living the Practices: Integrating Lectio and Visio Divina

To bring Lectio Divina and Visio Divina into daily prayer is to invite the Spirit to reshape your life from the inside out. These ancient practices, when woven into the rhythm of each day, have the power to transform fear into trust, distraction into stillness, and mere belief into a lived direction of love.

The journey begins by setting aside a sacred time and space. It does not need to be long or elaborate, but it must be intentional. A quiet corner, a candle, or a chair by the window can become a sanctuary. Stepping into this space each day is an act of faith, a declaration that God's presence matters.

Silence comes next—a few moments to still the noise within and without. This silence is not empty but expectant, like the pause before a symphony begins. It opens the heart, clears the mind, and prepares the soul for encounter.

With Scripture in hand, the practice of Lectio Divina unfolds. The text is read slowly, not rushed, as though each word were a gift to be savored. The words are allowed to echo in the heart. Reflection follows as the reader ponders how this passage intersects with life, stirring questions, hopes, or conviction. Prayer then rises naturally, a response born not of duty but of dialogue: "This is what I hear, Lord; this is where I am; this is what I long for." Finally, contemplation leads into stillness, a quiet resting in God's presence where the Word is no longer just read but received.

The practice continues with Visio Divina, turning from the written Word to the painted Word, from Scripture to sacred image.

An icon, a biblical scene, or a painting rich with symbol is chosen. The eyes linger, tracing the colors, gestures, and expressions. What stirs within? Awe, sadness, hope? Reflection deepens as the image tells its silent story, linking the holy past with the present moment. Prayer arises again, this time shaped by what the eyes have seen—gratitude, confession, longing, or intercession. And once more, silence completes the practice, a gaze of the heart resting in God.

When Scripture and image are prayed together, the two practices form a dialogue of Word and vision. The mirror reflects our own fears and desires, calling us to honesty. The window opens onto God's horizon, calling us to compassion. And the icon becomes a meeting place where the Spirit whispers love and reshapes the heart.

In time, this daily rhythm nurtures profound change. Fears lose their grip as we come to know ourselves embraced by God's unconditional love. False notions of God as distant or judgmental dissolve as we discover a God of tenderness and mercy. Reality itself begins to appear differently, not as fragmented and harsh but as interconnected and filled with grace.

Through these practices, we discover what it means to be fully human and fully alive. In Scripture and image, we see both our own story and the stories of others. We encounter Christ's compassion and justice. We are drawn toward a life of service and community. The virtues of faith, patience, humility, love, compassion, gratitude, wisdom, joy, hope, and peace begin to take root.

This integration does not end with the self. It shapes communities. As more hearts are opened through Lectio and Visio Divina, compassion flows outward, justice is sought more earnestly, and a sense of shared humanity is strengthened. The sacred practice of contemplation becomes the wellspring of action, grounding us in love that heals both souls and societies.

In the end, the daily weaving of Lectio and Visio Divina is not simply about prayer; it is about transformation. It is about learning to see ourselves truthfully, to see God lovingly, and to see the world as a place where love and justice can flourish. To live this way is to walk toward the fullness of life where every day becomes a sacred space, every encounter a window into grace, and every act an expression of God's love.

Lectio, Visio, and the Work of Justice

When practiced faithfully, Lectio Divina and Visio Divina do more than shape the inner life of prayer. They extend outward, planting seeds of compassion that grow into action. Together, these practices become a wellspring of social justice, reminding us that faith cannot be separated from love or contemplation from service.

Through Lectio Divina, Scripture speaks with fresh urgency. The prophets thunder again about justice rolling down like water. Jesus blesses the poor and challenges the complacent. The epistles call us to welcome the stranger and care for the vulnerable. Slowly, these words cease to be abstract teachings and become a living summons. In the silence that follows reading and meditation, hearts awaken to God's dream of equity and mercy.

Visio Divina works in a parallel way. Icons and sacred art portray Christ washing the disciples' feet, the Good Samaritan tending the wounded, or saints giving their lives in acts of love. These images do not simply decorate; they confront and inspire. As the eyes linger, compassion deepens; as the imagination engages, hope takes root. Through the beauty of sacred art, believers are drawn to see not only what is but what might be: a more just and merciful society.

Together, Lectio and Visio cultivate empathy. As we reflect on Scripture and sacred images, the suffering of others is no longer distant. Their pain becomes our pain, their longing our longing.

In this way, Spirit teaches us to feel with others, to recognize the humanity we share. From empathy flows the courage to act.

These practices also nurture community. When Scripture is read and icons contemplated in groups, new insights are shared, and collective vision emerges. What begins as silent prayer can blossom into common purpose. Believers find themselves moved not only to personal transformation but to communal action: advocacy, service, and solidarity with the oppressed.

There is also a challenging edge. Lectio and Visio invite us to look unflinchingly at the injustices of our time. In their light, excuses crumble and illusions are stripped away. The mirror of Scripture and image exposes our complicity, while the window opens to God's vision of a new humanity. Old assumptions about privilege and power are unsettled, making space for transformed perspectives.

At their deepest, these practices provide spiritual empowerment. In prayer, we remember that the work of justice is not ours alone but God's. Our small acts are caught up into God's greater purpose. In this way, Lectio and Visio free us from despair and instill hope. They grant us the courage to believe that another world is possible and that we are called to help shape it.

To practice Lectio and Visio daily is to live with a vision of a just society ever before us. The Word and the image remind us that God's kingdom is one of mercy, healing, and reconciliation. They insist that faith is not private sentiment but public witness, not mere reflection but embodied love.

In the end, the integration of these practices leads to transformation not only of the self but of the world around us. They deepen understanding, cultivate empathy, inspire action, and call forth community. They challenge injustice, empower faith, and sustain hope. Most of all, they remind us that to pray with Scripture and with images is to step into the story of God's justice and love—a story we are invited to live with our words, our hands, and our lives.

Lectio, Visio, and the Work of Justice

Meditation

"But let justice roll down like water and righteousness like an ever-flowing stream" (Amos 5:24).

Justice is not an optional add-on to faith. It is the river that flows from the heart of God, and through prayerful practices like Lectio and Visio Divina, we are invited to step into its current.

Narrative Reflection

When Scripture is read slowly through Lectio Divina, familiar words take on fresh urgency. The prophets thunder about justice, Jesus blesses the poor, and the apostles call us to welcome the stranger. These voices do not remain in the past; they speak into the present, summoning us to act with compassion and courage.

Similarly, Visio Divina opens another dimension of this call. Icons and sacred art tell stories of love and service in color and line. A painting of the Good Samaritan tending the wounded, an icon of Christ washing feet, or the image of saints giving themselves for others become a silent sermon. The longer we gaze, the more these images stir something within us: empathy, conviction, longing.

Together, these practices are not passive. They pull us into the world's pain and God's vision. They move us from reflection to action, from inward transformation to outward love.

Symbolic Reading

The River of Justice (Amos 5): A symbol of God's justice, ever-flowing, unstoppable, calling us to join its current

The Good Samaritan (Luke 10): A symbol of compassion that crosses boundaries, revealing that love is action, not sentiment

Christ Washing Feet (John 13): A symbol of humble service, the heart of discipleship and the essence of justice
Sacred Images of Saints: Symbols of courage, sacrifice, and hope, reminding us that ordinary people become extraordinary witnesses when shaped by love

These symbols, when contemplated through word and image, become mirrors of our own lives and windows into God's dream for the world.

Prayer

God of justice and mercy,
Open my eyes through Your Word
that I may see the cries of the oppressed.
Open my heart through sacred images
that I may feel compassion for the suffering.
Shape my hands for service,
my voice for truth,
and my life for love.
Let my prayer become action
and my reflection become justice.
Amen.

Reflection Questions

- Which biblical passages of justice or compassion speak most powerfully to me when prayed through Lectio Divina?
- How have sacred images—icons, paintings, even modern art—stirred my empathy or inspired me to act?
- Where do I see injustice in my community, and how might my prayer lead to concrete action?
- What fears or assumptions might I need to confront in order to live more justly?

- How can I practice justice not only as public advocacy but also in small, daily acts of compassion and service?

Lectio Divina and Visio Divina are not an end in themselves. These practices cultivate more than private devotion; they open us into a spiritual worldview where faith, compassion, and justice become inseparable. To linger with Scripture in prayer or to gaze upon an icon with love is to step into a vision of reality where God is present, the neighbor is beloved, and creation itself is sacred.

This worldview is integrative. It refuses to separate prayer from action, contemplation from compassion, or spirituality from justice. Through Lectio Divina, the Word of God becomes alive in our hearts, reminding us that the prophets' cries for justice and Jesus's call to love are not distant commands but present invitations. Through Visio Divina, sacred images reveal not only beauty but also responsibility—to see Christ in the poor, to notice God's presence in the suffering, and to respond with mercy.

An integrative worldview recognizes that personal transformation is never enough if it does not also lead to the transformation of relationships and communities. In this way, Lectio and Visio deepen our understanding of Scripture's call, cultivate empathy that stretches across boundaries, inspire action for those on the margins, foster communities of compassion, and empower us with the faith and hope necessary for the long journey toward justice.

To pray in this way is to see the world differently:

As Mirror: We see our fears, our longings, our complicity in injustice.
As Window: We glimpse God's vision of a reconciled world.
As Icon: We encounter the divine presence that transfigures reality.

In this worldview, prayer and justice are no longer two separate pursuits but one seamless movement. To encounter God in Word and image is also to encounter the neighbor in need. To contemplate Christ in Scripture or icon is to be sent forth to love Christ in the poor, the stranger, and the oppressed.

An integrative spiritual worldview anchors us in this truth: The contemplative life and the active life are not opposed but intertwined. Lectio and Visio lead us not away from the world but deeper into it with eyes of compassion, hearts of mercy, and hands ready to serve.

My interest in Eastern Orthodoxy was first piqued when I read Bishop Kallistos Ware's book *The Orthodox Way*. I remember feeling the same way John Wesley did when he encountered the writings of Macarius of Egypt. Wesley said his heart sang. When I read Macarius, my heart danced since I don't sing well but I do love to dance.

That moment lit a spark in me, one that eventually grew into my own work, Eastern Orthodoxy from a Wesleyan tradition. Out of that paper came reflections that have stayed with me, shaping not only my theology but also the way I see the Spirit moving in the world.

The Earth Has a Story: The Transformative Intersection of Wesleyan and Eastern Orthodox Spirituality

The Spirit has always moved through the world like wind across the waters—unseen yet shaping waves, stirring hearts, and sanctifying cultures. In the Eastern Orthodox tradition, this movement is not abstract; it is the living presence of the Holy Spirit weaving through history, animating each culture with its own song of praise. Tradition, then, is not a relic to be guarded but a living stream flowing fresh from the same source.

At the center of this stream is the Epiclesis—the invocation of the Spirit in the Divine Liturgy. In that sacred moment, ordinary bread and wine are transfigured into the body and blood of Christ. For me, this has always been more than symbol. It is a sign that the ordinary can indeed be transfigured, that all creation is meant to be drawn into divine life.

When I turn to Wesley, I see the same wind at work. Wesley, centuries apart, still found his heart stirred by Macarius and the desert fathers. In their words, he heard a familiar call—a call to holiness as Spirit-led transformation. His heart sang; mine danced. Here was a shared language of holiness, not as moralistic rule-keeping but as a baptism of love that consumes and reshapes the soul.

Both traditions, Wesleyan and Eastern Orthodox, affirm the same truth: the Spirit is not a distant observer but an active Presence guiding us into the life of God. Orthodoxy names this theosis, the call to become partakers of the divine nature. Wesley named it entire sanctification, the perfecting of love in the human heart. Two words, two traditions, yet the same vision: Salvation is not a single moment but a lifelong transformation, an ascent into Christ's likeness.

Both also share a love for community. In Orthodoxy, salvation is lived in communion through worship, sacraments, and the Body of Christ. In Methodism, salvation is nurtured in class meetings, societies, and mutual accountability. Orthodoxy offers the mystery of liturgy; Wesley offers the structure of disciplined discipleship. Yet both are rooted in the same reality that holiness is love and love is the very life of God poured into human hearts.

For me, the beauty of these traditions is how they converge. The Orthodox speak of deification, and Wesley speaks of sanctification, but both insist that to follow Christ is not simply to believe but to become like Him. Bread becomes body. A sinner becomes a saint. A heart becomes a dwelling place of God's perfect love.

The Rest of the Story

The Spirit's wind does not stop at borders of time or culture. It moved in the desert of fourth century Egypt, in the revival tents of eighteenth century England, and it still moves now. Macarius of Egypt spoke of holiness as God's fire dwelling in the depths of the human heart. Centuries later, Wesley read his words and felt his own heart leap with recognition. He knew the same truth: Holiness is not the fruit of human striving but the work of the Spirit in a heart yielded to God.

For me, reading Macarius alongside Wesley was like overhearing two friends praying side by side, one in a desert cell and one on horseback across the English countryside. Their words, though different, resonated with the same music. Their shared conviction has shaped my own journey that salvation is more than pardon; it is transformation. It is not only forgiveness but transfiguration.

Wesley's "second work of grace" mirrors the Orthodox vision of theosis. Both insist that salvation matures into love perfected—love for God and neighbor made whole. And both affirm that this work is impossible without grace but that grace is never imposed; it invites our cooperation. Prayer, sacraments, Scripture, daily choices of love—these are the places where divine and human meet, where the Spirit fills our sails and leads us toward holiness.

And so I hold this story close: two rivers flowing from the same source, meeting in the great sea of God's redeeming love. Macarius and Wesley, though separated by language and centuries, remind me that holiness is love, and love is holiness. The Spirit longs not only to forgive us but to transform us until our lives become radiant with God's love.

Introduction: My Heart Danced

My interest in Eastern Orthodoxy was first piqued when I read Bishop Kallistos Ware's *The Orthodox Way.* It eventually led me to write a paper titled "Eastern Orthodoxy from a Wesleyan Tradition." What follows is not an academic essay but a narrative reflection weaving together of two rivers of faith that share a common source.

The Earth Has a Story

The Spirit moves like wind across the waters—unseen yet shaping, stirring, sanctifying. Eastern Orthodoxy describes this movement not as history's backdrop but as the Spirit's living presence. Tradition is not a relic to be guarded but a living stream flowing with grace.

At the heart of this stream lies the Epiclesis, the invocation of the Spirit in the Divine Liturgy. In that moment, ordinary bread and wine are transfigured into the body and blood of Christ. The Spirit whispers: The ordinary can be transfigured; creation itself can be drawn into divine life.

A Wesleyan Dance with Macarius

John Wesley, centuries and cultures apart, found his own heart stirred by the same wind. He read the desert father Macarius, and his heart sang with recognition. When I read Macarius, my heart danced. Here was a shared language of holiness—a baptism of love consuming the heart and reshaping the soul.

For Wesley, this was not moralism. It was Spirit-led transformation. He called it entire sanctification, the perfecting of love in the heart. The Orthodox called it theosis, becoming partakers of the divine nature. Different words, same truth—holiness is love, and love is holiness.

A Communion of Traditions

Orthodoxy teaches that salvation unfolds in communion through liturgy, sacraments, and the Body of Christ. Wesleyan Methodism teaches it through class meetings and societies, with believers spurring one another toward love and good works.

Both insist salvation is not a legal pardon but a lifelong transformation into the likeness of Christ.

One tradition emphasizes mystery and rhythm; the other emphasizes accountability and discipline. Both depend on grace. Both require cooperation. Both see holiness as love poured into human hearts.

The Spirit's Wind Across Time

The Spirit's breath has never respected cultural borders. It moved in the desert of fourth century Egypt and in the revival tents of eighteenth century England, and it moves today.

Macarius prayed in a desert cell. Wesley preached from horseback. Yet both spoke the same truth: Holiness is not human striving but the Spirit's fire dwelling within. And that Spirit still whispers:

- You are not only forgiven, but you are also being transformed.
- You are not only pardoned, but you are also being made holy.
- You are being reshaped into love itself.

Reflection Questions

- When has your own heart sung or danced while encountering another tradition?
- How do you experience holiness, not as rule-keeping but as love being perfected in you?
- What practices (sacrament, prayer, accountability, community) have been streams of grace in your journey?

Symbolic Reading

The Spirit is the wind; the Church is the sail. Without the wind, the sail hangs limp. Without the sail, the wind passes by. Together, the wind fills the sail, and the ship moves toward God's horizon.

Prayer

Holy Spirit, wind of God,
breathe across my heart.
Sanctify me with love,
transfigure the ordinary,
and weave my story into the great stream
of Your redeeming grace.
Make me holy as You are holy;
make me love as You are love.
Amen.

Book 'Graphe' Seven

The Prophetic Mirror Amos 5; Isaiah 58; Luke 4

Here we stood before the prophets who would not let worship drift into empty ritual. Amos thundered against the people of Israel, exposing the disconnect between their songs and their lives: "Take away from me the noise of your songs. . . . But let justice roll down like water and righteousness like an ever-flowing stream" (Amos 5:23–24). In Amos's mirror, we saw ourselves: the ease with which we can sing hymns on Sunday and ignore injustice on Monday, the temptation to treat worship as performance rather than as covenant.

Isaiah, too, raised his voice: "Is not this the fast that I choose: to loose the bonds of injustice, to undo the straps of the yoke, to let the oppressed go free, and to break every yoke?" (Isa. 58:6). Here the mirror reflected our tendency to confuse piety with obedience, to substitute gestures of devotion for the harder work of compassion. The prophet would not allow us to look away. He held our gaze until we saw the truth: Faith divorced from justice is not faith at all.

And then, in the synagogue of Nazareth, Jesus unrolled the scroll of Isaiah and read, "The Spirit of the Lord is upon me, because he has anointed me to bring good news to the poor. He has sent me to proclaim release to the captives and recovery of sight to the blind, to set free those who are oppressed, to proclaim the year of the Lord's favor" (Luke 4:18–19). In that moment, the window opened wide. Worship was revealed not as escape from the world but as engagement with it. Liturgy led to liberation; prayer became proclamation; praise took flesh in the work of justice.

The prophetic mirror exposed our divisions between religion and righteousness, between ritual and mercy. But through the window we glimpsed another way: a worship inseparable from justice, a faith alive in compassion, a spirituality that joins God's dream for the world.

A broken mirror and window tell a different story. Richard Rohr reminds us, "Power distorts truth." Those who hold power—whether political, religious, or cultural—often reshape narratives to maintain control. The mirror then reflects not who we are but who the powerful want us to believe we are. The window no longer opens to God's horizon but to an illusion crafted for advantage. Such distortion is selective, silencing dissent and shaping perception for the sake of authority. Narrative spirituality resists this by truth-telling, by listening to voices on the margins, by questioning the narratives of dominance, and by reclaiming the gospel story as a mirror of honesty and a window of justice.

Symbolic Reading: A Broken Mirror and Window

The Broken Mirror: When power distorts truth, the mirror no longer reflects us honestly. Instead of revealing our dignity and our flaws, it projects an image shaped by manipulation. We begin to see ourselves through the eyes of dominance, measuring our worth by the standards of those in control. The broken mirror hides wounds, silences voices, and denies the full truth of who we are.

The Cracked Window: A window is meant to open onto God's horizon—wide, hopeful, expansive. But when power distorts truth, the window is cracked. The view becomes partial, blurred, and misleading. Instead of glimpsing the kingdom of justice and love, we see only what the powerful want us to see: illusions that justify oppression or maintain privilege.

Prophetic Repair: The work of prophets—ancient and modern—is to repair the mirror and window. Amos thunders against false worship. Isaiah cries out for justice. Jesus, in Luke 4, unrolls the scroll to declare release, healing, and liberation. They show us that God's truth is not the possession of the powerful but the inheritance of the poor, the oppressed, and the silenced.

Invitation: Narrative spirituality invites us to pick up the shards of the broken mirror and the cracked window. By listening to marginalized voices, by telling the truth of our wounds, by practicing justice, we participate in the mending. In this way, the mirror can again reveal us honestly, and the window can once more open onto God's horizon.

Prayer for Truth

God of light and justice,
You see through every distortion,
every false story, every broken reflection.
Where power has twisted truth,
set us free.
Where mirrors have lied to us,
show us who we really are:
Your beloved.
Where windows have been cracked and clouded,
clear our vision to see Your kingdom of love.
Give us courage to name falsehood,

wisdom to discern what is real,
and compassion to lift the voices
the world tries to silence.
Heal what is shattered,
restore what is broken,
and let Your truth shine
as mirror and window
so that we may walk in justice,
live in love,
and see Your face in every neighbor.
Amen.

Prophetic Consciousness: A Narrative of Transformation

At the heart of a spiritual worldview lies what I call prophetic consciousness. It is not merely an abstract idea but a way of seeing, a moral compass that helps us discern what is good and life-giving, and what is harmful and destructive. To cultivate such consciousness is to walk the long road of becoming a whole and holy person within community.

Yet many of us begin from a place of limitation. When our theory of mind is diminished, we confuse our perception with reality itself. We assume with certainty that the way we see the world is the way the world is. This illusion, unchecked, leads to destructive behaviors—unhealthy attachments to outcomes, addictions to ideology, and compulsions that harm both us and others. Nationalism of every kind, including Christian nationalism, becomes a prison of the spirit when perception masquerades as truth.

Strawn and Bland in *The Integrative Mindset* remind us that "all therapies or counseling models try to help the client understand the way they automatically see the world through their hermeneutical tradition and recognize that others see it differently." I would extend this to spiritual direction and teaching as well. At their best, they are journeys of companionship, walking alongside another until new horizons open and clarity comes into view.

What Strawn and Bland call a diminished mindset, I describe as a fixed or stuck mindset. It resists growth. It prevents the healing of relationships. By contrast, an open mindset, what I call a true theory of mind, cultivates awareness, understanding, and perspective. Narrative spirituality becomes the bridge, connecting our story to the gospel story so that prophetic consciousness may emerge. We're reminded again of what Anaïs Nin wrote, "We do not see the world as it is; we see it as we are."

A fixed mindset insists that my way of seeing is reality itself. But prophetic consciousness recognizes the humility in perspective. It acknowledges that perception is always in search of a greater perspective. This is not a one-time achievement but an ongoing process, an unfolding marked by curiosity, learning, and transformation.

At its core, prophetic consciousness is the deepening capacity for love and freedom. It is the ability to see through lenses of compassion rather than fear, through liberation rather than exclusion. Diarmuid O'Murchu reminds us that from humanity's very beginnings, spirituality has carried both light and shadow. Healing begins when we release our clinging to exclusion and anchor ourselves in the ethic of liberation.

In this light, intersections of difference no longer appear as battlegrounds but as thresholds—sacred places where transformation can begin. Carl Jung once observed, "The upheaval of our world and the upheaval in consciousness are one and the same." If this is true, then the healing of the world must begin with the transformation of our own consciousness.

Even history itself bears witness to this truth. Mark Twain once quipped, "History doesn't repeat itself, but it does rhyme." George Santayana countered, "Those who cannot remember the past are condemned to repeat it." Seemingly contradictory, these two insights together remind us that life unfolds in patterns—echoes and rhymes of what has been before. To avoid repeating mistakes, we must not only recognize these patterns but also apply the lessons they teach. Prophetic consciousness is precisely this: the integration of pattern and lesson, memory and vision.

And so the journey circles back to the heart. Ezekiel's words echo across time: "A new heart I will give you, and a new spirit I will put within you" (Ezek. 36:26). Prophetic consciousness is this gift of a new heart, a new spirit, and a fresh way of seeing. It is the courage to stand at the threshold of transformation, to let go of what is fixed and closed, and to step into the spacious freedom of God's unfolding love.

Meditation

"Take away from me the noise of your songs; . . . But let justice roll down like water and righteousness like an ever-flowing stream" (Amos 5:23–24).

The prophets remind us that worship without justice is hollow. God does not desire our performance but rather our compassion.

Symbolic Reading

Amos' River: Justice is not a trickle but a flood. The river becomes a symbol of God's unstoppable demand for equity and compassion.

Isaiah's Fast: True devotion is symbolized not by sackcloth or ritual but by breaking chains and lifting burdens.

Jesus's Scroll: The scroll in Nazareth is a symbol of fulfillment—the Word becoming flesh, the promise of liberation taking form in Christ's mission.

Together, these symbols invite us to see that worship without justice is like a song without breath: empty, hollow, lifeless.

Prayer

God of justice and mercy,
Strip away our empty songs and shallow rituals.
Open our eyes to the poor, the captive, the blind, the oppressed.
May our worship be more than words; let it become rivers of justice, streams of righteousness, a song that sets the world free.
Amen.

Reflection Questions

- Where do I notice the gap between my worship and my daily practice of justice?
- What "empty rituals" might God be asking me to release?
- How can my prayer life become more connected to the liberation of others?
- What does it mean for me, personally, to let justice roll down like water?
- How does Jesus's proclamation in Luke 4 reshape my understanding of what worship truly is?

This chapter shows how Scripture serves as a prophetic mirror, exposing our separation of faith from justice. It reveals that God's vision of worship is not performance but participation in liberation. Through Amos, Isaiah, and Jesus, we discover that true devotion is measured not by ritual but by righteousness, not by songs but by justice rolling down like water.

Theme: Justice as worship
Mirror: Our tendency to separate faith from justice, ritual from righteousness
Window: The prophetic voice reveals that to know God is to seek justice, defend the poor, and let righteousness roll down like water.
Arc: From hollow religion to living faith that heals community

Book 'Graphe' Eight

The Good News for the Poor
Luke 6:20–26; Matthew 25:31–46; James 2:1–7

Narrative Expansion

Here we face the uncomfortable truth of God's kingdom: it always bends toward the poor. Jesus blessed the hungry, the weeping, and the hated while warning the satisfied, the laughing, and the admired. His Beatitudes unsettled our assumptions, holding up a mirror to privilege and complacency.

Matthew's vision of the nation being judged by how they treat the hungry, the stranger, the sick, and the prisoner was a sobering reminder that faith is not abstract. It is embodied in how we treat the most vulnerable. James added his sharp rebuke: When we give the rich the best seats and tell the poor to stand aside, we dishonor the very ones chosen by God.

The mirror reflected our complicity in systems that favor the powerful and neglect the weak. Yet the window revealed a startling reversal: a kingdom where the last are first, where bread is shared freely, where the poor are honored, and where justice is made visible.

The Cure of the Soul Through Cultural Encounter

The cure of the soul is not found only in private prayer or personal reflection but also in the way we live with one another across the boundaries of culture, history, and tradition. The terms multicultures, multicultural, and intercultural name a progression of human possibility, one that belongs as much to the work of psychology and ethics as it does to theology and spirituality.

Multicultures point to the presence of many distinct cultural groups within a shared space. Each community carries its own stories, rituals, and worldview, existing side by side with others. The emphasis here is on diversity, the recognition that within a single society, multiple streams of meaning and practice flow at once.

Multiculturalism reaches further. It not only acknowledges diversity but actively values it. A multicultural environment promotes coexistence, fosters respect, and cultivates belonging. It recognizes that traditions are not simply tolerated but honored, each contributing to the richness of shared life.

Intercultural engagement deepens this movement into living exchange. It is not merely about recognizing or respecting difference but about entering encounters, dialogue, and transformation. In intercultural life, cultures interact in ways that change each other; they do not remain fixed but become a living process of growth. Here, differences are not threat but possibility, not division but discovery.

Strawn and Bland in *The Integrative Mindset* caution that therapeutic or educational practices rooted only in unexamined Western theories risk narrowing the field of vision. Such a diminished or fixed mindset blinds us to the depth of human wisdom across cultures, doing harm by excluding what does not fit the Western frame. It obscures the possibility of a more integrative worldview, one capable of expanding human horizons rather than constricting them.

From a theological perspective, such narrowing resists the work of the Spirit, who is ever drawing humanity into wider circles of love. Scripture tells of the nations' bringing their treasures into the New Jerusalem and of the tree of life whose leaves are for the healing of the nations. The cure of the soul, then, is not only an inward task but a communal calling. It arises as we join in God's work of reconciliation, learning to welcome one another and seeing the image of Christ in every face.

To recognize multicultures, to nurture multicultural belonging, and to practice intercultural encounters is to participate in this reconciling work. It is to embody the gospel's own rhythm of incarnation: God dwelling among us, crossing boundaries, speaking many languages, and healing divisions. In such practices, both the individual soul and the collective soul of humanity find their cure. The Spirit restores not only what is broken within but also what is torn between us, weaving diversity into a unity bound together by love.

Reflection

The cure of the soul calls us into both inner healing and cultural encounter. It is an invitation to broaden our worldview and to participate in God's reconciling work among the nations.

Reflection Questions

- Where in your own life have you experienced the reality of multicultures and the presence of different traditions and worldviews side by side?
- What practices or experiences have helped you move from simply recognizing diversity to truly valuing it in a multicultural way?
- How have you entered intercultural encounters that changed you? What did you learn about yourself and about God through those experiences?

- In what ways might your community embody the gospel's vision of reconciliation by creating spaces of belonging across cultural difference?
- How does your faith call you to see diversity not as division but as part of the Spirit's work of healing the nations and curing the soul?

Prayer

God of many nations and one human family,
You created us in diversity and call us into unity.
Heal the wounds of division within us and among us.
Teach us to see Your image in every culture,
to welcome one another as Christ has welcomed us,
and to walk together in the Spirit toward the healing of the nations.
Amen.

The Cure of the Soul and the Healing of the Nations

In the vision of quantum spirituality, the whole is greater than the sum of its parts, and yet in mystery, the whole also participates in each part just as each part participates in the whole. This mutual indwelling reveals the profound interconnectedness of all creation: Nothing exists in isolation, and every life is bound to every other.

Some have suggested that death enters whenever the human spirit becomes overly preoccupied with self-preservation or consumed by belonging to the whole at the expense of the self. Life, then, is held in a delicate tensional balance of individuality and communion.

Even science gives us images of this truth. When a single atom is split and its halves are sent light years apart, what happens to one is mysteriously experienced by the other. If one is wounded, the other shares in its pain. So it is with humanity: Harm done to one reverberates throughout the whole. Violence, war, oppression, and injustice are not isolated events; they damage the very soul of the human family. A diminished or fixed mindset—blind to this interconnectedness—multiplies division and leads to death.

The cure of the soul, therefore, is never private alone. It is also the healing of the nations. Scripture gives voice to this truth in God's promise: "If my people who are called by my name humble themselves, pray, seek my face, and turn from their wicked ways, then I will hear from heaven and will forgive their sin and heal their land" (2 Chron. 7:14).

Healing begins with humility, repentance, and prayer. It grows into a renewed way of seeing life, one in which the flourishing of each person is bound to the flourishing of all.

Reflection

The mystery of our interconnectedness calls us to humility and responsibility. To harm another is to harm ourselves; to heal another is to discover our own healing.

Reflection Questions

- How do you see the truth of interconnectedness in your own life and community?
- Where have you witnessed the tension between self-preservation and belonging to the whole?
- In what ways can humility and repentance open a path toward healing in your family, your community, or your nation?
- How does the promise of 2 Chronicles 7:14 shape your understanding of God's invitation to participate in the healing of the land?
- What practices can help you live more fully into the reality that harm to one is harm to all, and healing for one is healing for all?

Prayer

God of wholeness and peace,
You have woven all creation together in Your love.
Teach us to see our lives as bound to the lives of others,
and our healing as part of the healing of the nations.
Give us humility to repent, courage to pray,
and faith to seek Your face.
Hear from heaven, forgive our sin, and heal our land,
that all may live in the light of Your reconciling grace.
Amen.

Meditation

"Blessed are you who are poor, for yours is the kingdom of God" (Luke 6:20).

The good news of the gospel is not abstract but embodied. It is measured by how the least are treated.

Narrative Reflection

Jesus proclaimed blessings and woes that overturned every social expectation. Matthew's sheep and goats story made care for the least the very measure of discipleship. James reminded us that favoritism toward the rich is a denial of faith itself.

The mirror revealed our preference for comfort and privilege. Yet through the window we glimpsed the abundance of God's kingdom where scarcity is transformed into shared gift and the poor are honored as bearers of God's blessing.

Symbolic Reading

The Beatitudes: Symbol of reversal where the poor are lifted up and the rich are brought low

The Sheep and Goats: Symbol of judgment based on love in action, not belief in words

The Assembly (James 2): Symbol of the church itself, called to embody God's justice, but often mirroring society's favoritism

Together, these symbols reveal that God's economy is not scarcity but abundance, not hierarchy but dignity.

Prayer

God of abundance,
Open our eyes to see Your kingdom among the poor.
Forgive our favoritism, our comfort, our complicity.
Teach us to share bread, welcome strangers,
and honor the least as Your beloved.
Let our faith be made visible in love.
Amen.

Reflection Questions

- Who are "the poor" in my own community, and how do I encounter them?
- Where have I unconsciously given privilege to the powerful while neglecting the vulnerable?
- How does Jesus's blessing of the poor reshape my understanding of God's kingdom?
- What would it mean for me to practice abundance instead of scarcity?
- In what concrete way can I embody love as justice this week?

This chapter shows how Scripture unmasks our favoritism and reveals God's radical reversal: The kingdom belongs to the poor. It shows that discipleship is not measured by belief alone but by love expressed in justice, hospitality, and shared abundance.

Theme: God's preferential option for the poor
Mirror: Our complicity in systems of privilege and neglect
Window: Jesus's Beatitudes, the judgment of the nations, and James' warning about favoritism all show that God's kingdom reverses social hierarchies.
Arc: From scarcity and inequality to abundance shared as gifts

Book 'Graphe' Nine

Breaking Walls, Building Tables Ephesians 2:11–22; Acts 10; Galatians 3:23–29

Narrative Expansion

Here we enter the story of reconciliation. The mirror showed us the walls we build—walls of race, class, gender, religion, politics; walls that separate "us" from "them." These barriers often masquerade as protection but become prisons of fear and division.

Paul's letter to the Ephesians offers a bold vision: Christ Himself is our peace, who has broken down the dividing wall of hostility and created one new humanity. In Acts, Peter's rooftop vision shattered centuries of boundary-keeping, and Cornelius's welcome revealed the Spirit's impartial embrace. In Galatians, Paul declared that in Christ there is neither Jew nor Greek, slave nor free, male nor female, for all are one in Christ Jesus.

The mirror reflected our complicity in division, our tendency to exclude and label. But the window opened onto a wider horizon: a new community where the table is long enough for everyone, where reconciliation replaces hostility, and where love makes strangers into kin.

Meditation

"For he is our peace; in his flesh he has made both into one and has broken down the dividing wall, that is, the hostility between us" (Eph. 2:14).

Christ does not merely call us to peace; Christ is our peace.

Narrative Reflection

Walls rise quickly—some built of bricks, others of prejudice, fear, or history. But the gospel insists that every wall is already broken in Christ. Peter's vision widened his heart to embrace those once considered unclean. Paul's words reminded the Galatians—and us—that baptism unites us across every boundary the world imposes.

The mirror revealed the lines we draw to keep others out. The window revealed the Spirit's call to a reconciled community where the table grows longer and no one is left outside.

Symbolic Reading

The Dividing Wall (Ephesians): Symbol of hostility—both literal and metaphorical—that Christ tears down

Peter's Vision (Acts 10): Symbol of the Spirit's radical impartiality, calling us to welcome those we once excluded

"No longer Jew or Greek" (Galatians 3): Symbol of baptism's unity, dissolving divisions of culture, class, and gender

Together, these symbols reveal that reconciliation is not optional but central to the gospel.

Prayer

God of peace,
Break down the walls we build in fear and pride.
Tear away the barriers that divide Your children.

Make us one new humanity in Christ,
and seat us at one table
where strangers become neighbors,
and neighbors become family.
Amen.

Reflection Questions

- What "walls" do I notice in my own life, community, or church?
- Where do I resist reconciliation because it feels uncomfortable or threatening?
- How might I lengthen my table to welcome those I usually exclude?
- What does it mean that Christ Himself is our peace?
- How can my faith community live as a sign of reconciliation in a divided world?

This chapter shows how Scripture unmasks our walls of division and reveals God's vision of reconciliation. It shows that in Christ, hostility is overcome, the table is widened, and the Spirit creates one new humanity.

Theme: Reconciliation across differences
Mirror: Our divisions—ethnic, social, religious—and the barriers we erect
Window: In Christ the dividing wall falls; the Spirit calls us to a new humanity where all are welcome at the table.
Arc: From exclusion to communion

Book 'Graphe' Ten

Creation Groaning, Creation Renewed Genesis 1; Romans 8:18–25; Revelation 22:1–5

I believe the greatest healing necessary in this season of our political, economic, religious, and relational landscapes is the healing of fixed mindsets. What someone has called the "danger of a single story that becomes a fixed mindset shaped by our fragmented worldviews, narratives, and ethics."

The Rendezvous of Giving and Receiving: A Gift-Based Economics

At the crossroads of economics, environment, and public policy lies a contested intersection: a place where language itself becomes power. Whoever names the narrative often steers the outcome. Too often, the dominant mindset bows to self-interest or profit-only models, building walls of separation, isolating people from one another and from the earth itself.

But when anchored in a spiritual worldview, the conversation changes. Self-interest need not be denied, yet it is woven together with social responsibility. Preservation finds its partner in belonging, and the individual discovers wholeness.

Gift-based economics offers a glimpse of another way. Rooted in grace, it recognizes the gap between those who have and those who have not and dares to work at closing it. It envisions personhood not as isolated autonomy but as relational being, shaped through encounter with others and through the beauty of difference.

African theologian Faustin Ntamushobora gives us a luminous image: the "rendezvous of giving and receiving" across cultures. His words echo the potlatch festivals of the Pacific Northwest where entire communities once gathered to exchange gifts, not to compete but to honor one another, to affirm their relationship, and to celebrate the abundance of belonging.

Integration in this sense does not erase difference. It treasures it. A spiritual worldview embraces otherness not as a threat but as a sacred presence in the public square. Here, humility can breathe. Here, civility can hold space. Here, generosity can guide conversation. The intersection becomes not a battleground of domination but a meeting ground of mutual blessing.

The Potlatch as Sacred Economy

Among Indigenous peoples of the Pacific Northwest—including the Haida, Tlingit, Kwakwaka'wakw, and Coast Salish—the potlatch was not merely a celebration. It was a whole economic and spiritual system. At its heart was the redistribution of wealth where the host clan or family gave away goods—food, blankets, tools, carved art, even canoes—sometimes to the point of impoverishing themselves. This is not a loss but rather an honor. A status is measured not by accumulation but by generosity.

This turns modern assumptions upside down. In market-driven economics, to give away is to lose, and to hoard is to gain. In potlatch logic, to give away is to increase your standing and deepen your ties to the community. The wealth that circulates enriches the whole.

Lessons from the Potlatch: A Narrative of Gift-Based Economics

The potlatch whispers a counter-story to the economics we know. It begins by reminding us that wealth is not possession but relationship. Measuring abundance in blankets or canoes alone misses the point; true wealth is revealed in the strength of bonds, the trust exchanged, and the flourishing of the whole community. In this light, to give is not to lose but to extend the circle of belonging.

From this flows a deeper truth: The world is not defined by scarcity but by abundance. The potlatch reframes reality as a river of gifts. Salmon returns to the streams, cedar trees rise to offer shelter, and the cycles of the seasons speak of endless renewal. Human beings enter this dance not as takers but as participants in reciprocity, giving back to ensure that the circle remains unbroken.

Yet abundance without justice can still fracture a people. Potlatch reflects just redistribution. Those with greater means bear greater responsibility, not as an act of charity but as a moral obligation to the whole. In giving more, the powerful ensure that none are excluded, that all have a place at the table. Gift-based economics challenges systems that hoard and concentrate, choosing instead to level the ground on which we stand together.

And finally, the potlatch redefines honor. Where Western systems often prize accumulation—trophies of wealth and status—the potlatch celebrates generosity as the true measure of dignity. Prestige belongs to those who give, not to those who grasp. This ethic heals the corrosive culture of envy and competition by grounding dignity in mutual blessing where every gift strengthens the bonds of community.

The lessons of the potlatch, then, are not relics of the past. They are guideposts for a future in which economics is not about hoarding but about honoring, not about scarcity but about sharing, not about possession but about relationships.

Potlatch and Spiritual Worldview

A potlatch is also liturgy. It is storytelling, song, dance, feasting, and covenant renewal. It situates economics within spirituality. Likewise, a gift-based economy is more than market reform; it is a worldview anchored in grace, seeing creation itself as a gift, and our role as stewards and sharers, not dominators.

As Faustin Ntamushobora's phrase "the rendezvous of giving and receiving" reminds us, difference does not divide but enriches. In the spirit of potlatch, we meet one another not to dominate but to bless.

In this way, the Native American potlatch is not an artifact of the past but a prophetic signpost pointing us toward an economy of grace where giving and receiving are both sacred acts and where the true wealth of a people is measured in relationships, reciprocity, and shared abundance.

Liberation Theology and the Here and Now

One vivid example of an integrative worldview is found in the Eastern Orthodox perspective on liberation theology. Rather than deferring salvation to "the next world," this vision seeks liberation in the here and now, confronting structures of evil and extending preferential treatment to the least advantaged.

It hears the voices of the oppressed not merely as cries for justice, but as words from God. This approach reframes salvation: To be saved is to help others live fully, to dismantle systems of oppression, and to restore vitality to communities. In this light, the cross becomes not only a symbol of suffering but also a sign of giftedness, the grace that makes transformation possible.

Reflection Pause

Who in your community might be considered "the least advantaged"? How might your faith call you to address their needs as part of your own salvation story?

Read Luke chapter 4 verses 18–19, Jesus's proclamation of good news to the poor and freedom for the oppressed.

Personality, Freedom, and the Brain

This conversation inevitably raises questions about personality. Is it genetically a fixed mindset or shaped by learned behavior? Can it change?

Neuroscience suggests that much of our decision-making happens beneath conscious awareness, yet a spiritual worldview insists on the capacity for transformation, for the renewing of the mind. Adrian van Kaam calls this capacity "life form" rather than "personality," connecting it to the biblical image of being formed into the likeness of Christ. His work reminds us that spirituality must be studied with both academic rigor and personal involvement, integrating psychology, theology, social justice, and tradition.

Reflection Pause

Do you believe people can truly change? What does "renewing of the mind" look like for you at this stage of life?

Read 2 Corinthians 5:17. "If anyone is in Christ, there is a new creation."

Narrative Expansion

Here we pause to listen to the voice of creation. The mirror showed us our misuse of the earth—our consumerism, our pollution, our neglect of ecosystems that sustain life. We saw how easily we reduce creation to a backdrop for human activity rather than the sacred trust it was meant to be.

Genesis reminded us that creation is not possession but blessing, a gift entrusted to our care. Paul wrote that creation itself groans, longing with us for redemption, caught in the same labor pains of hope. And Revelation gave us a final vision: a river of life flowing from God's throne, watering the tree whose leaves are for the healing of the nations.

The mirror reflected our exploitation and blindness. Yet the window revealed a new horizon: creation renewed, restored, and reconciled with humanity. We were invited to see ourselves not as masters of the earth but as kin within it, sharing in creation's groaning and glory alike.

Meditation

"For the creation waits with eager longing for the revealing of the children of God . . . the whole creation has been groaning together as it suffers together the pains of labor" (Rom. 8:19, 22).

Creation's longing is bound to our own. We wait, we groan, we hope together.

Narrative Reflection

From the beginning, Genesis told us creation was good—very good. Yet we have treated it as a resource to consume rather than a gift to cherish. Paul gave voice to creation's groaning, as though the forests, rivers, and skies cry out with us for redemption. Revelation widened our imagination to see creation healed, with the river of life flowing endlessly and the tree of life bearing fruit for all.

The mirror showed us the wounds we have inflicted on the earth. The window revealed creation not abandoned but renewed in Christ, waiting with us for resurrection.

Symbolic Reading

Genesis' Blessing: Symbol of gift: creation as sacred trust, meant for delight and care

Creation's Groaning (Romans): Symbol of solidarity: Creation shares in our longing and our hope

The River of Life (Revelation): Symbol of renewal: creation healed, flowing with God's abundance, leaves for the healing of nations

Together, these symbols reveal that creation is not a backdrop but a participant in salvation's story.

Prayer

Creator God,
Forgive us for the ways we have wounded Your earth.
Teach us again to see the world as blessing, not possession.
Join our prayers to creation's groaning,
and hasten the day when rivers run clean,
forests rejoice, and the earth is renewed in Your glory.
Amen.

Reflection Questions

- How do I see creation as a gift rather than as property or resource?
- Where in my community is creation "groaning"—polluted, exploited, or neglected?
- How can I join my life to creation care and healing?
- What does it mean to see salvation as renewal of all creation, not just of human souls?
- How might my daily choices reflect hope for creation's restoration?

This chapter shows how Scripture unmasks our exploitation of creation and reveals God's vision of renewal. It shows that creation shares in our hope, longing for redemption, and that in Christ all things—earth, sky, rivers, trees, humanity—are being made new.

Theme: Ecological justice and creation's redemption
Mirror: Our exploitation of the earth, consumerism, and ecological blindness
Window: The groaning of creation is joined to our own, awaiting renewal in Christ. The river of life flows for the healing of nations and ecosystems alike.
Arc: From domination to stewardship, from groaning to glory

Book 'Graphe' Eleven

The Beloved Community
Micah 6:6–8; John 13:1–17, 34–35; Revelation 7:9–12

The Earth Whispers It May Be Fall, but Winter Is Coming: As Spiritual Reflection

From the quiet perch of my heart, I sense the earth's gentle whisper. A story unfolds as autumn paints the world in hues of gold and crimson. Yet a shadow dances in the breeze, for winter approaches, a silent reminder of the cycles that govern our souls.

In my hometown of Warren, Ohio, the air is thick with nostalgia, and voices echo the sentiment. "It's a beautiful time of the year," they say, their eyes glimmering with the warmth of the season, "but we know what's coming." The chill of winter with its cold fingers and long, dark nights lurks just beyond the vibrant foliage. Yet amidst this anticipation there lies peculiar joy; the snowflakes that blanket the earth during the holidays bring forth a shimmering light, a contrast to the bleakness.

It may indeed be fall, but winter is coming.

As I tread through the autumn of my own life, the meaning of winter transforms. It is a gentle nudge toward reflection, a recognition of the fleeting nature of this existence. In these twilight years, thoughts of the past weave into the fabric of my present, and I find myself pondering the paths I've walked. Some choose to live in denial, clutching the present tightly, leaving behind a tangled web of unfulfilled dreams for others to unravel. Yet a few of us yearn to embrace the transition with grace, crafting a legacy of love that celebrates life rather than surrendering to chaos.

It may be fall, but winter is coming.

In this sacred space of contemplation, I feel an urge to reconnect with those who have shaped my journey. Friends and family, echoing laughter and shared moments linger in the corridors of memory. I seek the warmth of love and joy, a celebration of the light that illuminates our shared existence. I miss those who have traveled beyond this realm—my parents, my aunts and uncles—each a thread in the tapestry of my life. I recall the innocence of childhood, the thrill of snow-laden days spent sledding and ice skating, the magic of Christmas at Grandma's home. I would wander through the woods, allowing the soft caress of snowflakes to kiss my cheeks, each flake a fleeting moment of bliss. But now, winter whispers a different truth.

It may be fall, but winter is coming.

In these recent years, the essence of winter has morphed into a reflection on how I wish to spend my remaining days. The dreams I once held now dance just beyond my reach, and I grieve not for the past but for the future that feels elusive. It's a song I long to sing, yet the melody remains unformed, waiting for the right moment to emerge. With every breath I find a deeper connection to those I cherish, realizing that true richness lies not in grand gestures but in the sacred act of simply being together sharing love, laughter, and the beauty of life itself.

It may be fall, but winter is coming.

"Blessed are the pure in heart, for they will see God" (Matt. 5:8) whispers the Scripture, and I ponder the essence of purity. Is it a striving for holiness, a distant goal to be achieved? Or is it found in the simple act of being authentically human? Holiness, in my understanding, is less about perfection and more about the grace of our shared humanity. It is in these moments of connection—wasting time with God and with one another—that we discover the divine in our midst. Winter, then, becomes an opportunity, a sacred time to dwell in the presence of love.

It may be fall, but winter is coming.

Perhaps purity and holiness are not rigid ideals but gentle invitations to see the divine in all beings. To embrace those who seem different and to share the vision of a compassionate humanity are to cultivate a pure heart.

Beloved, we are cherished children of the divine; our future remains a mystery yet to be revealed. What we do know is this: When the divine is revealed, we shall resonate with that essence, seeing and being seen in the purity of love. As we hold onto this hope, we are called to purify ourselves, embodying the grace that reflects the divine.

It may be fall, but winter is coming.

In the hushed tones of a snowy evening, I am reminded of Robert Frost's musing. The woods, lovely and dark, beckon me, yet I carry promises within me. Miles stretch ahead, waiting to be traversed, and I am called to heed the journey before I lay down to rest.

It may be fall, but winter is coming.
I have promises to keep,
And many miles to walk before I sleep.
Many miles to walk.

Narrative Expansion

Here we reach the horizon of love, the vision of God's Beloved Community. The mirror showed us how easily we reduce faith to sentiment, how quickly we speak of love but fail to embody it in justice, humility, and service.

Micah reminded us that God does not desire endless sacrifices or religious performance but a simple, profound way "to do justice and to love kindness and to walk humbly with your God" (Micah 6:8). John took us to the upper room where Jesus washed the disciples' feet and gave a new commandment: "Just as I have loved you, you also should love one another" (John 13:34). And Revelation lifted our eyes to a vast multitude, beyond counting, gathered from every tribe and nation, praising God together in one voice.

The mirror reflected our failures to embody justice and mercy. Yet the window opened wide to a community where love is more than word, where service is greatness, where diversity is not erased but embraced, and where the whole creation sings in harmony before God.

Meditation

"And what does the Lord require of you but to do justice and to love kindness and to walk humbly with your God?" (Micah 6:8).

Love is not sentiment but action: justice, mercy, humility.

Narrative Reflection

In the upper room, Jesus showed that love kneels, love serves, and love washes feet. In Revelation's vision, love draws the nations into a single chorus of praise, each voice unique yet united.

The mirror revealed our tendency to privatize faith, to reduce love to words alone. The window revealed God's dream of Beloved Community where justice and mercy shape daily life, where love becomes the sign of discipleship, and where diversity is gathered into unity without erasure.

Symbolic Reading

Micah's Call: Symbol of simplicity: true faith is measured by justice, mercy, and humility.

The Basin and Towel (John 13): Symbol of servant-love: leadership that bends low to wash feet.

The Multitude (Revelation 7): Symbol of fulfillment: God's vision of a reconciled, diverse, worshiping community.

Together, these symbols reveal that the gospel's end is not isolation but communion, not domination but service, not division but unity in love.

Prayer

God of justice and mercy,
Form us into Your Beloved Community.
Teach us to love as Christ loves,
in service, in humility, in courage.
Gather us with all nations and peoples
into one song of praise
until Your kingdom comes on earth as in heaven.
Amen.

Reflection Questions

- Where am I tempted to make faith private rather than communal?
- How can I practice Micah's call to justice, mercy, and humility in my daily life?
- What does servant-love look like in my relationships and community?

- How do I honor diversity as a gift of God rather than a threat to unity?
- What might it mean for my community to live as a sign of the Beloved Community here and now?

This chapter shows how Scripture unmasks our shallow notions of love and reveals God's dream of Beloved Community. It shows that discipleship is not sentiment but service; not division but unity; not private piety but justice, mercy, and humility lived in community.

Theme: God's vision of community and shalom
Mirror: Our reduction of love to sentiment, or our failure to embody it socially
Window: True greatness is found in service; discipleship is marked by love; the end of history is a multitude gathered in justice, praise, and peace.
Arc: From individual salvation to beloved community, from love in word to love in deed

Everyone who reads Scripture does so through their own lens, as if looking into a mirror. The way we interpret Scripture reflects the way we see the world. Yet some insist, "We don't interpret Scripture." That claim often disguises the fact that their own lenses blind them to alternative readings, leaving them locked into a single story and fearful of seeing a passage in a new light.

Reframing a story is like a football coach throwing a red flag, asking the referee to review the play. After further review, the referee makes the call. In much the same way, reframing a parable involves deconstructing and then reconstructing the story, looking again with fresh eyes so its meaning may be more fully revealed.

Narrative Spirituality as a Hermeneutic of the Spirit and of Love

When the Eastern Orthodox tradition speaks of a "hermeneutics of the Holy Spirit," it is not referring merely to a method of interpretation but to a way of seeing through the eyes of the Spirit with a heart transformed by love. In this view, Scripture cannot be grasped only by intellect or logic; it must be received with humility, prayer, and openness to the Spirit who breathes through the text.

To say that this is also a "hermeneutic of love" is to confess that the Spirit's guidance always leads toward communion—communion with God and communion with one another. Interpretation is not meant to divide or to weaponize words but to nurture compassion, unity, and healing. To read in the Spirit is to read with love, and love becomes both the key and the fruit of understanding.

This approach acknowledges that Scripture speaks with many voices and offers many depths. It is not a flat surface but a living text layered with meaning like an icon painted in colors and light. The Orthodox imagination has long understood Scripture in four interwoven senses:

1. At the surface lies the literal sense, the story as it unfolds in its historical and cultural setting.
2. Beneath it shimmers the allegorical sense, in which people and events are seen as signs pointing to Christ and His Body, the Church.
3. Flowing from there is the moral or tropological sense where the text begins to question and shape the reader's own life, calling us to live differently.
4. Finally, the anagogical sense lifts the eyes toward what is ultimate: the Kingdom of God, the hope of salvation, the end for which all creation groans.

Each layer enriches the other. The Spirit, in love, leads readers not only deeper into the story but also deeper into themselves, into their community, and into the mystery of God's future.

In this way, Scripture becomes both mirror and window. As a mirror, it reflects the truth of our own lives—our wounds, our hopes, our distortions, our possibilities. It shows us who we are and who we are called to be. As a window, it opens into the larger story of God's redeeming love, letting us glimpse the radiance of divine reality. And when read as an icon, Scripture becomes sacramental—not an object to be mastered but a doorway through which we encounter the living God.

Thus, to read the Bible in the Orthodox spirit is to embark on a pilgrimage of the heart. It is not a solitary journey of analysis but a communal act of prayer, worship, and love. The Spirit guides the Church into truth, not by flattening Scripture into a single voice but by letting its many layers sing together in harmony. And always, the song that emerges is love.

Narrative Spirituality as a Hermeneutic of the Spirit and of Love

When we speak of Narrative Spirituality as a hermeneutic, we are entering into the Eastern Orthodox conviction that Scripture is not simply a text to be studied but a living mystery to be encountered. To read the Bible in the Spirit is to allow the words to breathe with divine life, to open ourselves not only to knowledge but to transformation. It is to receive Scripture as gift-given through the Holy Spirit and to interpret it in the key of love.

In this way, Narrative Spirituality aligns with what the Orthodox tradition calls the "hermeneutics of the Holy Spirit." It is not enough to analyze grammar, history, or context; the heart must be softened, the mind illumined, and the community drawn together in the Spirit's embrace. Interpretation becomes less about mastering the text and more about being mastered by the Word of God, shaped and healed in love.

The Church has long recognized that Scripture speaks in many layers. Like a story rich with meaning, it unfolds differently depending on where you stand and how you listen. Four primary senses of interpretation are often named:

1. The Literal Sense grounds us in history. It reminds us that these words were first spoken to real people in real times and places. To understand the narrative as the authors intended is to honor the foundation of God's ongoing story.
2. The Allegorical Sense draws us deeper, showing us how people, events, and symbols point beyond themselves to Christ and His Church. The old stories become windows into new creation.
3. The Moral or Tropological Sense turns the mirror toward our lives, asking how this text calls us to live. It presses us into questions of conduct, compassion, and integrity—how love takes shape in the choices of each day.
4. The Anagogical Sense lifts our eyes beyond the present moment to the hope of God's ultimate fulfillment. It whispers of the kingdom to come, the destiny of humanity, and the glory yet to be revealed.

Together, these senses remind us that Scripture is not flat but layered like an icon painted with depth and light. To read only one layer is to miss the richness of the whole. Guided by the Spirit, love draws these layers into harmony, forming a holistic vision of God's Word that both grounds us in history and opens us to eternity.

Within Narrative Spirituality, this becomes a way of seeing Scripture as both mirror and window. As a mirror, the text reflects the truth of our lives—our fears and failures, our hope and hunger.

It reveals who we are and who we are becoming. As a window, it opens onto God's larger story, letting us glimpse a reality beyond ourselves, radiant with divine presence.

And like an icon, Scripture is not simply looked at but looked through. It is not a mere object of study but a doorway to encounter. Through its layered depths, we do not just read words on a page; we are invited into communion with the living Word, Christ Himself.

Thus, Narrative Spirituality as a hermeneutic of the Spirit and of love teaches us to read with open hearts, with reverence, and in community. It invites us to see our story mirrored in God's story, and to step through the window of Scripture into the light of God's love.

Narrative Spirituality: A Hermeneutic of the Spirit and of Love

To read Scripture through Narrative Spirituality is to read in the Spirit with love as both the key and the safeguard. This way of interpretation does not reduce the text to a single meaning, nor does it allow us to weaponize Scripture against others. Instead, it invites us to enter into God's story, to see our own story reflected there, and to be transformed in relationship with God and with the community of faith.

1. Scripture as a Mirror

When we hold the text before us as a mirror, we see our own lives reflected—our joys, our failures, our hidden motives, our longing for God. The Spirit illumines these reflections, not to condemn but to guide us toward repentance and growth. Reading as a mirror is personal and intimate. It presses us to ask, "Where do I see myself in this story? How does this passage invite me to become more fully alive in Christ?" The mirror invites vulnerability and honesty, but it also points us to healing and renewal.

2. Scripture as a Window

At the same time, Scripture opens outward like a window. Through it we catch glimpses of God's larger story, the life of Christ, the unfolding drama of salvation. The window expands our vision beyond ourselves, helping us see history, culture, and the community of faith through God's eyes. It draws us into compassion, teaching us that our story is never just our own; it is bound up with the stories of others and with God's ongoing work of love in the world.

3. Scripture as an Icon

Finally, in Eastern Orthodox spirituality, Scripture is understood as an icon. Like painted icons that draw us into the mystery of divine presence, Scripture is not simply read but prayed with, contemplated, and entered into. It is a doorway through which the Spirit leads us into communion with God. Reading this way is not an academic exercise but a sacred encounter. To stand before Scripture as an icon is to recognize that the words do not end on the page; they point beyond themselves, revealing Christ, the Word made flesh.

Safeguarding Against False Narratives

Because Scripture is rich, layered, and living, there is always the temptation to force it into a narrow frame or to use it to support our own agendas. Here is where love becomes the greatest safeguard. To read in love is to do no harm, to refuse to impose your own interpretation on others, and to remain open to the Spirit's guidance through community, dialogue, and prayer.

Safeguarding against false narratives involves humility and several practices:

- *Critical discernment:* Listening carefully to the text, its context, and its history

- *Communal wisdom:* Allowing interpretation to be tested in the life of the Church, not in isolation
- *Ethical responsibility:* Communicating truthfully, without manipulation or harm
- *Openness to the Spirit:* Remembering that the Holy Spirit is the true interpreter who reveals Christ and leads us deeper into God's love

Above all, love is the measure. If an interpretation divides, harms, or diminishes others, it fails the hermeneutic of the Spirit. But if it nurtures compassion, unity, and transformation, then it bears the fruit of truth.

Narrative: The Hermeneutics of the Holy Spirit as Love

To read Scripture in the Spirit is to enter a rhythm of both Logos and Rhema. These two dimensions of God's Word are not in opposition but in harmony, one laying the foundation and the other quickening the heart. Together, they safeguard our narratives in love and keep us from distortion.

Logos: The Eternal Word

In the beginning there was the Logos. For the Orthodox mind, this is not simply text on a page but the eternal Word of God, Christ Himself—the One through whom all things were made and in whom all things hold together. The Logos is universal, timeless, and unchanging. It is the framework of truth that grounds our faith. It is the voice of God echoed through prophets, apostles, and the Church's living witness. To read Scripture in the Logos sense is to enter into that grand story, to hear the heartbeat of God's covenant, and to anchor your life in the eternal Word that transcends all cultures and times.

Rhema: The Word That Speaks Now

The Word of God is not only timeless; it is timely. Rhema is the Spirit's whisper in the present moment, the word that takes the eternal truth of Logos and applies it to our particular lives, our struggles, our decisions, and our seasons of joy or grief. Where Logos forms the foundation, Rhema opens the door of encounter. It is when a passage suddenly burns within us as if written for this very day. It is when the Spirit personalizes Scripture, not to bend it to our will but to draw our hearts into God's will for us here and now.

The Dance of Logos and Rhema

Narrative Spirituality as a hermeneutic of the Spirit and of love depends on both. If we cling only to Logos, our reading risks becoming abstract, rigid, or disconnected from lived experience. If we chase only Rhema, we risk fragmenting truth into private impressions without grounding. But together, Logos and Rhema embody a divine dance: the eternal Word becoming flesh in our lives, the timeless truth finding expression in our daily story.

This is why love becomes the safeguard. The Spirit of Love ensures that our Rhema does not contradict the Logos and that our Logos does not suffocate without Rhema's breath of life. In love, interpretation does no harm but instead builds up, heals, and unites.

Mirror, Window, Icon Revisited

As a mirror, Logos grounds us while Rhema exposes the truth about ourselves and calls us to transformation.

As a window, Logos opens onto the great story of God's salvation, while Rhema presses our nose to the glass and shows us where we stand in that story now.

As an icon, Logos reminds us that Scripture always points beyond itself to Christ, while Rhema draws us through that icon into living communion with Him.

Thus, Narrative Spirituality becomes more than an interpretive method; it becomes a way of living in the Spirit where love interprets all things. To read with the Spirit is to let the eternal Logos shape our worldview and let the Rhema of the Spirit speak directly into our lives. Both together mirror who we are, open a window to who God is, and invite us through the icon of Scripture into the transforming presence of divine love.

Logos and Rhema - The Word as Spirit and Love

Meditation

"In the beginning was the Word, and the Word was with God, and the Word was God" (John 1:1).

The eternal Word—Logos—stands as the foundation of all creation and all truth. Yet the Word also comes alive in each moment as Rhema, the Spirit's living voice that speaks into our unique circumstances. Together, Logos and Rhema invite us into a relationship where Scripture is not merely read but encountered, where the eternal Word becomes present in the here and now.

Narrative Reflection

I have often found myself reading Scripture with two different kinds of eyes. At times, I am rooted in the Logos, the great story of God's covenant with humanity—truth that is universal, timeless, and unshaken. At other times, the words seem to leap from the page as if written for me in that very moment. That is the Rhema—God's Word speaking personally, drawing my life into God's larger story.

The Logos steadies me. It keeps me from drifting into private interpretations unmoored from the Body of Christ. The Rhema quickens me. It keeps me from treating Scripture as a static relic of the past. Both together, grounded in love, become a hermeneutic of the Spirit—faithful to truth yet alive in experience.

Symbolic Reading

Logos as the Mirror: When I look into Scripture, the Logos reflects eternal truth back to me, showing where my life aligns—or does not—with God's Word.

Rhema as the Window: The Spirit opens a window into my present, letting me glimpse how God is guiding me right now in my relationships, struggles, and hopes.

Together as Icon: Logos and Rhema unite to form a sacred icon. Through it, I do not just study Scripture; I step through it into the presence of Christ, the living Word.

Reflection Questions

- When have you experienced Scripture as Logos, a universal truth that grounded or corrected you?
- When have you experienced Scripture as Rhema, a word that spoke directly into your present situation?
- How do you safeguard your interpretations so that Rhema remains faithful to Logos?
- In what ways does love guide your reading of Scripture as both Logos and Rhema?
- How does thinking of Scripture as mirror, window, and icon shape the way you approach your own spiritual journey?

Prayer

Holy Spirit, Breath of God,
You inspired the Word from the beginning,
and You speak still today.
Let Your Logos be the foundation of my life,
firm and unshaken.

Let Your Rhema be the living voice in my heart,
timely and true.
Through both, guide me in love
that I may reflect Your light as a mirror,
see Your vision as through a window,
and encounter You as through a holy icon.
Amen.

Introduction: Encountering the Living Word

Scripture is more than ink on paper; it is the living Word of God. The Orthodox tradition gives us two lenses—Logos and Rhema—to help us grasp the depth of this mystery. Logos is the eternal Word, the foundation of truth, Christ Himself who "was in the beginning with God" (John 1:2). Rhema is the Spirit's personal word, the timely whisper that brings the eternal Word into our present life.

When read together, Logos and Rhema form a dialogue: the timeless Word and the timely word, the grand story and the intimate message. Narrative Spirituality as a hermeneutic of the Spirit and of love invites us to listen for both at once. Logos roots us in God's eternal faithfulness; Rhema awakens us to God's immediate presence.

Meditation: The Dance of Eternal and Present Word

Imagine standing at the edge of a great river. The riverbed itself is ancient, carved into the earth through ages. That is the Logos—stable, universal, unchanging. Within that riverbed flows living water, fresh and renewing each day. That is the Rhema—personal, immediate, responsive to the season.

When we read Scripture, we need both. If we drink only of Logos, we risk abstraction and distance, a Word that feels eternal but not alive. If we drink only of Rhema, we risk subjectivity, a Word that feels personal but unanchored. The Spirit of Love teaches us to hold both together. Logos provides the context and framework; Rhema makes the Word come alive in the here and now.

Symbolic Reading: Mirror, Window, Icon

1. Scripture as a Mirror

With Logos, the eternal Word shows us the truth about human nature, sin, grace, and salvation.

With Rhema, the Spirit reflects our own story back to us, showing where this truth intersects with our daily lives.

Reading as mirror means asking, "What does this passage reveal about me—my heart, my choices, my need for God's grace?"

2. Scripture as a Window

With Logos, we see the wide sweep of God's salvation history, the covenant promises fulfilled in Christ.

With Rhema, the Spirit positions us in that window, showing how our own story connects to the larger narrative.

Reading as window asks, "How do I see God's purposes beyond myself, and what is my part in this story?"

3. Scripture as an Icon

With Logos, we recognize that Scripture always points beyond itself to Christ, the eternal Word.

With Rhema, the Spirit draws us through the icon into communion with Christ in the present moment.

Reading as icon asks, "How does this passage draw me into the presence of Christ right now?"

A Narrative Example: Logos and Rhema on the Emmaus Road

In Luke 24, two disciples walk a lonely road, hearts heavy after the crucifixion. Jesus Himself walks beside them, but they do not recognize Him. He opens the Scriptures—this is Logos, the eternal

Word interpreted considering Christ. Later, when He breaks bread, their eyes are opened and their hearts burn within them—this is Rhema, the Word made personal and alive in their moment of despair.

The Emmaus story teaches us that Logos and Rhema are inseparable. The Scriptures reveal Christ, and the Spirit makes that revelation burn within our hearts. The eternal Word becomes a present encounter.

Safeguards: Love and "Do No Harm"

Because Scripture is layered and alive, it is always vulnerable to distortion. That is why love is the ultimate safeguard. Love insists on humility, on listening, on refusing to impose your interpretation as final.

Love as safeguard means to interpret in ways that build up, heal, and unite.

Do no harm means avoiding weaponizing Scripture or using it as a tool of control.

Non-imposition means to respect that the Spirit may speak Rhema differently to another, while never contradicting the Logos that is Christ.

Narrative Spirituality reminds us that Scripture is not meant to be possessed but to be entered into. It belongs not to the interpreter but to the Spirit who speaks through love.

Reflection Questions

- Recall a time when Scripture anchored you with Logos, a truth that felt timeless and unshakable. What was that experience like?
- Recall a time when Scripture spoke to you as Rhema, a personal word for a particular season. How did it change you?
- Which of the three perspectives—mirror, window, icon—do you most often experience in your reading? Which might you need to lean into more?

- How can you practice "love as safeguard" in your engagement with Scripture?
- What would it mean to let Scripture not only reflect (mirror) or reveal (window) but actually draw you through into the presence of Christ (icon)?

Prayer

Eternal Logos, Word of God,
anchor me in the truth of who You are
so that my life may rest on Your eternal promises.
Living Rhema, Spirit's Whisper,
speak to me in the quiet of my heart.
Let the Word become alive in me today,
not only for my comfort but for my transformation.
Holy Spirit of Love,
teach me to read Scripture as mirror, window, and icon.
Keep me from false narratives;
guide me in love that does no harm.
Draw me ever deeper into the presence of Christ,
the Word made flesh.
Amen.

Introduction: Encountering the Living Word

I still remember the first time a student in my MBA ethics class asked, "Professor, how do we know if a principle is universal or just personal preference?" Their question pierced deeper than they realized. It was not only about business ethics but about how we discern truth itself. In Scripture, the Orthodox tradition offers us a way to hold both universality and particularity together through Logos and Rhema.

Logos is the eternal Word, Christ Himself, the foundation of truth that applies across time and culture. Rhema is the personal whisper of the Spirit, a timely word that speaks into our unique lives and circumstances. Both are necessary, and both are gifts of love.

Narrative Spirituality as a hermeneutic of the Spirit teaches us to hold Logos and Rhema together in love. The eternal Word provides the framework; the Spirit personalizes it for the moment. Without Logos, we drift. Without Rhema, we wither. With both, we live in the story of God.

Meditation: The Dance of Eternal and Present Word

Years ago, while serving in my first church, I found myself in the living room of a grieving widow. She held a Bible in her lap, but it seemed like only words on a page. I read Psalm 23 aloud: "The LORD is my shepherd; I shall not want."

In that moment, the Logos—an eternal promise spoken across centuries—became Rhema, a personal word of comfort in her tears. She clutched those words as if they had been written for her that very morning.

That is the dance of Logos and Rhema. Logos assures us of God's unchanging truth. Rhema breathes that truth into our present need. Both are the work of the Spirit; both are expressions of divine love.

Symbolic Reading: Mirror, Window, Icon

1. Scripture as a Mirror

In my early ministry, I often interpreted Scripture to "teach" others. But then, during a retreat, a mentor reminded me, "Ken, the first person the Word addresses is you." Reading as mirror forced me to stop using Scripture as binoculars for others and start using it as a mirror for myself.

With Logos, I see humanity's universal condition—our sin, our need for grace, God's covenant of love.

With Rhema, the Spirit shines a light on my particular impatience, pride, or fear.

The mirror confronts me, but it also heals me. Logos tells me "all have sinned." Rhema whispers, "Yes, Ken, even here in this struggle of yours, grace abounds."

2. Scripture as a Window

During my years teaching cross-cultural ethics, I often told students, "The shortest distance between difference and similarity is a story." When I read Scripture as a window, I am drawn beyond myself into God's larger narrative.

With Logos, I see the grand story of Israel, the ministry of Christ, the mission of the Church.

With Rhema, I hear the Spirit nudging me into that story, perhaps as the Samaritan who must cross the road or the prodigal who must come home.

Scripture as window reminds me that I am not the center of the story. God is. My role is to locate myself within that drama, to see with God's eyes and to live with compassion for others.

3. Scripture as an Icon

I recall standing before an icon of Christ Pantocrator in Oxford one summer. The gold background seemed to shimmer as if lit from within. Icons are not meant to be stared at like pictures; they are meant to be prayed with, looked through.

So it is with Scripture.

With Logos, the text points beyond itself to Christ, the eternal Word made flesh.

With Rhema, the Spirit draws me into communion with Christ here and now so reading is not just study but encounter.

When I read Scripture as an icon, I no longer ask, "What does this mean for me?" but rather "How is Christ revealing Himself through this Word today?"

A Narrative Example: Emmaus Road

Luke 24 gives us the perfect picture. The disciples walk home discouraged, their dreams shattered. The Logos walks beside them, opening the Scriptures and showing them how everything pointed to Jesus. But it was not until Jesus broke bread that they recognized Him—their Rhema moment when the Word became alive and burning in their hearts.

We, too, need both: the Logos that anchors us in the truth of Christ and the Rhema that awakens us to His presence now.

Safeguards: Love and Do No Harm

I have seen Scripture used to wound as well as to heal. A church member once confided, "Pastor, every time I hear the Bible quoted, I feel judged, not loved." That broke my heart, and it reminded me that the safeguard of all interpretation is love.

Love as safeguard: We interpret in ways that build up, not tear down.

Do no harm: We avoid weaponizing Scripture to control or exclude.

Non-imposition: We allow the Spirit freedom to speak Rhema differently to others while always tethered to the Logos of Christ.

Narrative Spirituality as a hermeneutic of love keeps us grounded in humility. It reminds us that the Word is not ours to possess; it is God's gift to share.

Reflection Questions

- When has Scripture spoken to you as Logos, a timeless truth that anchored your faith?
- When has Scripture become Rhema, a word that felt written for your exact situation?
- Which of the three perspectives—mirror, window, icon—do you find most natural? Which one challenges you?

- How might you practice the principle of "do no harm" in your interpretation of Scripture?
- In what ways do Logos and Rhema together help you avoid false narratives and live in the Spirit of love?

Prayer

Eternal Logos, Christ the Living Word,
anchor me in the truth of Your eternal love.
Keep me steady when the world shifts,
and root my soul in Your unchanging presence.
Speaking Rhema, Spirit's Whisper,
speak into my heart today.
Make the Word alive and personal
so I may walk in Your guidance and grace.
Holy Spirit, Hermeneutic of Love,
teach me to read Scripture as mirror, window, and icon.
Protect me from false narratives;
let love be my safeguard and humility my posture.
Draw me ever closer into Christ,
the Word made flesh,
in whose name I pray.
Amen.

The Word as Spirit and Love

The Intersection of Integrated Mindsets and Worldview

Philosophical and Theological Roots

Statement of the problem: Wounds need healing and mending mindsets that are addicted to and attached to unethical and unhealthy outcomes. Mindsets cause harm to others by exclusion based on gender, race, political views, wealth, and religious intolerance.

Worldview and Mindsets as the Fragmented Human Condition

The whole is greater than the sum of its parts, and yet the whole participates in each part. What does the whole mean relative to a spiritual worldview and an ethic of liberation? Eastern Orthodoxy may help clarify how these terms are used for the purpose of this book. This tradition helps us understand how the whole relates to the parts if, in fact, the whole is greater than its summary.

In Eastern Orthodoxy, the essence of God is unknown. However, accordingly God is known in God's energies. Many may differ on the question as to how God's essence and God's energy are connected, but that is beyond the scope of this book. However, to gain perspective, it is worthwhile to elaborate the difference between apophatic theology, which is referred to as "negative theologies," and cataphatic theology. The word *negative* may be misleading. An analogy may help clear some of the fuzziness about what is meant by negative here.

Suppose a patient went to see a doctor about some pain issue that might be symptomatic of a critical illness. The physician orders an X-ray to see what cannot be seen by the naked eye. What the doctor sees on the X-ray and what a layperson sees, of course, are different. However, as a patient, all you want to hear is "the results are negative" because that's good news. It means whatever was feared—cancer or a tumor—is not there. Apophatic theology says simply, "This is not God" but rather a figment of the text or a projection of an image. This does not mean that texts or forms are wrong but rather that it would be more appropriate to think in terms of it is not this but rather it is that. This, for Christian spirituality apophatic theology, is God's essence, which cannot be known in text or image. Rather God is that which is known in God's energy-cataphatic.

Apophatic spirituality tells us what God is not. To say it's not this but rather that is cataphatic spirituality in texts and image-icons.

A spiritual worldview as a process, in light of these two poles, says, "God is that," in which case that becomes this—apophatic and unknown in terms of the whole. However, in an integrated process, this becomes that—cataphatic in text and image through vision and language (or some other version of communication such as sound or sign language). The analogy is that what apophatic is to the whole, cataphatic is to each part. A spiritual worldview is a quest or process that vitiates all epistemological assumptions, metaphysical propositions, and axiological maxims. However, a mindset as an anchor, rooted in an ethic of liberation, enables a dialogical process through different sounds, silence, texts, and images.

From the perspective of a spiritual worldview, an anchor is the consciousness of the whole, which is greater than its sum parts and yet paradoxically participates in each part. The underlying epistemological assumption is self-knowledge, place and space awareness, perception in quest of a perspective, and discernment of otherness and the different. A second layer to a spiritual worldview is a metaphysical shift from literal language to symbolic language of text and image, dealing specifically with freedom and being.

Spiritual worldview axiological considerations of an ethic of liberation has three caveats: mind-talk about what is the good, soul-talk about being good, and spirit-talk about the meaning of the beautiful-aesthetics. Ethics and aesthetics as an integration is descriptive of the whole from the point of view of a mindset as a part, in which the whole paradoxically participates.

The fragmented human condition subverts mindsets, which become attached and/or addicted to outcomes that are unhealthy and unethical. The first step is to identify and distinguish worldviews and mindsets. The second step is transformation through spiritual worldview as a process wherein mindsets become anchored. That becomes a natural spirituality anchored into a spiritual worldview as a process of being and becoming a self/soul in relationship to otherness and the different.

In order to address the problem of fragmentation, Diarmuid O'Murchu's book *In the Beginning was the Spirit: Science, Religion and Indigenous Spirituality* says quantum theology calls for a new paradigm for understanding worldview: "Jesus was embracing and emulating the creative wisdom of the Sophia tradition which is the more ancient and foundational version of the Greek Logos, and that the deeper meanings of the Logos in John's gospel can best be accessed by grounding them in the Hebrew concept of Sophia Wisdom."

The wisdom tradition has implications for the environment and the economy calling for ecotheology. According to O'Murchu, "The Sophia tradition is a basis for the interface between religious wisdom and the pressing ecological and environmental issues of our time."

How worldviews and mindsets present a problem is the critical assessment of the following example. "This ancient wisdom poses quite a threat to the conventional patriarchal worldview," says O'Murchu, "especially as articulated in religion, and not surprisingly tends to be ridiculed and dismissed out of hand in several major religious traditions." A patriarchal outlook is more properly a mindset instead of a worldview. A spiritual worldview and an ethic of liberation functions as an anchor and is the standard by which human ideas and behavior are evaluated.

To critically assess mindsets requires a spiritual worldview and ethics of liberation, and it becomes a way of describing, analyzing, and evaluating actionable, measurable, and goal-oriented human behavior. A spiritual worldview is used here in a particular fashion to describe epistemological assumptions and metaphysical propositions with regard to religious language, freedom, and being. Finally, axiological maxims deemed as core values will be assessed. A spiritual worldview functions as a process, and mindsets elicit nature and validity of knowledge (i.e., perceptions of what is real and what is valuable in terms of what it aesthetically means to do good or be a good person).

This book calls for a spiritual worldview and an ethic of liberation as a process that is adequate to deal with issues confronting the tension between localization and globalization relative to the economy, ecology, and public policy, as well as how these are shaped and formed by unhealthy and unethical mindsets attached to certain outcomes. Public policy, in order to be healthy and ethical, must comport with a spiritual worldview and ethics of liberation. That raises another question for consideration, which has to do with personal/private epiphanies (referred to as place and public space).

A spiritual worldview as process and ethics of liberation critically integrates the external world and the internal world by means of dialogical self-awareness and in doing such becomes a living soul. The Logos becomes sarx, translated into a dialogue, and becomes a self when the Spirit transforms the self into the external God-communicator. The Jesus event of history is a metaphor for the external dialogue (God-eye view) that becomes internalized as a dialogical new humanity. A new humanity heals, transforms, and mends the self to become a living soul. The transformation of the self that I am to the Self-God is connected in a global spiritual worldview, as a process of becoming self-transcendent. A natural and narrative spirituality develops a God-eye spiritual view of reality.

A spiritual worldview is interconnected and global, whereas different cultures, including different traditions, values, and practices, impinge upon all of humanity. In the interface of different cultures, a new self emerges with the world's complexities, contradictions, oppositions, and encounters. Integrations are part of society at large and at the same time answer to those influences from its own particular point of view (i.e., mindsets).

A traditional understanding of worldview is used in connection with reality, the God question. Worldview as a philosophical category includes assumptions about what the nature and validity of knowledge is, what reality is, and asks what is valuable about both ethics and aesthetics. The way in which humans answer this question provides a structure for how you believe and behave in public—mindsets. Mindsets are the building blocks hidden much like a frame of a house, which one cannot see, but it holds the space, which is visible.

The problem arises when a mindset, which is unseen, often attached to or addicted to certain outcomes in religion, politics, and moral behavior, is confused for a worldview. Mindsets are driving beliefs, and behavior systems and are unseen. There is no one particular worldview but rather particular mindsets justified as worldviews. A worldview as a connected process is therefore spiritual. The difference between worldview and mindset from this perspective understands a worldview as a spiritual worldview, as process, and mindsets as particular, either attached or addicted to certain closed outcomes.

Mindsets anchored into a worldview as dynamic and lucid are open to transformational functions like a stream that flows through landscapes on a journey to a sacred space. In his book *The New Testament and the People of God*, N. T. Wright avers that a worldview includes narrative-story, questions, symbols, and praxis. My hypothesis is that a worldview as a process is compatible with a spiritual and natural worldview.

What is the connection between mindsets and worldviews? Diarmuid O'Murchu, in his book *Quantum Theology, Spiritual Implications of the New Physics* explains mindsets and worldview connection when he says, "The whole is greater than its sum parts." That is, the sum parts do not equal the whole. The particulars as parts equal mindsets and, when considered as the whole, become either addicted or attached to certain outcomes, confused for a spiritual worldview as a process. In biblical terms, that would be tantamount to idolatry. However, O'Murchu goes on to postulate that the whole participates in each part.

My thesis is that when we are considering the issue of spiritual worldview, the parts are to the whole what mindsets are to worldview as a process, a spiritual worldview. Flawed mindsets that are addicted and attached to certain outcomes are static and, therefore, subvert and undermine a spiritual worldview as a process. That in turn causes confusion and a flawed mindset that is particular and local for a worldview with global implications.

In contrast, a mindset that serves as an anchor in a worldview is interconnected, and therefore the intersection of localization and globalization is more open to dialogue. For Eastern Christian spirituality, mindsets are anchored functions as cataphatic epistemology—a model or metaphor for knowledge. A spiritual worldview or worldview as process functions similarly to apophatic epistemologies, a negative theology. A simple way to understand apophatic epistemology is to think critically, a way of thinking about models or forms as not what is real but rather a means to talk about reality meaningfully rather than literally or linearly. Knowledge and language are necessary for communication, but at the same time they are not absolute in scope. Rather, they are traces or pointers in the right direction. To hold both cataphatic knowledge and apophatic epistemologies is, then, critical thinking about mindsets and a spiritual worldview in terms of localization and globalization issues of wealth, poverty, disparity, nuclear proliferation, violence, and environmental sustainability.

An anchor is a moment in which anxiety, fear, and panic may cause addiction or attachments to certain outcomes due to angst, pain, and suffering about the future. A spiritual worldview leaves one place (a mindset), and the journey is often fraught with anxiety because we don't know what's around the bend or what lies ahead. Ahead may be a space for globalization that becomes a new place, which includes the different and otherness. Paul Tournier in his book *A Place for You*, refers to this experience of anxiety as "the middle of the road anxiety." When we leave a place but haven't quite reached our goal, we become anxious and panic about the future. Anchors along the way are necessary to help us calm our fears and anxieties before going on toward the unknown.

That leads us to consider how mindsets and worldviews function as essence and energies. In Eastern Orthodoxy theology, God is not known in God's essence but in God's energies.

A real distinction between the essence (*ousia*) and the energies (*energeia*) of God is a central principle of Eastern Orthodox theology. Eastern Orthodox theology regards this distinction as more than a mere conceptual distinction. This doctrine is most closely identified with Gregory Palamas. The teachings of Palamas were made into dogma in the Eastern Orthodox church by the Hesychast councils.

Historically, Western Christianity has tended to reject the essence-energies distinction as real in the case of God, characterizing the view as a heretical introduction of an unacceptable division in the Trinity and suggestive of polytheism. Further, the associated practice of hesychasm used to achieve theosis was characterized as "magic." More recently, some Roman Catholic thinkers have taken a positive view of Palamas' teachings, including how he understood the essence-energies distinction, arguing that it does not represent an insurmountable theological division between Roman Catholicism and Eastern Orthodoxy.

To know God in God's energies is visible and measurable in human praxis, in worship, spiritual disciplines, creation, and God-talk. Wesley's quadrilateral primacy of Scripture, tradition, reason, and experience is helpful in this discussion. A spiritual worldview and ethics of liberation is a natural spirituality that acts dialogically to integrate theology, psychology, and philosophy with a "difference principle" where science and spirituality meet and do not meet. The intersection of these various landscapes becomes an opportunity for transformation, and therefore, transformative intersections are those spaces where a table of inclusion sets the agenda.

When we attach ourselves to only a certain way of knowing, a mindset emerges; it excludes others who sit at the table of globalization and defines reality from its particular lenses that it's either attached to or addicted to certain outcomes. A spiritual worldview is a metaphysical shift in language, freedom, and being. It embraces the limitations and weakness of any given perception of reality and mindset to gain a new perspective, which then forms a new perception in need of perspective, an ongoing dynamic process.

A spiritual worldview acknowledges the distance between perception and the reality to which perception points as the "difference principle." The difference principle, according to John Rawls, "removes the indeterminateness the inequalities of a basic structure of economic inequalities that are to be judged."

Rawls goes on to say, "Assuming the framework of institutions required by equal liberty and fair equality of opportunity, the higher expectations of those better situated are just if and only if they work as a part of a scheme which improves the expectations of the least advantaged member of society."

The function of the difference principle is to close the gap in an in-between space; that is, whatever obfuscates truth and reality. In actuality, the potential difference principle acts as a prophetic conscience and a goal toward perfection, as a process that will be realized in the now/not yet tension of the coming of the Reign of God. That is to say, the table we set is all-inclusive, holding the bread we eat for our bodies as well as the bread we consume for our spiritual sustenance. There are no unequal humans before the face of God.

> *But now that faith has come, we are no longer subject to a disciplinarian, for in Christ Jesus you are all children of God through faith. As many of you as were baptized into Christ have clothed yourselves with Christ. There is no longer Jew or Greek; there is no longer slave or free;, there is no longer male and female; for all of you are one in Christ Jesus. And if you belong to Christ, then you are Abraham's offspring, heirs according to the promise.*
>
> —Gal. 3:25-29

Before God we all stand naked and equal; however, diversity and difference are marks of unity and tension; the different and similar are held together in tension as a response to grace.

A spiritual worldview, as process, includes epistemology as defined by the nature and validity of knowledge. It includes metaphysics, including ontology (meaning and being), language, and freedom. Axiology, what is valuable, ethics and aesthetics notwithstanding, shapes morality and core values that are measurable, actionable, and goal-oriented. Through moral imagination, humans grow in self-awareness, understanding, and the perspective of mindsets that obfuscates a spiritual worldview and liberation of ethics. Mindsets when attached or addicted to certain outcomes are closed, static, and localized. A mindset anchored into a spiritual worldview and ethics of liberation is more open and moves to otherness and the different by embracing the tension between localization and globalization issues that are ultimate concerns. Religion is defined by Paul Tillich as human response to ultimate concerns, and therefore, whatever ultimately concerns you is your religion.

In the intersection of mindsets and spiritual worldview, a worldview essentially has three philosophical components: epistemology, metaphysics, and axiology. All of them point to ultimate concerns. A mindset addicted and attached to certain outcomes is a religion that subverts a spiritual worldview as a process by making local and self-interest the ultimate concern. A spiritual worldview and an ethics of liberation is rooted in the particular or localization concerns and at the same time moves out to engage the issues of globalization by examining epistemological assumptions and critically assessing the nature and validity of knowledge. This is explained in the ideas of metaphysics and axiology. Metaphysics generally deals with natural and supernatural realities, and axiology explores values; that is, morality, ethics, and aesthetics; what is deemed praiseworthy, who is the good person, and ultimately what is beautiful and who is beautiful.

Ancient and traditional spiritual disciplines enhance a spiritual natural worldview. Rather than a fixed notion, the spiritual natural worldview becomes a process, a goal-oriented journey similar to the ancient process of becoming through purification, illumination, and union with God's transcendence and immanence. This process enables you to more fully engage the Reign of God and act more as a citizen of the reign. That allows you to, in turn, act as a citizen in the global world context and rooted in the localization as citizen of the content of your world. A spiritual worldview and an ethic of liberation hold in balance the tension between the poles of local and global concerns. In quantum spirituality, the tension between a preoccupation with self-preservation and the preoccupation with belonging to the whole creates a connection of vitality. When one or the other pole becomes predominant in quantum terms, death occurs because there is a disconnection. Spirituality, then, is about being connected to otherness and the different.

The transcendent God is wholly other and unknowable. The immanent God is close and known through God's self-revealing presence in the Christ event. Immanence in this context is not to be confused with the Trinitarian immanence of the relationship within the Godhead, which has more to do with how Father, Son, and Holy Spirit are related through perichoresis. The early church used this term to describe the relationship between the divine and human natures of Christ. Moreover, it became useful among contemporary persons such as Jürgen Moltmann and John Zizioulas as a term to describe the relationship of the Trinitarian God. The energies of God are then known in relationship, similar to the way God relates to the triune ideas of God, creation, and humanity. A spiritual worldview and an ethic of liberation act in human relationships of otherness and the different, which has global implications.

The complex relationship between mindsets and the spiritual worldview, energy as theological praxis, and essence as metaphysical/theological concept can be further explored in regard to brain-based reality and quantum theology. Spirituality and ethics connect brain-based reality and quantum theology, according to O'Murchu. This has spiritual implications and consciousness in connection with the moral values within the heart, a pneumatic expression of transformation, for which wholeness and sacred places are possible.

An intersection where mindsets and worldview clash must become transformative to prevent a collision. In traffic intersections, a decision is necessary, depending on what rules are in place such as a red light or a stop sign. The rules for the most part are in place to prevent a crash. In a similar way, a spiritual worldview, as process, and the ethics of liberation prevent a crash at the intersection of localization and globalization of otherness and the different. Mindsets fixated (addictions and attachments) on certain ideologies such as politics, economics, environmental issues, and religion—including social issues racism, sexism, violence, and distribution of wealth—become idols that cause crashes and potentially cause great harm to humans flourishing.

How do we maintain integrity with personal mindsets and engage a worldview as process that enables civility? That is, how do we connect personal place with public space in a way that is congruent and wholesome? Quantum spirituality suggests that all of life is interconnected, and change occurs when particles bump up against one another. This fits with natural spirituality in which different mindsets could bump up against one another rather than crash in a destructive way. We can learn through the spiritual disciplines to bump up against otherness through dialogue and integration as a preventive to crashing, which causes harm, pain, and suffering to humans who think and believe differently.

An important aspect of the relationship between worldview and mindsets focuses on differentiation. We see this clearly in Eastern Orthodoxy's deification process (theosis), the understanding of cataphatic and apophatic, in relationship to God's essence and energies regarding the Imago Dei that guides us through the roles of ethics and spirituality.

The Imago Dei, the image and likeness of God expressed through human anthropology and social relationships, is infused by divine attributes: What can be known of God's activity and presence among humanity. The central epistemological assumption between humans and God is represented by Hans Urs von Balthsasar and Catherine Mowry LaCugna, proponents of such a view in the perspective of celebrating the mysteries of the Eucharist.

From one perspective, what's at stake is the entire notion of spiritual worldviews and mindsets. That indicates that transformation is never easy. It is, at best, difficult to understand how different theologies are entrenched in worldviews and mindsets, especially when the differences are grounded in diverse mindsets anchored into a spiritual worldview. All we can hope for is civility, humility, and generosity in diversity, while exemplifying the virtue to love when separated by difference. In the issue of mindsets and spiritual worldviews, the idea is not that we must agree on everything but rather that we must embrace otherness and maintain integrity through the virtue of love.

Part one of LaCugna's book deals with the emergence and defeat of the doctrine of the Trinity, while part two reconceives the doctrine in light of the mystery of salvation. In the process, she places the emphasis on who God is for us in historical, liturgical, and traditional ecclesial experience.

The nuances of ontology and epistemology are complex, which has to do with God's essence and energies, mindsets, and worldviews. For LaCugna's mindset, a shift from God's essence to God's energy has to do with epistemology; whereas, for the Eastern Church's mindset, any shift would disrupt God's essence (apophatic), which is ontological and cannot be known. Language, words, and symbols shape our perception of reality. Therefore, God's energies are not ontological but rather cataphatic as revealed in text, image, and, in particular, icons. Both mindsets are anchored into spiritual worldviews that are different and diverse, which is good insofar as the relationship between persons are authentic and maintain integrity through humility. The outcome will then be inclusive: unity and diversity.

One example of an integrative moment that illustrates the intersection between mindsets, a spiritual worldview, metaphysics, and ontology is the Eastern Orthodox perspective of liberation theology. A spiritual worldview as a process and an ethics of liberation focuses on liberation in the "here and now" world of social justice and countering the structures of evil rather than salvation in the next world. Salvation of the soul is, then, defined as liberating others to a vitality living. Ethics of liberation deal with human relationships to provide preferential treatment to the least advantaged rather than to the privileged. The voices of the oppressed are heard as a word from God. The intersection of language as literal and symbolic, freedom and determinism, being and consciousness, calls for a metaphysical shift from supernatural divine intervention to spirituality and ethics of liberation.

Freedom from oppression becomes the occasion for freedom and healing to both the oppressed and the oppressors; the liberation is for both victims and perpetrators. The Reign of God's central goal is freedom from evil, both cosmic and structural, in law and policies. This is the message Jesus proclaims; the symbol of the cross becomes a gift-based reality in blessings and grace. The tension that holds polar opposites becomes the occasion for the cross: the symbol of giftedness, the grace necessary for transformation.

We need to consider how, why, and what are the issues that shape mindsets. What drives a worldview is not theology but rather mindsets that shape text and images of who God is for us. America's four Gods suggestion that mindsets are shaped by previous experience of religion is essentially a projection of our self-image of what God is for us, but not necessarily informed. "Do we create our own reality?" asks O'Murchu. He provides us with some insight. "In the quantum worldview, nothing makes sense in isolation; basically, there are no boundaries, and influences can emerge from several sources."

According to quantum theory, not only is the observer involved, but the observer actually brings about what is being observed. We become the god we imagine. And, therefore, O'Murchu says, "Our very act brings reality into being."

A spiritual worldview as a process discerns and strives to distinguish between projections of the self, becoming through grace what God is by nature. The logos of a spiritual worldview functions in two ways: first, as a universal affirmation of God's love and acceptance, and second, as an affront to the human condition. A spiritual worldview develops a prophetic consciousness as a moral compass of wisdom, a gift of discernment, as well as a skill to distinguish good and evil, and appropriate behavior to any given situation, especially in relationships to others. O'Murchu is helpful when he writes, "From the beginning of our evolution as a species, we have been exploring and expressing our spirituality with both its light and shadow."

Transformative intersections are places where we can let go of our particular mindsets, which for the most part are attached to beliefs that exclude others. It is a distinction between mindsets that are anchored into a worldview and mindsets that are addicted and attached to particular outcomes. For example, a student from China taking my business ethics course said to me, "My Chinese ethical worldview is utilitarian and survival of the fittest, but my American worldview is virtue ethics and a moral imperative."

I asked him why he thought he had two worldviews. He responded by saying that he thought his government had no soul because he had no other choice in his country. This is a prime example of how mindsets and worldviews are confused. In actuality, he was learning to distinguish mindsets by process of a spiritual worldview in which two very different ideas about business ethics enter into his intersection of Chinese and American experiences. He thought critically through how a worldview is not a particular way of viewing life but rather a process by which we can evaluate the global economy and how politics operates under different circumstances. The fact that he could make that distinction suggests that he was able to process two different outcomes. Ultimately, choices are made, but the consequence of our choice is something we often can't control. A spiritual worldview simply embraces that knowledge is possible; that is, knowledge grounded in science, reason, and personal epiphanies of consciousness of God-communication, revealing the divine human encounter with Logos. This dialogue leads to integration of the epistemologies of science, reason, and self-revealing encounters with consciousness.

When we attach ourselves only to a certain way of knowing, a mindset emerges. When the mindset excludes, it's either attached or addicted to certain outcomes. A spiritual worldview is a metaphysical shift in language, freedom, and being, embracing the limitations and weakness of any given perception of reality in order to gain a new perspective, which then forms a new perception in need of perspective in an ongoing fluid dynamic process. Often a crash in the intersection of opposing theologies does not seem like a shock but rather rational arguments for or against (rather than a dialogue leading to integration). The outcome of dialogue and integration transforms individuals and the world.

Intersections where different core values bump up against one another are actually opportunities for transformative action, and therefore, not all conflicts are necessarily destructive. The intensity of the integrative process of a spiritual worldview and archetypal intersections of a worldview are identical. According to Jung, "The upheaval of our world and the upheaval in consciousness are one and the same."

To be human is spiritual, and therefore humanity is connected, albeit unconsciously. According to quantum theology, all of life is interconnected. Do humans become spiritual, or are they spiritual beings having a human experience? How we answer this question reveals much about mindsets and worldviews. However, there is another aspect that has to do with human praxis: actionable and measurable human behavior. The practice of spirituality shapes and forms humans around knowledge, reality, and values: a worldview in the process of becoming and awakening to otherness, God, and humanity (hence a spiritual worldview). "The human being is defined through otherness," writes Zizioulas.

A spiritual worldview and an ethics of liberation assumes the human capacity for choice. Accordingly, Zizioulas postulates that the meaning of freedom has to do with the drive to ontological otherness: "The drive of the human being towards otherness is rooted in the divine call to Adam, which implies three qualities revealing the Imago Dei: relationship, freedom, and otherness."

What is the meaning of freedom, then? In some way, humans live an answer to this question. "To recognize that all human experience, including transcendence, religious and aesthetic experience is brain-based, is not to embrace a reductionist position in which higher consciousness is somehow explained away a series of events in the cerebral cortex," asserts McGrath.

Natural spirituality does not rule out the reality of transcendence but rather is consistent with a shift in metaphysics from literal language to symbolic language and asserts incarnational/natural spirituality that for human beings in this world is accessed through the "medium of our material bodies."

Mindsets and worldview are ways of talking about personhood, or your personality, in which the way we talk about ultimate concerns religiously or politically expresses our view of life. A mindset anchored into a spiritual worldview as process and the ethics of liberation define personhood. Mindsets that are addicted or attached create an illusion of reality, sometimes confused with a worldview, but instead undermine and subvert personhood.

Adrian van Kaam would rather use the term "life form" than the word "personality." He does so because "personality" describes a humanistic notion rather than religious spiritual vitality. For van Kaam, life form is more in keeping with the Judaean-biblical concept of human life as the image, or form, of God to the concept of the Christ-form of the soul, implied in the New Testament.

van Kaam is unique in that he has developed a language for his "Science of Foundational Formative Spirituality." He provides one way in which self-discovery and human praxis discern the difference between a mindset that is anchored and a mindset that is addicted and attached to certain outcomes, undermining a developmental aspect to a natural spiritual worldview.

van Kaam legitimizes the process of spirituality within an academic setting by indicating that we cannot study spirituality without a self-referential and interdisciplinary approach. He writes, "The term 'science' is not used in its restricted sense, in which the word applies exclusively to the physical science, but in its original and wider sense of any systematic body of data and insights validated by its own proper research methodology, including inter-subjective methods of validation by trained researcher in the same field."

An academic study of spirituality involves self-referential or self-implication, which van Kaam means when he discusses science as intersubjective and interdisciplinary. We cannot study spirituality as a disinterested observer. He goes on to write, "A rigorous method guarantees the science's objectivity, it therefore secures the identification and validation of foundational data and insights of Western and Eastern form traditions, arts, and sciences."

An academic study of spirituality is an interdisciplinary approach and critically integrative in the research. We must remain disinterested in the research so we can remain as objective as possible and allow the data to lead to its logical conclusion. In the study of spirituality, we cannot remain aloof, however, as the discipline calls for self-implication in praxis. van Kaam says there are six basic assumptions of the science of foundational human formation:

1. Natural development evolution
2. Human developmental psychology
3. Spiritual religious experience, transcendence dynamic theological, and Scripture
4. Social justice, local and international foundational for human spirituality confronting structures of evil, as in St. Ignatius discerning of spirits
5. Tradition: wisdom of religious and cultural formation in virtue of love and compassion
6. Praxis and pedagogy: academic and professional training

Considering our discussion above and integrating van Kaam's assumptions, we see that a worldview as a transformative process is a pneumatic expression, a vital life-form that integrates the six assumptions that van Kaam articulates. Spirituality and ethics guide us through an intersection where natural, human, spiritual, social justice, tradition, and praxis crash, becoming transformative through "bumping up" against one another in quantum theology. A destructive crash occurs, however, when worldview ceases as process and becomes attached or addicted to mindsets as walls of separation, independence, and isolation. Mindsets build walls, whereas a worldview as process builds bridges to connect—a form of spirituality. In this equation, ethics provide a measurable and actionable way of life that reflects in "human formation which may be complemented and perfected by the graced formation that is the gift of the Holy Spirit." Graced formation is van Kaam's way of articulating what Athanasius said in antiquity:

> By grace we become what God is by nature. . . . Such insight into the harmonization of the human and graced formation of transcendent and pneumatic formation may help to deepen our own spiritual life to make us more integrated, less tense and anxious, more appreciative, poised, form potent, and attractive in our whole personality.

Spirituality and ethics, accordingly, shape not only identity but human behavior, inwardly as well as outwardly. Faustin Ntamushobora in his book *Transformation Through the Different Other* sees the primary problem that divides people is the "heart."

He continues, "that race, tribe, and worldview differences can widen the gap among people's relationships, thus leading to exclusion, even for faith-based Christians." Ntamushobora is saying that mindsets attached or addicted to worldviews create gaps because of personal place; when normative for public space, it is a mindset that builds isolation and alienates otherness. Ntamushobora uses the language of a "rendezvous of giving and receiving among people from different cultures." The rendezvous describes perhaps more adequately an intersection where decisions are called for, which then reflects either a conflict leading to independence or a dialogue leading to integration. Integration respects difference by embracing otherness as a place in public space.

Ntamushobora understands that transformation takes place through giving and receiving, much like a potlatch festival in the Native American tradition of the Pacific Northwest.

A potlatch is a gift-giving festival and primary economics system practiced by Indigenous peoples of the Pacific Northwest Coast of Canada and United States. The word comes from the Chinook jargon, meaning "to give away" or "a gift"; originally from the Nuu-chah-nulth word that means to make a ceremonial gift.

The stage is set for three social issues as economics, environment, and public policy are transformed by a spiritual worldview as process and the ethics of liberation. This intersection can be shaped, however, by mindsets through assumptions about what we know: perceptions of reality shaped by narrative, and religious beliefs. Whoever controls the language has the power to affect public policy in ways that are based on self-interest and for profit. Culture, environment, and economics are often at odds in the intersection where all people of goodwill decide the fate of a world in transition.

The transformation of public policy journeys through a transformative intersection of a mindset that is addicted and attached to certain outcomes that run contrary to a mindset anchored in a spiritual worldview. The addicted mindset is absorbed in self-interest without regard for those who are less fortunate. It takes a spiritual awakening that embraces a gift-based economics to understand and negotiate the tension that exists between the for-profit and ecological realms.

This awakening understands the gap between those who have and those who have not, and is best suited for purposeful public policy. Self-interest, based on for-profit models, builds walls of separation and isolation. The tension between a preoccupation for self-preservation and the need to belong to the whole is then critically integrated, mixing self-interest and social responsibly. Spirituality connects the self to the greater whole without losing the sense of identity of our rootedness and personhood because personhood is best understood in relation to the different and otherness.

When the Word Became Rhema in the Rain

One morning, I sat on the deck as rain fell steadily on the earth. The drops tapped the railing like a thousand tiny fingers keeping time with my heartbeat. I opened the Scriptures, and my eyes fell on these familiar words: "He makes His sun rise on the evil and on the good and sends rain on the righteous and on the unrighteous" (Matt. 5:45).

At first, I read it as Logos—an eternal truth about the character of God: impartial, generous, ever faithful. I thought of the universality of that promise, spoken across generations.

But as I listened to the rain striking the leaves and streaming into the soil, it became Rhema. The Spirit whispered, "This rain is for you too. I am watering the dry ground of your soul. Even the places you think are barren are being nourished."

I felt tears mix with the rain, and suddenly Scripture was not abstract theology but a living word. The Logos of God's faithfulness had become Rhema in my weakness, speaking directly into my season of thirst.

It was mirror, showing me my dryness.

It was window, reminding me of God's larger story of blessing.

It was icon, drawing me into the presence of the Living Word who rains love upon us all.

On the deck that morning, I realized again: the Spirit interprets Scripture not only in study or the sanctuary but also in the soil, the sky, and the quiet whispers of creation. The Word is alive—always Logos, always Rhema, always love.

Tillich, Kierkegaard, and the Paradox of Grace

The human encounter with God is never one-dimensional. Paul Tillich described this relationship in paradoxical terms: God is at once the universal affirmation of humanity and the universal affront to humanity. Søren Kierkegaard, in a different key, spoke of the divine paradox where faith lives in the tension between the finite and the infinite, the temporal and the eternal, the human and the divine. Together, their voices remind us that to know God is to live within contradiction where love comforts and truth unsettles.

Tillich's paradox insists that God affirms us in our very being. We are accepted, embraced, and upheld by grace. Yet the same divine presence confronts us by exposing our limitations, our moral failures, and our tendency to evade responsibility. God's "yes" gives us dignity; God's "no" calls us to transformation.

Kierkegaard spoke of the paradox differently but no less profoundly. For him, faith meant embracing the absurd, that the eternal became temporal, that God took on flesh in Christ. This paradox cannot be solved by reason alone; it must be lived. The leap of faith is not a denial of contradiction but a surrender to it, trusting that divine love holds together what human reason cannot.

Grace stands at the intersection of these paradoxes. To accept grace means to believe that we are accepted by God despite our flaws and failures. This is both liberating and deeply challenging. It liberates us from guilt, shame, and the relentless demand for perfection. It challenges us because it requires surrendering—letting go of self-judgment, pride, and the illusion of self-sufficiency. Accepting grace demands that we allow ourselves to be loved, which for many is the hardest step of all.

The experience of grace reshapes self-perception. It leads to greater self-acceptance, resilience, and compassion. It quiets the voice of perfectionism and frees us from the burden of endless striving. It fosters authenticity, forgiveness, and belonging. Yet grace also unsettles us, confronting our doubts, fears, and resistance to vulnerability. It calls us into responsibility, not as a condition for love but as the natural fruit of being loved.

Tillich and Kierkegaard both insist that faith is forged in this tension: affirmation and affront, comfort and challenge, love and paradox. The one who accepts grace discovers a new freedom—the freedom to be fully human, fully alive, and fully embraced by God. But they also discover a new calling—to live beyond the self, in love, justice, and compassion for others.

In this way, the paradox is not an obstacle to faith but its very heartbeat. To live within it is to be drawn deeper into the mystery of God, whose love is both gift and demand, both comfort and confrontation, both affirmation and affront.

Meditation

"But he said to me, 'My grace is sufficient for you, for power is made perfect in weakness.' So I will boast all the more gladly of my weaknesses, so that the power of Christ may dwell in me" (2 Cor. 12:9).

Grace is both comfort and confrontation. It affirms us in love and challenges us into transformation.

Symbolic Reading

Mirror: Grace affirms our dignity yet reflects our brokenness, showing us both belovedness and need for change.

Window: Grace opens outward, offering us God's horizon of hope while revealing the gap between the world's injustice and God's dream.

Icon: Grace confronts us with Christ himself, both gentle shepherd and crucified Lord—the One who embraces and demands, comforts and transforms.

Paradox: Affirmation and affront held together in love form the living pulse of authentic faith.

Prayer

God of grace and truth,
Speak Your "yes" over my life
that I may rest in Your love.

Speak Your "no" to my pride and fear
that I may walk in Your way.
Help me to live within the paradox,
affirmed yet confronted,
comforted yet challenged.
Form me in your grace, until my life becomes
a witness of Your love and justice.
Amen.

Reflection Questions

- When have I most clearly experienced God's "yes" of affirmation in my life?
- When have I felt God's "no," confronting me with truth or calling me to change?
- How does Kierkegaard's "leap of faith" resonate with my own spiritual journey?
- In what ways has grace liberated me from shame or perfectionism?
- How might living in paradoxes both affirm and affront—deepen my faith and shape my engagement with the world?

Fivefold Arc of the Second Half (Books 6–10)

1. From prophetic judgment to healing justice.
2. From privilege unmasked to good news for the poor.
3. From dividing walls to a shared table.
4. From creation's groaning to creation's renewal.
5. From individual faith to the Beloved Community.

Together, these next five "graphia" carry the reader into the social, communal, and ecological implications of a spiritual worldview, completing the tenfold journey from mirror and window to integrated justice and communion.

The following represents the entire work.

One Gospel Story, Tenfold Graphia

Scripture, like a mirror and a window, reflects who we are and reveals who we can become. Across these ten graphia we have not read isolated texts but have walked pathways woven together into a single garment of grace. Each book has its own story, yet together they form one narrative—a tenfold journey of love, justice, and communion.

Book One: Samaria (Luke 10; John 4)

Here we saw ourselves in the Samaritan and the woman at the well—our prejudices, our thirsts, our single stories. Yet the mirror became a window, and the stranger's face revealed the very face of God.

Book Two: Echoes of the Innocents (Matthew 2; Mark 4; John 11)

Here we entered the extremities of the human condition: violence, grief, storm, and death. Yet lament became love's deepest prayer, and the command to "unbind him and let him go" echoed as God's invitation to us all.

Book Three: Night Conversations (John 3)

Here, with Nicodemus, we wrestled in the shadows. We discovered that being "born again" was less formula than awakening, less doctrine than dawn breaking in the soul.

Book Four: The Christ Event and the Gap (Mark 8; Exodus 3; John's I AM)

Here we faced the question of discipleship: "Who do you say that I am?" Peter's confession showed both faith and fragility. In transfiguration, cross, and resurrection, we found that grace heals the gap between our words and our lives.

Book Five: From Confession to Communion

Here we entered the heart of the mystery. Confession led to cross; cross to resurrection; resurrection to Spirit; Spirit to communion.

Faith was revealed not as possession but as process—ever-deepening, ever-opening.

Book Six: The Prophetic Mirror (Amos 5; Isaiah 58; Luke 4)
Here we stood with the prophets. The mirror showed our worship without justice. The window revealed God's desire for mercy, liberation, and a faith inseparable from love.

Book Seven: Good News for the Poor (Luke 6; Matthew 25; James 2)
Here the kingdom turned our world upside down. We saw privilege unmasked and abundance shared. The poor became honored guests at God's feast, and justice became love in action.

Book Eight: Breaking Walls, Building Tables (Ephesians 2; Acts 10; Galatians 3)
Here we saw the barriers of race, class, and creed crumble. In Christ there is no division, only a widened table where all belong and peace is born in reconciliation.

Book Nine: Creation Groaning, Creation Renewed (Genesis 1; Romans 8; Revelation 22)
Here creation itself became our companion in prayer. We heard its groaning, joined to ours, awaiting redemption. And we glimpsed the river of life, watering the tree whose leaves heal nations and ecosystems alike.

Book Ten: The Beloved Community (Micah 6; John 13; Revelation 7)
Here we arrived at the horizon of love. The mirror showed our failures to embody justice, mercy, and humility. But the window opened onto the Beloved Community—a multitude reconciled, diverse and united, serving and praising together.

The Arc of Tenfold Grace

- From mirror to window
- From innocence lost to lament voiced
- From night's searching to morning's new birth
- From confession's gap to Spirit's communion
- From prophetic judgment to healing justice
- From privilege unmasked to good news for the poor
- From dividing walls to shared tables
- From creation's groaning to creation's renewal
- From individual faith to Beloved Community

All of it is one gospel story: love that reflects us truthfully, heals us mercifully, and calls us into God's greater horizon of justice and peace.

And so, dear reader, the journey does not end here. For every time you open the Scriptures with an integrative worldview anchored in love, committed to justice, alive to the Spirit, you are writing the next chapter of this gospel story with your own life.

The Intersection of Mindsets and Worldviews

Is there a difference between a worldview and a mindset? Once when I was attending a lecture at Oxford, the speaker used the words mindset and worldview interchangeably. So, I asked, "What is the difference between a mindset and a worldview?"

The professor answered, "I've never been asked that question before; I don't know."

During my undergraduate studies, I was taught to distinguish mindset as the particular and worldview as a universal toward which the particular pointed. But this was not satisfactory to me. Pressing further into the distinction between mindset and worldview on several layers, the multi-tiered question became this: Is there such a thing as a particular worldview? Is there a Christian worldview, a biblical worldview, and a cultural worldview?

The answer contains three layers. One of my international students said, "In Chinese worldview I would reason this way, but in my American worldview I would reason that way." Understood in these terms, it is actually a mindset as used in this book and not a worldview. So the first layer is confusion about how these words are used semantically.

The second understanding of how worldview must be used is process. The process philosophically, as used for purposes of clarification, is asking open-ended questions: How do we know, what is real, and what do we value? These questions are assumptions about epistemology and metaphysical ontology, and are axiological in scope. Providing answers to these questions reveals mindsets.

The third consideration defines a worldview as spiritual, and mindsets that are attached and addicted to certain assumptions as unhealthy and unethical. A spiritual worldview is an open-ended process that engages interdisciplinary studies and dialogical process, and integrates through self-critical thinking and reflection. The process is inclusive both in personal and social fields and horizons of cognitive thought. It is expressed through the humanities, sciences, and art in religious and political life, toward ethical and healthy human praxis.

Finally, a spiritual worldview anchored in a mindset is to what apophatic and cataphatic are to an Eastern Orthodox perspective. As a metaphor, the difference is, in essence and energies, what we can know and not know. A metaphysical shift in language from literal to symbolic provides a descriptive, analytical, and prescriptive of moral core values.

The four moral theories—utilitarian, deontological, libertarian, and virtue/communal ethics—are inadequate to deal with globalization on their own merits. Through critical integration of the four moral theories, an ethic of liberation functions as a healthy and ethical mindset. A mindset that is anchored in a spiritual worldview is an ethic of liberation which is adequate to deal with the issues of localization and globalization both religiously and politically.

Frameworks

Transformational intersections begin with radical uncertainty, identify crisis and disorientation, and are painful at best. Mindsets are about change, which is difficult, and that is why attachments and addictions are seemingly comfortable. However, attachments are unhealthy and unethical, and could possibly lead to violence. According to Charles Taylor in his book *Sources of the Self: The Making of the Modern Identity*, "In general one might try to single out three axes what can be called in moral thinking, which are respect for human life, what kind of life is worthy, and dignity an attitude of commanding respect."

An anchored mindset is what Taylor calls a framework. The transformation from mindsets that are addicted and attached to certain unhealthy and unethical outcomes is to embrace the radical uncertainty. The framework that Taylor provides is similar to an ethic of liberation, respect for human life, worth or fulfillment, and dignity. Why are frameworks necessary? The answer to that question involves the role of a spiritual worldview as a process.

The framework that Taylor employs functions as an anchored mindset connected to a spiritual worldview. A spiritual worldview as a process reflects the whole, which is greater than its sum of the parts and yet paradoxically participates in each part. At this juncture, a spiritual worldview is similar to apophatic theology, the whole or ontological essence that cannot be known. A mindset that is anchored as an ethic of liberation is connected and therefore reflects cataphatic theology—the energies of essence that are visible and measurable human action. (Energies are fields or horizons of vitality as cosmic spirit in the transformative process.) Mindsets that are addicted or attached to certain outcomes are liberated to authentic ontological being, a new humanity anchored in a spiritual worldview as an ongoing fluid and dynamic life of vitality. This mindset for what Taylor calls framework has many colors and contours rooted in religion, culture, family, and human experience. "In the language of modern physics, the whole is greater than the sum of the parts, and it is primarily in the whole that the eroticism of the Great Spirit births the non-duality that holds all life in creative unison," writes O'Murchu.

An understanding of the whole and the parts in quantum spirituality is essential to this book. "We see with different eyes," O'Murchu postulates. We can see past our differences and see the whole, which is connected beyond dualism that "fragments and violently divides." The radical uncertainty of crisis, disorientation, and pain calls for a quantum leap of faith as mystical experience that is not, says O'Murchu, "about transcending life's struggles but rather abiding more deeply within them."

Catherine Keller, in a foreword to Shelly Rambo's book *Spirit and Trauma: A Theology of Remaining*, says, "By translating the Greek *menein* as 'remaining' rather than 'abiding,' Rambo inspires an inter-human capacity to stand by each other in our sufferings—especially those who cannot be victoriously fixed." Rambo's theological exegesis of John's vine and the branches is the context for her translation of John 15:1–5, "Abide in me as I abide in you."

Celtic spirituality is akin to what quantum suggests. "Though the human body is born complete in one moment, the birth of the human heart is an ongoing process. It is being birthed in every experience of your life," says John O'Donohue, "and everything that happens to you has the potential to deepen you." O'Donohue also believes that the heart is the inner face of our life. The heart, for him, is a place where attachments and addictions potentially begin with an unhealthy and unethical outcome. The heart, then, is a window into the soil of your soul, liberated from mindsets addicted or attached to certain outcomes, transformed from an anchored mindset into a spiritual worldview.

"What is emerging here," says Keller, "under the sign of the middle Spirit, is a pneumatology that may actually hold up in the face of personal and collective suffering, for it frees us from the dishonest resolutions, the grim guarantees, and the disappointing promise, this Spirit breathes, witnesses, and remains, and it lures us as well." A cosmic spirit remains in the radical uncertainty of crisis and disorientation, and its painfully liberating mindsets that are attached and addicted to certain outcomes. The cosmic spirit is transformed from an anchor into a spiritual worldview transforming human fragmented souls with respect, a life worth living, and dignity.

Landscapes

This narrative is divided into three landscapes. Part one is rooted in philosophical and theological discussions about the fragmented human condition. The first part deals with worldviews and mindsets, as well as the fragmented human condition. The fragmented human condition subverts mindsets, which become attached and/or addicted to outcomes that are unhealthy and unethical. Natural spirituality, on the other hand, is anchored into a spiritual worldview as a process of being and becoming a self/soul in relationship to otherness.

The next part posits that moral theories and a transformative intersection of localization and globalization through core values inventory analysis indicate that the lens through which ethics shape and form the landscapes of the soul reinforce the fragmented human condition. A transformative intersection of locality and globalization calls for a new vision of the ethics of liberation to deal adequately with issues confronting ecology, economics, and public policy. Here, results, reputation, relationships, rights, and responsibility represent the four moral theories of utilitarianism, deontological, libertarianism, and virtue/communal ethics.

Part two describes, analyzes, and prescribes a spiritual worldview and ethic of liberation as a process of healing and mending mindsets. Mindsets are fragmented, unhealthy, and unethical. Christian spirituality, however, from a natural, narrative, and scriptural perspective, is compatible with a spiritual worldview and ethic of liberation. A spiritual worldview and ethic of liberation are anchors in the light of mystery and observable human behavior.

The third part discusses natural spirituality and Scripture while exploring Christocentric teachings of Scripture. An ethic of liberation through positive emotions transforms mindsets that are addicted and attached to certain outcomes. A new humanity is an ontological being. Ontological being within this context of Christian spirituality is Christocentric and authentic. Interconnecting a spiritual worldview as a process and a mindset of liberation, then, becomes a vision for a new humanity. A spiritual worldview and an ethic of liberation critically assess and integrate core values of results, relationships, reputation, rights, and responsibility to deal more adequately with issues of localization and globalization.

Next, the concerns are with the role of the cosmic Holy Spirit and Scripture, which are vital to the transformation of humanity toward theosis. The divine-human dialogue is narrative spirituality. The following part uses the ideas of quantum leap of faith, transformative spirituality, and an ethic of liberation as a window to narrative spirituality. Through transformative intersections, mindsets confused for worldviews potentially become people in community with a new vision for the transformation of the world. The discussion then continues through dialogical self-theory, mindfulness, and ethics of liberation of soul-talk for otherness and different, as a vision for a new humanity.

The third part suggests that applied spirituality and the ethics of liberation are key in the process of becoming an ethical agent. The focus is working toward a goal of healthy and ethical spiritual worldviews and an ethic of liberation with a dialogical application.

The final part deals with a spiritual worldview and an ethic of liberation as applied ethics in business, the workplace, and church organization. The conclusion theologizes human experiences as an ecumenical and pneumatic expression of a spiritual worldview and ethic of liberation for the landscapes of all human experience.

Philosophical and Theological Roots

Statement of the problem: Wounds need healing/mending mindsets that are addicted and attached to unethical and unhealthy outcomes. Mindsets cause harm to others by exclusion based on gender, race, political views, wealth, and religious intolerance.

The first time I held a broken piece of stained glass in my hand, I remember how sharp it felt, how fragile and yet strangely beautiful it was. The fragment had once belonged to a window that told a larger story. Alone, it could only reflect a fraction of the light. But placed back within its frame, surrounded by other colors and shapes, it became part of a radiant design.

So it is with us. Humanity has always known itself in fragments—cultures divided, hearts divided, faiths divided. Each person carries splinters of memory, identity, and longing. We stumble into life carrying pieces of a whole we can barely imagine. We search for meaning in traditions, philosophies, and spiritual practices that give us glimpses of the greater window. But too often those fragments cut against one another, leaving wounds instead of beauty.

My own journey into this question began not in a library but in the lived intersections of culture, faith, and personal history. Growing up, I learned that people do not always see the same world, even when they are looking at the same landscape. A mindset (how we habitually think) and a worldview (the deep frame through which we perceive) can shape what we believe is true, what we value, and how we act. And when those mindsets and worldviews collide, something breaks.

Yet there is hope in the breaking. At the intersection of different worldviews and mindsets, a transformative possibility emerges. Like shattered glass meeting light, the fragments can create a vision more luminous than any single pane. This is the heart of what follows: a search for healing the fragmented human condition, not by erasing difference but by learning how the intersections themselves can become transformative.

The whole is greater than the sum of its parts, and yet the whole participates in each part. What does the whole mean relative to a spiritual worldview and an ethic of liberation? Eastern Orthodoxy may help clarify how these terms are used for the purpose of this book. This tradition helps us understand how the whole relates to the parts if, in fact, the whole is greater than the sum of its parts.

In Eastern Orthodoxy the essence of God is unknown. However, accordingly God is known in God's energies. Many may differ on the question of how God's essence and God's energy are connected, but that is beyond the scope of this discussion. However, to gain perspective, it is worthwhile to elaborate the difference between apophatic theology, which is referred to as "negative theologies," and cataphatic theology.

Apophatic spirituality tells us what God is not. To say it's not this but rather that is cataphatic spirituality in texts and image-icons. A spiritual worldview as a process, in light of these two poles, says, "God is that," in which case that becomes this—apophatic and unknown in terms of the whole. However, in an integrated process, this becomes that—cataphatic in text and image through vision and language (or some other version of communication, such as sound and/or sign language). The analogy here is that what apophatic is to the whole, cataphatic is to each part. A spiritual worldview is a quest or process that vitiates all epistemological assumptions, metaphysical propositions, and axiological maxims. However, a mindset as an anchor, rooted in an ethic of liberation, enables a dialogical process through sounds, silence, texts, and images of the different.

From the perspective of a spiritual worldview, an anchor is the consciousness of the whole, which is greater than its sum parts and yet paradoxically participates in each part. The underlying epistemological assumption is self-knowledge, place and space awareness, perception in quest of a perspective, and discernment of otherness and the different. A second layer to a spiritual worldview is a metaphysical shift from literal language to symbolic language of text and image, dealing specifically with freedom and being.

Spiritual worldview axiological considerations of an ethic of liberation have three caveats: mind-talk about what is the good, soul-talk about being good, and spirit-talk about the meaning of the beautiful-aesthetics. Ethics and aesthetics as an integration is descriptive of the whole from the point of view of a mindset as a part, in which the whole paradoxically participates.

The fragmented human condition subverts mindsets, which become attached and/or addicted to outcomes that are unhealthy and unethical. The first step is to identify and distinguish worldviews and mindsets. The second step is transformation through spiritual worldview as a process wherein mindsets become anchored. This becomes a natural spirituality anchored into a spiritual worldview as a process of being and becoming a self/soul in relationship to otherness and the different.

In order to address the problem of fragmentation, Diarmuid O'Murchu's book *In the Beginning Was the Spirit: Science, Religion, and Indigenous Spirituality* says quantum theology calls for a new paradigm for understanding worldview: "Jesus was embracing and emulating the creative wisdom of the Sophia tradition which is the more ancient and foundational version of the Greek Logos, and that the deeper meanings of the Logos in John's gospel can best be accessed by grounding them in the Hebrew concept of Sophia Wisdom."

The wisdom tradition has implications for the environment and the economy calling for ecotheology. According to O'Murchu, "The Sophia tradition is a basis for the interface between religious wisdom and the pressing ecological and environmental issues of our time."

How worldviews and mindsets present a problem is the critical assessment of the following example: "This ancient wisdom poses quite a threat to the conventional patriarchal worldview," says O'Murchu, "especially as articulated in religion, and not surprisingly tends to be ridiculed and dismissed out of hand in several major religious traditions." A patriarchal outlook is more properly a mindset instead of a worldview. A spiritual worldview and an ethic of liberation functions as an anchor and is the standard by which human ideas and behavior are evaluated.

To critically assess mindsets requires a spiritual worldview and ethics of liberation, and it becomes a way of describing, analyzing, and evaluating actionable, measurable, and goal-oriented human behavior. A spiritual worldview is used here in a particular fashion to describe epistemological assumptions and metaphysical propositions with regard to religious language, freedom, and being. Finally, axiological maxims deemed as core values will be assessed. A spiritual worldview functions as a process, and mindsets elicit nature and validity of knowledge (i.e., perceptions of what is real and what is valuable in terms of what it aesthetically means to do good or be a good person).

Narrative spirituality calls for an integrated spiritual worldview and an ethic of liberation, as process, that is adequate to deal with issues confronting the tension between localization and globalization relative to the economy, ecology, and public policy, as well as how these are shaped and formed by unhealthy and unethical mindsets attached to certain outcomes. Public policy, in order to be healthy and ethical, must comport with a spiritual worldview and ethics of liberation. That raises another question for consideration, which has to do with personal/private epiphanies (referred to as place and public space).

A spiritual worldview as process and ethics of liberation critically integrates the external world and the internal world by means of dialogical self-awareness, and in doing such becomes a living soul. The Logos becomes sarx, translated into a dialogue and becomes a self, when the Spirit transforms the self into the external God-communicator. The Jesus event of history is a metaphor for the external dialogue (God-eye view) that becomes internalized as a dialogical new humanity. A new humanity heals, transforms, and mends the self to become a living soul. The transformation of the self that I am to the Self-God is connected in a global spiritual worldview as a process of becoming self-transcendent. A natural and narrative spirituality develops a God-eye spiritual view of reality.

A spiritual worldview is interconnected and global, whereas different cultures, including different traditions, values, and practices, impinge upon all of humanity. In the interface of different cultures, a new self emerges with the world's complexities, contradictions, oppositions, and encounters. Integrations are part of society at large and at the same time answers to those influences from its own particular point of view (i.e., mindsets).

A traditional understanding of worldview is used in connection with reality, the God question. Worldview as a philosophical category includes assumptions about what the nature and validity of knowledge is and what reality is, and asks what is valuable about both ethics and aesthetics. The way humans answer this question provides a structure for how we believe and behave in public, or mindsets. Mindsets are the building blocks hidden much like a frame of a house, which one cannot see, but it holds the space, which is visible to the eye.

The problem arises when a mindset, which is unseen, often attached to or addicted to certain outcomes in religion, politics, and moral behavior, is confused for a worldview. Mindsets are driving beliefs and behavior systems, and are unseen. There is no one worldview but rather particular mindsets justified as worldviews. A worldview as a connected process is therefore spiritual. The difference between worldview and mindset from this perspective understands a worldview as a spiritual worldview, as process, and mindsets as particular, either attached and/or addicted to certain closed outcomes.

Mindsets anchored into a worldview as dynamic and lucid are open to transformational functions, like a stream that flows through landscapes on a journey to a sacred space. In his book *The New Testament and the People of God*, N. T. Wright avers that a worldview includes narrative-story, questions, symbols, and praxis. The hypothesis here is that a worldview as a process is compatible with a spiritual and natural worldview.

What is the connection between mindsets and worldviews? Diarmuid O'Murchu, in his book *Quantum Theology: Spiritual Implications of the New Physics*, explains mindsets and worldview connection when he says, "The whole is greater than its sum parts." That is, the sum parts do not equal the whole. The particulars as parts equal mindsets and, when considered as the whole, become either addicted or attached to certain outcomes, confused for a spiritual worldview as a process. In biblical terms, this would be tantamount to idolatry. However, O'Murchu goes on to postulate that the whole part participates in each part. My thesis is that when we are considering the issue of spiritual worldview, the parts are to the whole what mindsets are to worldview as a process, a spiritual worldview. Flawed mindsets that are addicted and attached to certain outcomes are static and, therefore, subvert and undermine a spiritual worldview as a process. This in turn causes confusion and a flawed mindset, which is particular and local, for a worldview that has global implications.

In contrast, a mindset that serves as an anchor in a worldview is interconnected, and therefore the intersection of localization and globalization is more open to dialogue. For Eastern Christian spirituality, mindsets are anchored functions as cataphatic epistemology—a model or metaphor for knowledge. A spiritual worldview or worldview as process functions similarly to apophatic epistemologies, a negative theology. A simple way to understand apophatic epistemology is to think critically, a way of thinking about models or forms as not what is real but rather a means to talk about reality meaningfully rather than literally or linearly. Knowledge and language are necessary for communication but at the same time not absolute in scope; they are rather traces or pointers in the right direction. To hold both cataphatic knowledge and apophatic epistemologies is then critical thinking about mindsets and a spiritual worldview in terms of localization and globalization issues of wealth, poverty, disparity, nuclear proliferation, violence, and environmental sustainability.

An anchor is a moment in which anxiety, fear, and panic may cause addiction or attachments to certain outcomes due to angst, pain, and suffering about the future. A spiritual worldview leaves one place (a mindset), and the journey is often fraught with anxiety because we don't know what's around the bend or what lies ahead. Ahead may be a space for globalization that becomes a new place, which includes the different and otherness. Paul Tournier, in his book *A Place for You*, refers to this experience of anxiety as "the middle of the road anxiety"; when we leave a place but haven't quite reached our goal, we become anxious and panic about the future. Anchors along the way are necessary to help us calm our fears and anxieties before going on toward the unknown.

This leads us to consider how mindsets and worldviews function as essence and energies. In Eastern Orthodoxy theology, God is not known in God's essence, but in God's energies. A real distinction between the essence (*ousia*) and the energies (*energeia*) of God is a central principle of Eastern Orthodox theology. Eastern Orthodox theology regards this distinction as more than a mere conceptual distinction. This doctrine is most closely identified with Gregory Palamas, whose teachings were made into dogma in the Eastern Orthodox church by the Hesychast councils.

Historically, Western Christianity has tended to reject the essence-energies distinction as real in the case of God, characterizing the view as a heretical introduction of an unacceptable division in the Trinity and suggestive of polytheism. Further, the associated practice of hesychasm used to achieve theosis was characterized as "magic." More recently, some Roman Catholic thinkers have taken a positive view of Palamas' teachings, including how he understood the essence-energies distinction, arguing that it does not represent an insurmountable theological division between Roman Catholicism and Eastern Orthodoxy.

To know God in God's energies is visible and measurable in human praxis, worship, spiritual disciplines, creation, and God-talk.

Wesley's quadrilateral primacy of Scripture, tradition, reason, and experience is helpful in this discussion. A spiritual worldview and ethics of liberation is a natural spirituality that acts dialogically to integrate theology, psychology, and philosophy with a "difference principle" where science and spirituality meet and do not meet. The intersection of these various landscapes becomes an opportunity for transformation, and therefore, transformative intersections are those spaces where a table of inclusion sets the agenda.

When we attach ourselves to only a certain way of knowing, a mindset emerges; it excludes others who sit at the table of globalization and defines reality from its particular lenses. It's either attached or addicted to certain outcomes. A spiritual worldview is a metaphysical shift in language, freedom, and being. It embraces the limitations and weakness of any given perception of reality and mindset to gain a new perspective, which then forms a new perception in need of perspective, an ongoing dynamic process.

A spiritual worldview acknowledges the distance between perception and the reality to which perception points as the "difference principle." The difference principle, according to John Rawls, "removes the indeterminateness the inequalities of a basic structure of economic inequalities that are to be judged."

Rawls goes on to say, "Assuming the framework of institutions required by equal liberty and fair equality of opportunity, the higher expectations of those better situated are just if and only if they work as a part of a scheme which improves the expectations of the least advantaged member of society."

The function of the difference principle is to close the gap in an in-between space; that is, whatever obfuscates truth and reality. In actuality, the potential difference principle acts as a prophetic conscience and a goal toward perfection as a process that will be realized in the now/not yet tension of the coming of the Reign of

God. That is to say, the table we set is all-inclusive, holding the bread we eat for our bodies as well as the bread we consume for our spiritual sustenance. There are no unequal humans before the face of God.

> *But now that faith has come, we are no longer subject to a disciplinarian, for in Christ Jesus you are all children of God through faith. As many of you as were baptized into Christ have clothed yourselves with Christ. There is no longer Jew or Greek; there is no longer slave or free; there is no longer male and female, for all of you are one in Christ Jesus. And if you belong to Christ, then you are Abraham's offspring, heirs according to the promise.*
>
> —Gal. 3:25–29

Before God we all stand naked and equal; however, diversity and difference are marks of unity and tension. The different and similar are held together in tension as a response to grace.

A spiritual worldview, as process, includes epistemology as defined by the nature and validity of knowledge; it includes metaphysics, including ontology (meaning and being), language, and freedom. Axiology, what is valuable, ethics and aesthetics notwithstanding, shapes morality and core values that are measurable, actionable, and goal-oriented. Through moral imagination humans grow in self-awareness, understanding, and the perspective of mindsets that obfuscates a spiritual worldview and liberation of ethics. Mindsets when attached and/or addicted to certain outcomes are closed, static, and localized. A mindset anchored into a spiritual worldview and ethics of liberation is more open and moves to otherness and the different by embracing the tension between localization and globalization issues that are ultimate concerns. Religion is defined by Paul Tillich as human response to ultimate concerns, and therefore whatever ultimately concerns you is your religion.

In the intersection of mindsets and spiritual worldview, a worldview essentially has three philosophical components: epistemology, metaphysics, and axiology, all of which point to ultimate concerns. A mindset addicted and attached to certain outcomes is a religion that subverts a spiritual worldview as a process by making local and self-interest the ultimate concern. A spiritual worldview and an ethics of liberation is rooted in the particular or localization concerns and at the same time moves out to engage the issues of globalization by examining epistemological assumptions and critically assessing the nature and validity of knowledge. This is explained in the ideas of metaphysics and axiology. Metaphysics generally deals with natural and supernatural realities, and axiology explores values; that is, morality, ethics, and aesthetics—what is deemed praiseworthy, who is the good person, and ultimately what is beautiful and who is beautiful.

Ancient and traditional spiritual disciplines enhance a spiritual natural worldview. Rather than a fixed notion, the spiritual natural worldview becomes a process, a goal-oriented journey similar to the ancient process of becoming through purification, illumination, and union with God's transcendence and immanence. This process enables us to more fully engage the Reign of God and act more as a citizen of the reign. That allows us to, in turn, act as a citizen in the global world context and rooted in the localization as citizens of the content of our world. A spiritual worldview and an ethic of liberation hold in balance the tension between the poles of local and global concerns. In quantum spirituality, the tension between a preoccupation with self-preservation and the preoccupation with belonging to the whole creates a connection of vitality. When one or the other pole becomes predominant in quantum terms, death occurs because there is a disconnection. Spirituality, then, is about being connected to otherness and the different.

The transcendent God is wholly other and unknowable. The immanent God is close and known through God's self-revealing presence in the Christ event. Immanence in this context is not to be confused with the Trinitarian immanence of the relationship within the Godhead, which has more to do with how Father, Son, and Holy Spirit are related through perichoresis. The early church used this term to describe the relationship between the divine and human natures of Christ. Moreover, it became useful among contemporary persons such as Jürgen Moltmann and John Zizioulas as a term to describe the relationship of the Trinitarian God. The energies of God are then known in relationship, similar to the way God relates to the triune ideas of God, creation, and humanity. A spiritual worldview and an ethic of liberation act in human relationships of otherness and the different, which has global implications.

The complex relationship between mindsets and the spiritual worldview, and energy as theological praxis and essence as metaphysical/theological concept, can be further explored in regard to brain-based reality and quantum theology. Spirituality and ethics connect brain-based reality and quantum theology, according to O'Murchu. This has spiritual implications and consciousness in connection with the moral values within the heart, a pneumatic expression of transformation for which wholeness and sacred places are possible.

An intersection where mindsets and worldview clash must become transformative to prevent a collision. In traffic intersections, a decision is necessary, depending on what rules are in place, such as a red light or a stop sign. The rules for the most part are in place to prevent a crash. In a similar way, a spiritual worldview, as process, and the ethics of liberation prevent a crash at the intersection of localization and globalization of otherness and the different. Mindsets fixated (addictions and attachments) on certain ideologies such as politics, economics, environmental issues, and religion, including social issues such as racism, sexism, violence, and distribution of wealth, become idols that cause crashes and potentially cause great harm to humans flourishing.

How do we maintain integrity with personal mindsets and engage a worldview as process that enables civility? That is, how do we connect personal place with public space in a way that is congruent and wholesome? Quantum spirituality suggests that all of life is interconnected, and change occurs when particles bump up against one another. This fits with natural spirituality in which different mindsets could bump up against one another rather than crash in a destructive way. We can learn through the spiritual disciplines to bump up against otherness through dialogue and integration as a preventive to crashing, which causes harm, pain, and suffering to humans who think and believe differently.

An important aspect of the relationship between worldview and mindsets focuses on differentiation. We see this clearly in Eastern Orthodoxy's deification process (*theosis*) understanding of cataphatic and apophatic in relationship to God's essence and energies regarding the Imago Dei that guides us through the roles of ethics and spirituality.

The Imago Dei, the image and likeness of God expressed through human anthropology and social relationships is infused by divine attributes: what can be known of God's activity and presence among humanity. The central epistemological assumption between humans and God is represented by Hans Urs von Balthsasar and Catherine Mowry LaCugna, proponents of such a view in the perspective of celebrating the mysteries of the Eucharist.

From one perspective, what's at stake is the entire notion of spiritual worldviews and mindsets. This indicates that transformation is never easy. It is, at best, difficult to understand how different theologies are entrenched in worldviews and mindsets, especially when the differences are grounded in diverse mindsets anchored into a spiritual worldview. All we can hope for is civility, humility, and generosity in diversity, while exemplifying the virtue to love when separated by difference. In the issue of mindsets and spiritual worldviews, the idea is not that we must agree on everything but rather that we must embrace otherness and maintain integrity through the virtue of love.

Part one of LaCugna's book deals with the emergence and defeat of the doctrine of the Trinity, while part two reconceives the doctrine in light of the mystery of salvation. In the process, she places the emphasis on who God is for us in historical, liturgical, and traditional ecclesial experience.

The nuances of ontology and epistemology are complex, which has to do with God's essence and energies, mindsets and worldviews. For LaCugna's mindset, a shift from God's essence to God's energy has to do with epistemology; whereas, for the Eastern Church's mindset, any shift would disrupt God's essence (apophatic), which is ontological and cannot be known. Language, words, and symbols shape our perception of reality. Therefore, God's energies are not ontological but rather cataphatic as revealed in text, image, and in particular icons. Both mindsets are anchored into spiritual worldviews that are different and diverse, which is good insofar as the relationships between people are authentic and maintain integrity through humility. The outcome will then be inclusive: unity and diversity.

One example of an integrative moment that illustrates the intersection between mindsets, a spiritual worldview, metaphysics, and ontology is the Eastern Orthodox perspective of liberation theology. A spiritual worldview as a process and an ethics of liberation focuses on liberation in the "here and now" world of social justice and countering the structures of evil rather than salvation in the next world. Salvation of the soul is, then, defined as liberating others to a vitality living. Ethics of liberation deal with human relationships to provide preferential treatment to the least advantaged rather than to the privileged. The voices of the oppressed are heard as a word from God. The intersection of language as literal and symbolic, freedom and determinism, being and consciousness, calls for a metaphysical shift from supernatural divine intervention to spirituality and ethics of liberation.

Freedom from oppression becomes the occasion for freedom and healing to both the oppressed and the oppressors; liberation is for both victims and perpetrators. The Reign of God's central goal is freedom from evil, both cosmic and structural in law and policies. This is the message Jesus proclaims: The symbol of the cross becomes a gift-based reality, in blessings and grace. The tension that holds opposites becomes the occasion for the cross—the symbol of giftedness, the grace necessary for transformation.

We need to consider how, why, and what the issues are that shape mindsets. What drives a worldview is not theology but rather mindsets that shape text and images of who God is for us. America's four Gods suggestion that mindsets are shaped by a previous experience of religion is essentially a projection of our self-image of what God is for us, but not necessarily informed. "Do we create our own reality?" asks O'Murchu. He provides us with some insight. "In the quantum worldview, nothing makes sense in isolation; basically, there are no boundaries, and influences can emerge from several sources."

According to quantum theory, not only is the observer involved, but the observer actually brings about what is being observed. We become the god we imagine. And therefore, O'Murchu says, "Our very act brings reality into being."

A spiritual worldview as a process discerns and strives to distinguish between projections of the self becoming, through grace, what God is by nature. The Logos of a spiritual worldview functions in two ways: first, as a universal affirmation of God's love and acceptance, and second, as an affront to the human condition. A spiritual worldview develops a prophetic consciousness as a moral compass of wisdom and a gift of discernment, as well as a skill to distinguish good and evil, appropriate behavior to any given situation, especially in relationships to others. O'Murchu is helpful when he writes, "From the beginning of our evolution as a species, we have been exploring and expressing our spirituality with both its light and shadow."

Transformative intersections are places where we can let go of our particular mindsets, which for the most part are attached to beliefs that exclude others. It is a distinction between mindsets that are anchored into a worldview and mindsets that are addicted and attached to particular outcomes. When we attach ourselves only to a certain way of knowing, a mindset emerges. When the mindset excludes, it's either attached or addicted to certain outcomes. A spiritual worldview is a metaphysical shift in language, freedom, and being, embracing the limitations and weakness of any given perception of reality in order to gain a new perspective, which then forms a new perception in need of perspective in an ongoing fluid dynamic process. Often a crash in the intersection of opposing theologies does not seem like a shock but rather rational arguments for or against (rather than a dialogue leading to integration). The outcome of dialogue and integration transforms individuals and the world.

Intersections where different core values bump up against one another are actually opportunities for transformative action, and therefore, not all conflicts are necessarily destructive. The intensity of the integrative process of a spiritual worldview and archetypal intersections of a worldview are identical. According to Jung, "The upheaval of our world and the upheaval in consciousness are one and the same."

To be human is spiritual, and therefore, humanity is connected, albeit unconsciously. According to quantum theology, all of life is interconnected. Do humans become spiritual, or are they spiritual beings having a human experience? How we answer this question reveals much about mindsets and worldviews. However, there is another aspect that has to do with human praxis: actionable and measurable human behavior. The practice of spirituality shapes and forms humans around knowledge, reality, and values—a worldview in the process of becoming and awakening to otherness, God, and humanity (hence a spiritual worldview). "The human being is defined through otherness," writes Zizioulas.

A spiritual worldview and an ethics of liberation assumes the human capacity for choice. Accordingly, Zizioulas postulates that the meaning of freedom has to do with the drive to ontological otherness: "The drive of the human being towards otherness is rooted in the divine call to Adam, which implies three qualities revealing the Imago Dei: relationship, freedom, and otherness."

What is the meaning of freedom, then? In some way, humans live an answer to this question. "To recognize that all human experience, including transcendence, religious and aesthetic experience is brain-based, is not to embrace a reductionist position in which higher consciousness is somehow explained away a series of events in the cerebral cortex," asserts McGrath.

Natural spirituality does not rule out the reality of transcendence but rather is consistent with a shift in metaphysics from literal language to symbolic language and asserts incarnational/natural spirituality that for human beings in this world is accessed through the "medium of our material bodies."

Mindsets and worldview are ways of talking about personhood, or our personality, in which the way we talk about ultimate concerns religiously or politically expresses our view of life. A mindset anchored into a spiritual worldview as process and the ethics of liberation define personhood. Mindsets that are addicted or attached create an illusion of reality, sometimes confused with a worldview, but instead undermine and subvert personhood.

Accordingly, spirituality and ethics shape not only identity but human behavior, inwardly as well as outwardly. Faustin Ntamushobora, in his book *Transformation Through the Different Other*, sees that the primary problem that divides people is the "heart."

He continues, "that race, tribe, and worldview differences can widen the gap among people's relationships, thus leading to exclusion, even for faith-based Christians." Ntamushobora is saying that mindsets attached or addicted to worldviews create gaps because of personal place. When normative for public space, it is a mindset that builds isolation and alienates otherness. Ntamushobora uses the language of a "rendezvous of giving and receiving among people from different cultures." The rendezvous describes perhaps more adequately an intersection where decisions are called for, which then reflects either a conflict leading to independence or a dialogue leading to integration. Integration respects difference by embracing otherness as a place in public space.

The stage is set for three social issues as economics, environment, and public policy are transformed by a spiritual worldview as process and the ethics of liberation. This intersection can be shaped, however, by mindsets through assumptions about what we know, perceptions of reality shaped by narrative, and religious beliefs. Whoever controls the language has the power to affect public policy in ways that are based on self-interest and for profit. Culture, environment, and economics are often at odds in the intersection where all people of goodwill are to decide the fate of a world in transition.

The transformation of public policy journeys through a transformative intersection of a mindset that is addicted and attached to certain outcomes that run contrary to a mindset anchored in a spiritual worldview. The addicted mindset is absorbed in self-interest without regard for those who are less fortunate. It takes a spiritual awakening that embraces a gift-based economics to understand and negotiate the tension that exists between the for-profit and ecological realms. This awakening understands the gap between those who have and those who have not, and is best suited for purposeful public policy. Self-interest, based on for-profit models, builds walls of separation and isolation. The tension between a preoccupation for self-preservation and the need to belong to the whole is then critically integrated, mixing self-interest and social responsibility. Spirituality connects the self to the greater whole without losing the sense of identity of our rootedness and personhood, because personhood is best understood in relationship to the different and otherness.

This discussion of mindsets and worldviews leads us to ask if there is a connection between a mindset and personality. Exactly what is a personality? Is personality genetically conditioned, or is personality learned behavior, and what defines who is a person? Can a person change their personality?

The answers to these questions are complex and can be effectively approached through the terms we have explored up to this point. We can helpfully formulate the question in this way: What prevents persons from fulfilling their potential for growing into a spiritual worldview and an ethic of liberation? The solution is a spiritual worldview that transforms mindsets from addiction and attachments to a certain outcome to anchors that connect to a process of becoming or fulfilling our potential.

> *I appeal to you therefore, brothers and sisters, on the basis of God's mercy, to present your bodies as a living sacrifice, holy and acceptable to God, which is your reasonable act of worship. Do not be conformed to this world, but be transformed by the renewing of the mind, so that you may discern what is the will of God—what is good and acceptable and perfect.*
>
> —Rom. 12:1–2

This work describes a personality in terms of worldview and mindsets so we can begin to understand that similarities and differences in personalities can grow toward a natural spirituality, transforming addicted/attached mindsets that have a direct effect on public policy. All assumptions, how one interprets reality and embraces a set of values, motivate a person to certain kinds of actions.

Often personality disorders describe criminal activity, harm to another, or perhaps inappropriate behavior. For example, a continuum of neurosis and displacement describes a mind within a certain range of normal behavior; whereas crossing a certain line will either describe a psychosis or sociopathy. The question as to whether these patterns are brain-based or a matter of choice is an ongoing debate. The upshot of this has implications for talk therapy or use of medication to enable a more normal range of human activity that is consistent with a spiritual worldview and ethic of liberation.

A person's moral development at best is often difficult to gauge. How free are humans to make changes that match a moral development of character? Neuroscience seems to suggest human action is brain-based rather than free will. If John Wesley was a neuroscientist, his question would undoubtedly be not "how is it with your soul?" but rather "how is it with your brain?"

Recent neurological findings have led to the twofold conclusion that my choice at any given moment is restricted by my particular brain-stat with a particular set of environmental conditions and that the decision-making process generally occurs at a level beneath personal awareness.

How then can we build a bridge between what we know from science and how we theologize about the soul? The core values inventory test describes four possibilities: results, relationships, rights/responsibilities, and reputation that can shape our mindsets.

I often return in memory to a day when I walked through the ruins of an old church. Its stained-glass windows had long since shattered, their colors scattered across the ground. As the sunlight poured through the empty frames, I imagined what once was—a window alive with story, light, and beauty. Now, only fragments remained—sharp-edged, disconnected, vulnerable to being trampled underfoot.

For me, that window has become a living metaphor of the human condition. We are a fractured species. Our histories are scarred by war, prejudice, and mistrust. Families splinter, cultures collide, and faith traditions divide. Each fragment of humanity carries color and potential, yet when torn from the whole, it reflects light only in part.

I grew up surrounded by these fragments—different worldviews, different mindsets, each claiming truth, each shaping how people thought, felt, and acted. A mindset determines how we interpret the world, the habitual lens through which we see. A worldview is deeper still, the framework that holds our sense of meaning and reality. Both can be powerful forces of belonging and identity. Both can also blind us, creating walls that divide.

But at the points where worldviews and mindsets meet—often uncomfortably—something profound can happen. Intersections can wound, yes. But they can also transform. When fragments meet light, they can form a new mosaic. When people allow themselves to stand at the crossroads, they begin to see beyond the narrow boundaries of their inherited frame.

We begin here in the tension between fragmentation and possibility. We will explore the philosophical and theological roots of our broken condition, not as abstract ideas but as lived realities. To speak of a "transformative intersection" is to speak of those moments when different ways of seeing them crash against each other and, in the collision, open a doorway to something new.

Philosophical Roots: The Divided Self

Long before psychology named the divided mind, Augustine confessed in *Confessions*, "I had become a question to myself." His words echo the universal experience of fragmentation. Augustine saw within his own soul a restless war—desire pulling in one direction, conviction pulling in another. The divided self was not simply weakness of will but evidence of humanity's deeper wound.

Centuries later, René Descartes would search for certainty by separating mind from body, thought from matter. In doing so, he gave the modern West a framework that sharpened analysis but also intensified fragmentation. Humanity was now split between subject and object, inner and outer, sacred and secular. What was once whole became divided by philosophy's scalpel.

Other voices pushed back. Kierkegaard described the "sickness unto death" as despair, the refusal to be oneself before God. Nietzsche lamented the "death of God," seeing a culture collapsing under the weight of its contradictions. These thinkers, though worlds apart, recognized that fragmentation is not simply individual but cultural, woven into the very ways societies imagine themselves.

Theological Roots: Sin, Brokenness, and Hope

The Bible itself is a story of fragmentation and restoration. From the shattering of Eden's harmony to the scattering at Babel, humanity is pictured as divided between God and creation, between one another, and even within ourselves. Paul names this inner fracture in Romans: "I do not do what I want, but I do the very thing I hate" (Rom. 7:15).

Yet woven into this diagnosis is also a vision of healing. The prophets cry out for a time when justice and peace will embrace. The psalmists lament division but cling to hope. In the Gospels, Jesus meets the fragmented—the cast-out lepers, the despised tax collectors, the sinners broken by shame—and restores them to community, to dignity, to wholeness.

In this light, the "transformative intersection" is not merely a philosophical puzzle; it is a theological promise. God meets us at the crossroads of our contradictions. Grace does not erase the fragments but gathers them into a new whole.

Mindsets and Worldviews in Collision

In our own day, fragmentation appears in the clash of cultures, religions, and political ideologies. A globalized world brings people into constant intersection, but not always into understanding. The local village mindset meets the global marketplace worldview. Ancient traditions collide with secular rationalism. Western individualism strains against communal worldviews of the Global South.

These collisions can generate violence, but they can also spark transformation. When a community learns to see beyond the limits of its own lens, something new becomes possible: a mosaic of meaning richer than any single piece.

Toward Transformation

The challenge before us is not to deny fragmentation but to learn to dwell within it, to see the intersections as sacred spaces rather than battlegrounds. Transformation is not achieved by retreating into the safety of our fragments or by demanding uniformity. It emerges when we dare to let light pass through our brokenness and refract into something beautiful.

This, then, is the task of philosophy, theology, and spirituality in dialogue: to help us imagine how fractured humanity can move toward wholeness.

I want to explore the connection between false narrative and conspiracy theories and moreover, how a spiritual narrative is no less than truth-telling. We begin with the creation story.

The tree of life and the tree of knowledge of good and evil: "You will not die," said Satan (Gen. 3:4). This is a false narrative—the seduction—seduced to a false notion of God, self, and reality. "Where are you?" God said (Gen. 3:9). The fear of being discovered is hiding and afraid of being unmasked from evil.

A false narrative and conspiracy of Satan is the seduction to believe what is not true. That's why Jesus said to Peter, "Get behind me, Satan! You are a hindrance to me" (Matt. 16:23). Peter was on the side of a false conspiracy theory and not on the side of God's revealed truth, even if we confess that truth as did Peter, "You are the Messiah, the Son of the living God" (Matt. 16:16).

There's enough truth hidden in the lie that makes it a deception to seduce others into false narratives and conspiracy theories. Spiritual narrative intrinsically unmasks evil because spirituality is grounded in the Holy Spirit of truth.

Someone can be sincere about a lie they believe in, and that makes it even more difficult to unmask the evil. Explicate and elucidate the follow from Wittgenstein: "Words don't have inherent meaning, but only mean something given the context in which they are used."

And what does it mean when Wittgenstein talks about a mistaken family resemblance and confusion of tongues? Wittgenstein's assertion that "words don't have inherent meaning, but only mean something given the context in which they are used" speaks to the essence of language as a social tool rather than a fixed system of signs. This perspective is crucial in understanding how meaning is constructed in communication.

Wittgenstein suggests that the meaning of a word is not intrinsic to the word itself but is shaped by the context in which it is employed. This implies that the same word can carry different meanings depending on various factors such as the situation, the speaker's intent, and the listener's interpretation. For example, the word "bank" can refer to a financial institution or the side of a river, and its meaning becomes clear only through contextual clues.

Mistaken Family Resemblance

The concept of "family resemblance" addresses the issue of categorizing concepts and words. Rather than there being a single essence that defines each term, Wittgenstein suggests that words are connected by overlapping similarities, much like members of a family share various traits but not a single defining characteristic. For instance, the term "game" encompasses a wide variety of activities (sports, board games, etc.) that share some features but do not necessarily fall under a strict definition. This illustrates how our understanding of words can be fluid and interconnected rather than rigidly defined.

Confusion of Tongues

The "confusion of tongues" refers to miscommunication that arises when people use the same words but mean different things. This can happen when individuals come from different backgrounds, cultures, or contexts, leading to misunderstandings. For instance, technical jargon in specialized fields may confuse those outside that field. This phenomenon emphasizes the importance of context in communication; without awareness of the underlying meanings and implications, conversations can lead to confusion.

Conclusion

Wittgenstein's insights challenge the notion of fixed meanings in language, highlighting the importance of context and the relational aspects of words. By recognizing that meanings are context-dependent and that our understanding of language is shaped by social interactions, we can navigate the complexities of communication more effectively, reducing the potential for misunderstanding that arises from mistaken family resemblances and the confusion of tongues.

Part Two Question

How does this fit with "the danger of a single story, which fosters a false narrative?"

The concept of "the danger of a single story," popularized by Chimamanda Ngozi Adichie, aligns closely with Wittgenstein's insights about the contextual nature of meaning in language. Both ideas emphasize the risks associated with oversimplification and the importance of recognizing multiple perspectives.

The Single Story and False Narratives

Adichie warns that when only one narrative is presented about a person, group, or culture, it can lead to stereotypes, misunderstandings, and a limited view of reality. This "single story" creates a false narrative, reducing the complexity of individuals and cultures to a single dimension. For example, depicting a culture solely through the lens of poverty or conflict neglects its richness, diversity, and resilience.

Connection to Contextual Meaning

Wittgenstein's notion that words derive meaning from their context complements this idea by illustrating how language can similarly contribute to the creation of "single stories." When we use language without acknowledging the broader context, we risk oversimplifying complex ideas and experiences. Just as a single narrative can distort understanding, using words in a way that lacks context can lead to misinterpretations and a failure to grasp the full picture.

Implications for Communication

Both concepts highlight the importance of multiple viewpoints and the richness of dialogue. In communication, recognizing that words and stories are shaped by diverse contexts encourages us to seek a more comprehensive understanding. By being aware of the limitations of a single narrative and the context-dependent nature of language, we can foster more nuanced discussions that appreciate complexity rather than reduce it.

Conclusion

In essence, both Wittgenstein's insights on language and Adichie's caution against the single story serve as reminders of the complexities inherent in communication. They encourage us to embrace diversity in narratives and meanings, promoting a more holistic and empathetic understanding of the world around us. This approach not only enriches our conversations but also helps dismantle stereotypes and foster genuine connections among individuals and cultures.

Narrative Spirituality, False Narratives, and the Work of Truth

Narrative spirituality begins with a conviction that stories shape who we are, how we see the world, and how we live within it. Stories can heal, but they can also wound. They can reveal truth, or they can conceal it. In this light, the question arises: How can narrative spirituality heal a false narrative? And even more, what makes a spiritual narrative authentic?

Healing False Narratives

A false narrative is one that distorts reality, reducing people to stereotypes, flattening experience into oversimplifications, or exploiting fear and division. Narrative spirituality responds not with arguments but with stories—stories that restore depth, complexity, and truth.

Personal storytelling becomes an act of healing. When individuals share their lived experiences, the single story is disrupted. Struggles, joys, losses, and hopes come to light, reminding us that every human being is more than the labels imposed upon them.

Collective storytelling expands this healing further. Communities gather to tell and hear diverse experiences, weaving together a tapestry of voices. This shared story fosters empathy and belonging, dismantling the false narratives that isolation and misunderstanding create.

Contextual storytelling situates these narratives within broader social, historical, and cultural frameworks. It reminds us that our stories are never told in isolation but in relation to the world around us.

Restorative storytelling, whether through reflective writing, communal rituals, or group conversations, honors the wounds of the past, validates the pain of the present, and opens the possibility of reconciliation and hope.

Truth-Telling and Authentic Narratives

Authentic narrative spirituality insists on truth-telling. It is not content with polished, sanitized stories. It calls for honesty, vulnerability, and courage.

An authentic narrative admits struggle and doubt as well as joy and faith. It embraces diverse perspectives, recognizing that truth is never exhausted in a single telling. It is transformative, sharing stories of growth, resilience, and healing that invite others into the same possibility. And always it is aligned with values: compassion, justice, humility, and love.

In this way, truth-telling becomes both mirror and window. The mirror reflects who we are with honesty, while the window opens onto a horizon of what, by grace, we might yet become.

Unmasking Conspiracy Through Narrative Spirituality

Another pressing question arises: How can authentic narrative spirituality unmask the evil of conspiracy theories?

Conspiracy theories are false narratives that thrive on fear, suspicion, and division. They offer oversimplified answers to complex realities. Authentic narrative spirituality can counter these distortions in several ways.

First, it nurtures critical thinking. By questioning assumptions, examining context, and embracing the complexity of truth, it helps individuals resist the lure of simplistic explanations. Second, it fosters empathy and connection. Shared stories draw people out of isolation and into community, dismantling the "us versus them" mentality that conspiracy theories exploit. Third, it grounds us in values: compassion, justice, and honesty. Where conspiracy thrives on suspicion and hate, authentic spirituality insists on love and truth. Finally, it offers meaning and resilience. When people find purpose through faith and community, they no longer need the false comfort of fear-driven narratives.

Conspiracy theories isolate and divide; authentic narrative spirituality restores connection and belonging. It is not merely an intellectual counterpoint but a spiritual antidote.

False Narratives and the Fallen Human Condition

It is fair to say that false narratives, whether simple distortions or complex conspiracies, reveal the depth of the fallen human condition. Humanity has always longed for control in the face of chaos. False stories offer that illusion—neat explanations in a world that is messy and uncertain.

They thrive on fear, mistrust, and the desire to find scapegoats. They exploit confirmation bias, reinforcing what people already believe rather than inviting them into deeper truth. And they reveal alienation—the human tendency to withdraw into suspicion, self-interest, and division.

This, too, is why narrative spirituality is so vital. By reclaiming stories rooted in honesty, compassion, and hope, it exposes the false narratives for what they are: fragile attempts to mask fear, distrust, and brokenness. In the gospel story, by contrast, we find the deeper truth: a God who redeems, reconciles, and calls us into love.

The Role of Fear

At the heart of conspiracy theories lies fear. Fear magnifies uncertainty and drives people toward simplistic answers. Fear distorts perception, manipulates emotions, and fuels division. It erodes trust in institutions and relationships, leaving people vulnerable to suspicion. It isolates individuals but also binds them into closed communities defined by anxiety and resentment.

Fear creates fertile soil for false narratives. But narrative spirituality offers another way. By sharing stories of courage, resilience, and hope, communities can confront fear rather than feed it. By telling the truth in love, they can create belonging and trust, grounding people not in suspicion but in faith.

Narrative spirituality is both mirror and window. It reflects our false narratives honestly and opens us to God's larger story of truth and love. It heals distortion with authenticity, unmasks conspiracy with compassion, and confronts fear with faith.

False narratives reveal the fragility of the human condition, but authentic narratives—especially when joined to the gospel story—reveal a deeper reality: that we are not abandoned to fear, mistrust, or division. We are invited into a story that tells the truth, heals the past, and transforms the present.

To live within this story is to resist distortion and embody hope. It is to see the world and us through the mirror and window of God's love.

Narrative Spirituality: Healing False Stories, Unmasking Fear

Meditation

"You will know the truth, and the truth will make you free" (John 8:32).

False narratives imprison us in fear and distortion. Authentic stories, grounded in love, open the way to healing and freedom.

Narrative Reflection

Narrative spirituality reminds us that every life is a story and that stories can heal or harm. False narratives reduce people to stereotypes, oversimplify complexity, and often thrive on fear or mistrust. They can lead to deeper distortions such as conspiracy theories, isolating individuals and dividing communities.

But authentic spiritual narratives have the power to heal. When individuals share their personal stories with honesty and vulnerability, the single story is broken open. When communities weave their stories together, and empathy and belonging grow. When stories are told in context—social, historical, cultural—we begin to see the larger forces that shape our lives. And when these stories are told in rituals, writing, or communal practices, they become restorative, bringing reconciliation and hope.

Authenticity matters. True spiritual narratives do not hide doubt, pain, or struggle. They embrace honesty and complexity, transforming wounds into wisdom. They align with values of compassion, justice, and humility, and they point toward God's story of redemption. In this way, narrative spirituality is both mirror and window—a mirror reflecting who we are with truth and a window opening to what, by grace, we are called to become.

Symbolic Reading

Mirror: False narratives reflect distortion and fear; authentic stories reflect honesty, dignity, and healing.

Window: False narratives narrow our sight; authentic stories open us to God's horizon of compassion and justice.

Icon: The gospel story becomes the living image, exposing the fallen condition while revealing the possibility of redemption.

Fear and Faith: Fear fuels false stories; faith sustains true ones.

Prayer

God of truth and compassion,
shine Your light upon the stories we tell.
Heal what is distorted,
restore what is broken,
and unmask what is false.
Give us courage to speak with honesty,
to listen with empathy,
and to live as people of Your truth.
Let our stories join Your gospel story,
that love may overcome fear
and truth may set us free.
Amen.

Reflection Questions

- What false narratives have shaped me, and how have they limited my vision of myself or others?
- When have I experienced the healing power of telling or hearing an authentic story?
- How might fear distort the way I interpret events or people in my life?
- In what ways does the gospel story reframe and redeem my personal story?

- How can I contribute to communal storytelling that fosters compassion, justice, and truth?

Narrative spirituality heals false stories and unmasks the fear that fuels conspiracy theories. It teaches that authentic narratives—honest, vulnerable, and grounded in love—can dismantle distortions, foster empathy, and reconnect us to community. As mirror, narrative spirituality reflects the truth of who we are; as window, it opens us to God's greater story. In this way, it cultivates an integrative spiritual worldview where truth-telling becomes an act of love, and storytelling becomes a pathway to healing, justice, and hope.

Healing False Narratives Through Story

Meditation

"Putting away falsehood, let each of you speak the truth with your neighbor, for we are members of one another" (Eph. 4:25).

Authentic stories do more than describe life; they heal what false stories have distorted.

Narrative Reflection

False narratives are everywhere. They reduce people to caricatures, simplify complex realities, and often perpetuate prejudice or fear. These stories create division because they are less about truth and more about control.

Narrative spirituality responds by reclaiming story as a sacred act. When individuals share personal stories with honesty, they resist the flattening power of the single story. When communities gather their stories together, they weave a richer tapestry of truth, one that nurtures empathy and belonging. Context matters too. Stories gain depth when placed within their cultural, social, and historical settings, allowing us to see how larger forces shape our journeys.

Restorative practices—reflective writing, communal rituals, shared testimony—provide safe spaces to process pain, reconcile differences, and honor each other's journeys. In these ways, narrative spirituality serves as both mirror and window: a mirror reflecting our struggles with honesty and a window opening to God's healing horizon.

Symbolic Reading

Mirror: Stories reveal both wounds and the possibility of healing.

Window: Stories open onto the larger vision of God's reconciling love.

Icon: Christ as the Living Word, whose story reframes all stories.

Prayer

God of healing, teach us to tell our stories in truth.
Where falsehood has wounded, bring restoration.
Where silence has isolated, bring connection.
Let our words and our lives mirror Your grace
and open a window to Your love.
Amen.

Reflection Questions

- What false narratives have I believed about myself or others?
- How has telling my story—honestly and vulnerably—brought healing?
- Where do I see God weaving my personal story into a larger one?

Narrative spirituality heals false stories by lifting honest, contextual, and restorative storytelling. In doing so, it reclaims truth as an act of love and story as a path to healing.

Unmasking Fear and Conspiracy Through Story

Meditation

"For God did not give us a spirit of cowardice but rather a spirit of power and of love and of self-discipline" (2 Tim. 1:7).

Fear distorts truth into falsehood. Love restores truth through community.

Narrative Reflection

Conspiracy theories are among the most destructive false narratives of our time. They thrive on fear, suspicion, and division. By offering oversimplified answers to complex problems, they lure people into mistrust and alienation.

Authentic narrative spirituality offers another way. By encouraging critical thinking and embracing the complexity of truth, it resists the oversimplifications of conspiracy. By fostering empathy through shared stories, it counters the "us versus them" mentality. By grounding stories in values of compassion and justice, it unmasks narratives of hatred and division.

Most importantly, narrative spirituality gives people a sense of purpose. Conspiracy theories feed anxiety; authentic stories nurture resilience and hope. They confront fear not by denying it but by transforming it into courage and trust.

Symbolic Reading

Mirror: Conspiracy exposes our fallen tendency to fear, control, and mistrust.

Window: Authentic stories reveal a horizon of compassion, justice, and belonging.

Icon: Christ unmasks fear and calls us to truth, even when it is costly.

Prayer

God of truth,
expose the lies that feed on fear.
Break the chains of distortion,
and open our hearts to honesty,
compassion, and courage.
Teach us to live as people of light
whose stories resist fear
and reflect Your love.
Amen.

Reflection Questions

- How have I seen fear distort the way people tell or believe stories?
- Where am I tempted to settle for oversimplified explanations instead of deeper truth?
- How can my community practice truth-saying that resists fear and builds trust?

This shows how authentic narrative spirituality unmasks conspiracy and fear by cultivating honesty, empathy, and community. It reveals that the antidote to distortion is not argument alone but storytelling grounded in love, justice, and trust.

Closing: The Story We Continue to Write

Throughout these pages, we have investigated Scripture as mirror and as window, as icon that both affirms and confronts us. We have traced our way through personal stories, communal stories, false narratives and authentic ones, conspiracies and fears, affirmation and affront, faith and paradox. What emerges is not a tidy doctrine but a living testimony: Scripture is not finished with us. It continues to read us even as we read it.

The stories we tell matter. They heal or they wound, they bind or they set free. And yet every story, no matter how fractured, can be gathered into God's greater story—the gospel of love, justice, and reconciliation. Narrative spirituality, then, is not simply a method of interpretation. It is a way of life, a posture of truth-telling, an openness to paradox, and a willingness to see ourselves and our world through the eyes of grace.

Conclusion: Mirror, Window, Icon

In the end, the metaphor holds. Scripture is a mirror, reflecting back to us our dignity and our distortions, our beloved and our brokenness. It is a window, opening onto the horizon of God's kingdom, inviting us into justice, mercy, and compassion. And it is an icon, drawing us into the presence of the One who is both comfort and challenge, both "yes" and "no," both grace and truth.

To read Scripture with an integrative spiritual worldview is to refuse the false separation of prayer and justice, of contemplation and action, of personal healing and communal responsibility. It is to embrace the wholeness of faith where story, symbol, and Spirit weave together to form a life that is fully human and fully alive in God.

Epilogue: The Next Chapter Is Yours

Books end, but stories do not. The story of God and humanity continues—in your life, your community, and your world. Each time you open the Scriptures, you are not only reading ancient words; you are also stepping into a living conversation. Each time you tell your story with honesty, you add a thread to the tapestry of God's redemption. Each time you listen to the story of another with compassion, you participate in healing what is broken.

The invitation now is simple: to live as both mirror and window. Let your life reflect truth, humility, and love. Let your life open outward toward justice, reconciliation, and hope. Let your story join the greater story of God's love—a story that affirms our worth, confronts our fears, and transforms the world.

And so, dear reader, this book closes not with a period but with an open sentence. The next chapter is yours to write—with your prayers, your courage, your compassion, and your love.

Benediction

May the God who is both mirror and window,
affirmation and affront,
grace and truth,
bless you and keep you.
May your story be healed by love,
your voice strengthened by hope,
your heart opened to justice.
And as you go,
may your life itself become a mirror of God's compassion
and a window into God's kingdom
for the sake of the world God loves.
Go in peace,
and write the next chapter with your life.
Amen.

A Reader's Prayer

God of Story and Spirit,
I have looked into Your Word as a mirror,
and I have seen both my need and Your grace.
I have gazed through it as a window,
and I have glimpsed Your kingdom of justice and love.
Now send me forth
to live the story You are writing in me.
Heal the false narratives I have carried,

and teach me to walk in truth.
Open my eyes to the stories of others
that I may listen with compassion
and act with courage.
Let my life become
a mirror of Your love
and a window of Your hope—
a living testimony to Your grace.
Through Christ, who is Word made flesh,
Amen.

About the Author

The Rev. Dr. Ken Macklin, Ph.D. is an adjunct professor and ordained United Methodist clergy with over four decades of pastoral and academic experience. He teaches spirituality, theology, and ethics at California Lutheran University, where he is known for integrating faith, ethics, and professional practice in both graduate and undergraduate programs. Dr. Macklin holds advanced degrees in theology, Christian spirituality, and Eastern Orthodox studies, including a Ph.D. in Theological Studies from the Graduate Theological Foundation with Oxford Summer Programs. His publications include Mirror & Window: Narrative Spiritual Reading with an Integrative Mindset, Narrative Spirituality and Healing, Mark: The Inverted Gospel, and the novel The Echoes of the Innocents. His scholarship bridges theology, psychology, and spirituality, emphasizing relational, dialogical, and interdisciplinary approaches. Married to Anna, with whom he shares three adult sons and several grandchildren, he enjoys hiking, dancing, reading, and motorcycling.

www.ingramcontent.com/pod-product-compliance
Lightning Source LLC
LaVergne TN
LVHW010555100826
845148LV00014B/2728

* 9 7 8 1 6 8 4 8 8 1 6 5 9 *